GREAT HOUSES OF BRITAIN

ENDPAPERS A perspective view of Castle Howard, Yorkshire, taken from
Colen Campbell's *Vitruvius Britannicus* published in 1715

GREAT HOUSES OF BRITAIN

NIGEL NICOLSON

PHOTOGRAPHS BY KERRY DUNDAS

G.P. PUTNAM'S SONS 200 MADISON AVENUE NEW YORK

For Dan and Dorothy

© 1965 by George Weidenfeld and Nicolson Ltd, London

Library of Congress Catalog Card Number: 65-19760

Designed by Colin Banks and John Miles for George Weidenfeld and Nicolson Ltd

Full colour gravure illustrations and text printed in England

Monochrome gravure illustrations printed in Ireland

Contents

Foreword

With very few exceptions, every chapter in this book has been written in the house which it describes, and the author and photographer have accompanied each other from house to house, and almost room to room. Our pleasant collaboration was duplicated by that between ourselves and the owners, and this is the place in which to put on record not only our gratitude for their hospitality and help, but our admiration for the care with which they have maintained these exquisite buildings often in face of great difficulties. Thirteen of the houses now belong to the National Trust, two are in the care of municipalities, and one, Sulgrave Manor, has been acquired and furnished by joint Anglo-American enterprise. All the others are privately owned and in almost every case privately occupied. Most of them are regularly or periodically open to the public, and one purpose of this book is to encourage readers to see for themselves what text and photographs can only summarily describe. In order to save both owners and public from misguided intrusion, it should be said that three of the houses are not normally shown to strangers: Groombridge Place, Easton Neston and Heveningham.

The choice of these houses could easily be criticised by those readers who regret, like the author, that certain favourites are left out. But the choice was not haphazard. The first essential was that each house should be in perfect condition, either as it was built, or as it was later transformed without too much damage to its original character. Secondly, an attempt was made to choose examples representative of each main architectural style and period between the fourteenth century and the early nineteenth. Thirdly, a balance has been kept between large houses and small, the famous and the less familiar. Finally, it was the intention, not wholly fulfilled, to distribute the houses with fair equality over the whole country; if there is a close grouping of houses, like a marksman's shots on a target, in Norfolk, Derbyshire, Northamptonshire and Kent, it is because those counties are unusually rich in the type of house for which we were seeking.

Only country-houses are described. Although Mompesson House lies in the middle of Salisbury and the Royal Pavilion is in Brighton, neither of them has an urban character. Town-houses are not included, partly in order to limit the choice and partly because one of the characteristics of English domestic architecture is that so much of it belongs to the countryside. The patricians of the great centuries saw no disadvantage in planting their grandest houses alongside their farms, in robbing agriculture of sufficient land to form their gardens and parks and in burying their works of art a week's journey or more from London. Nor were they in the least shy of experimenting with new architectural fashions, often foreign, in the middle of their native fields.

If there is any emphasis in this book it is one that has emerged naturally as it was being written – an emphasis upon the continuity of family and taste. The people who could afford to build such houses formed a very small circle. They all knew each other, and their children intermarried down the generations. In one house you will find a portrait of a girl who reappears as châtelaine of another and whose daughter becomes mistress of a third, like the three-generation link between Althorp, Chatsworth, Blenheim and Castle Howard, or Lady Anne Clifford's switch from Knole to Wilton. The relationship between the houses also meant that fashions in architecture and decoration spread rapidly from one to another, and the names of the same architects and artists recur frequently in this narrative as their post-chaises criss-cross the country in execution of their extravagant commissions. The history of the great houses is a slowly turning wheel which will never make more than one revolution, and it was completed a hundred and fifty years ago. It is a happy chance that when people could afford to build like this, they did build like this, and that so many of them realised the merits of styles that had gone out of fashion when they had so much to contribute themselves.

Apart from emphasizing the architectural inventiveness of the British, these houses also illustrate how our ancestors lived and, to some extent, how they thought. Fly over almost any part of Great Britain and you will see below you the social system of past centuries showing between the modern grid of housing estates and railway-sidings. It could be no other country. The great houses have left a cultural pattern around them, descending in a measured scale from palace to manor, surrounded by park and lake or fields and pond, and detached, but not offensively, from the neighbouring villages. There is some arrogance, certainly, in their situation, and the legend of the local lord frequenting the village pub and hunting with the hounds is more apparent in sentimental fiction than in fact. The houses have imposed upon their owners a status that the last hundred years of social change have not shaken fundamentally. Even to those who now pay to enter, the owners are still the hosts, 'the people in the big house'.

What is different is the concern which many of them now feel for the future, not for their own sakes or their children's so much as for the house itself. It could be argued that a house, like a beech-tree, has a natural term of years and that the time must come when it would be absurd to prop it up further. This could be true if the houses were replaceable or in poor condition. They are not replaceable; they form collectively Britain's greatest contribution to the visual arts. They are not in poor condition; they are magnificently kept up. When private capital fails, the State, as it has already done in so many cases, must move to the rescue.

NIGEL NICOLSON
Sissinghurst Castle, Kent

ST MICHAEL'S MOUNT

CORNWALL

A mediaeval island-priory, now a country house

Few notable houses in Britain lie within sight of the sea. It provided too spectacular and competitive a background for the taste of the sixteenth to eighteenth centuries, when proprietors preferred to look landwards over their farms and parks, the source and symbol of their wealth. The sea was hostile, public and cold. In their eyes St Michael's Mount would have combined every possible disadvantage as a gentleman's seat. It was difficult of access, swept by gales, exposed to piratical attack and the gaze of the curious, and absurdly unsuited to the architecture and landscape-gardening of the times. Besides, the place was not a house at all. It was a fortified monastery, grim and melancholy in its associations and aspect.

In the nineteenth century the reputation of the Mount changed completely, and today we are the inheritors of the romantic tradition that no place in England is more dramatic in its situation nor more subtle in the composition of its different parts. St Michael's Mount is an island – and yet not quite an island, for twice in every twenty-four hours the tide sweeps back from its northern side to expose a causeway, a quarter of a mile long, over which you can walk dryshod to Marazion on the mainland shore. At high spring-tide eighteen feet of water cover the causeway, and this diurnal ebb and flow, controlled as it seems by distant sluice-gates, governs the life of the St Aubyn family who have lived here for over three hundred years.

At the full tide no island appears more perfectly insular, cupped in the inner curve of Mount's Bay like a Hebridean fortress. Its form is that of a nearly symmetrical cone, a mile in circumference at its base and rising in rocky and partly wooded slopes to a peak three hundred feet high. On the summit stands the church with the house below it, extending by their granite walls and towers the upward sweep of the rock, so that from a distance it is almost impossible to tell where the rock ends and the building begins. From Marazion the house has the appearance of a coronet of stone, less a structure than a sudden tightening of the natural rock.

Once ashore, an entirely new aspect of the Mount is revealed. It is now seen to be semi-tropical in its flowers and vegetation. The sturdy little harbour, with the white boatmen's cottages,

St Michael's Mount looking west towards Penzance, from a drawing made by Richard Scadden in the late seventeenth century. The height and cragginess of the Mount are considerably exaggerated

opposite Looking outwards through the west door, down the pilgrims' steps towards the sea. The massive stonework and portcullis illustrate the double role of the Mount as priory and fortress

A drawing made in about 1810 showing the original appearance of the summit of the Mount before additions were made later in the century

opposite top An air view of the Mount looking north-east at high tide, when the rock is completely cut off from the mainland. The harbour (left) dries out at low tide

opposite bottom St Michael's Mount at low tide seen from Chapel Rock. The causeway (left) is open. The harbour and boatmen's cottages are on the right

is everybody's dream picture of a Cornish fishing village. As one climbs the steep cobbled pathway to the summit, following the pilgrims' route to St Michael's shrine, one is back again in the Middle Ages. Each difficult step upwards is both a penance and a pleasure. The view widens over the great sweep of the bay. Overhead, a Cornish cross on a jutting rock, the ruins of a watch-tower, a battery of guns, the solid soaring walls of close-set masonry, make one wonder what place this can be – a church, a castle, a relic or a private house? The Mount is all these things. Apart from its incomparable situation, its chief fascination lies in the mingling of truth with fantasy, as its history emerges from legend into recorded fact.

St Michael's Mount has been known by that name, *Mons Sancti Michaelis de Cornubia*, since at least the time of Edward the Confessor. By lifting one of the pew-seats in the choir of the church, one can expose a tight spiral staircase leading downwards to a vaulted cell cut in the rock. Only surmise can supply an explanation of it. It could be a hermit's cell dating from the darkest ages of English history, or a priest's hole, or a dungeon, or even a tomb, for a skeleton was found in it when the cell was discovered in 1720. But there is no doubt about the significance of the lovely cruciform church above it. In 1070 St Michael's Mount was granted by Robert, Count of Mortain, to Mont Saint Michel in Normandy, the great abbey which resembles the Cornish Mount not only in name but in situation, for it too is built on the summit of a rock which becomes an island at high tide. St Michael's Mount was one of its dependent priories, and a church was built there in 1135 by Bernard, Abbot of Mont Saint Michel. It had a Prior and twelve monks, selected from the brothers of the French abbey, to which it owed obedience and sixteen marks a year. For nearly 350 years, until 1414, the Cornish Mount remained attached to the Norman Mount, the strength of the ties between them varying with the current state of tension between England and France. In wartime the priory was taken into the hands of the English king; with the return of peace, it was honourably restored to the French. Without intermission, it was a place of pilgrimage, for it contained important relics, and from the revenues of the farms, harbour, annual fair, and the offerings of the pilgrims, it prospered greatly.

The existing church is not Abbot Bernard's original, which was destroyed by an earthquake in 1275. A new church was raised on the foundations of the old late in the fourteenth century, and the present windows were added about fifty years later, together with the Lady Chapel, a lovely casket of carved stone which stands on the highest point of the Mount beside the church. By this time St Michael's Mount had passed by the gift of Henry VI from the French abbey into the hands of the Bridgettine convent of Syon, Middlesex. The Abbess of Syon held it for over a hundred years until the dissolution of both foundations in 1539. This disaster did not affect the Mount as much as its mother convent, since the number of monks had

declined to as few as two or three, and for many years its importance as a fortress had overshadowed its religious significance. Occupying a strategic and almost impregnable position near the south-west tip of England, it became a gateway for revolution and a bastion of defence. It was first seized by the king's enemies in 1194, recaptured, fortified, garrisoned, attacked by pirates, corsairs, pretenders and English rebels, a bone of contention in the Hundred Years' War, the Wars of the Roses and the Civil War – one must picture the Mount throughout these centuries as fulfilling a double role, the priory sheltering behind the garrison, the Prior and Governor, monks and soldiers, sharing the cramped quarters folded round the upper part of the rock. It was here that the Earl of Oxford landed from France in 1471 with a posse of men disguised as pilgrims; here that Perkin Warbeck raised the standard of his ill-fated revolt; from here that Humphrey Arundell launched the Cornish rebellion of 1549; and from here that the Spanish Armada was first sighted, according to Macaulay,

> For swift to east and swift to west the ghastly war-flame spread.
> High on St Michael's Mount it shone; it shone on Beachy Head.

Queen Elizabeth sold the Mount to Robert Cecil, first Earl of Salisbury, in 1599, and from the Cecils it passed to Francis Basset, who held it for the King in 1646. It came to the Cornish family of St Aubyn in 1657, and the garrison was soon afterwards disbanded. For many years the Mount remained virtually unoccupied. But during the eighteenth century the St Aubyns began to use it as an occasional summer home, and converted the Lady Chapel into the charming drawing-rooms that one sees today. But it was too small a house, too inconvenient in its site and monastic-military layout, for use as a permanent residence by a landed family. It was not until 1875 that the old rock was scoured and blasted to provide the foundations for a great new block of rooms which make the Mount, in spite of its exposure to the Atlantic winds, one of the most comfortable houses in the country.

This latest phase in the history of St Michael's Mount is usually dismissed as a misfortune or unworthy of serious attention. In fact its Victorian additions are among the greatest achievements of nineteenth-century domestic architecture. The architect was Piers St Aubyn, a cousin of the owner, who is otherwise known for his restorations of Cornish churches and the Temple Church in London. His problem was both aesthetic and structural. The top of the Mount was hallowed ground, not only for its religious and historical associations, but for the world-famous silhouette which it presented from the mainland shore. It could not be radically disturbed. But below the parapet level there was nothing but precipitous rock. St Aubyn solved the problem by erecting his new building in the form of a tall, wide tower set against the south-eastern face. Its foot rests upon the bedrock halfway down the slope, its summit rises almost, but not quite, to the level of the original buildings, which are thus left

opposite Looking up towards the west door approached by the pilgrims' steps. Until the late nineteenth century this was the only entrance to the Mount

A drawing of the south-eastern additions designed by Piers St Aubyn in 1875, when the old priory-fortress was transformed into a comfortable private house

opposite The interior of the fourteenth-century church which stands on the summit of the Mount and replaced an earlier church built in 1135 by the Abbots of Mont St Michel in Normandy. Services are still held here every Sunday

below The arms of St Aubyn and Godolphin at the opposite end of Chevy Chase, with a detail of the frieze below. St Michael's Mount has been owned by the St Aubyn family since 1657

above Chevy Chase, the former refectory of the monks. The room takes its name from the frieze of scenes of the chase made in late Elizabethan or early Stuart times.

untrammelled by modern additions and continue to crown the Mount as they have for the previous seven hundred years. The workmanship is everywhere superb. The whole is built of silver-coloured granite which outcrops into the body of the house as staircases, cornices and window-frames, so that the visitor feels himself suspended in a huge cage of stone. Outside the double-windows is the cry of gulls and the continuous rumble of the sea.

Most great houses are fusions of different styles of architecture. St Michael's Mount is a fusion of functions dictated by the extraordinary nature of the site. Because it is all built of the same granite, and because its shiplike exposure necessitated at every period the same massiveness of construction, every part of it from the twelfth century to the nineteenth blends into a whole. From the terraces contrived on the knobbly summit of a Gibraltar one looks across and downwards at a scurry of small boats or at a procession of approaching visitors. It is not difficult to translate this view into the mediaeval terms of carracks and pilgrims. If a rock is a symbol of permanence, a house on a rock is a symbol of continuity. This is the dominant impression left by St Michael's Mount. It is gay on a summer's day, and majestic in a storm. It can never have been very different.

16

opposite The Blue Drawing Room, originally the fifteenth-century Lady Chapel, which was converted in 1740. The decoration is an early form of eighteenth-century Gothic

IGHTHAM MOTE

KENT

A fourteenth-century moated manor house

One of the happiest of the many legends about Ightham Mote is that Cromwell's soldiers, intent on destroying it as a Royalist stronghold, got lost in the deep wooded valleys of the Weald and ransacked another house of lesser interest instead. Thus Ightham passed safely through another crisis in its remarkably long life. It was saved on this occasion by its seclusion. Between two main roads from London to the Kentish coast a network of lanes increases more than clarifies the intricacies of this rich country-side of arable and fruit. So deep have the old drovers' tracks been worn by centuries of traffic that they have become less like roads than tunnels through the woods. At the foot of one of them the screen parts for an instant to reveal a house wholly in keeping with the privacy of its approach. It is deliberately hidden, hugging the ground like an animal its den.

Ightham is built round four sides of a courtyard and is sur-rounded by a moat. The moat is so much part of it – indeed almost the essence of it – that the casual visitor could be forgiven for imagining that the 'Mote' of its name is an earlier spelling of the word. It is nothing of the sort. It recalls the *moot* or local council which in the Middle Ages met in the most prosperous house of each neighbourhood, and the name alone would be a sufficient indication of its antiquity. But the buildings themselves proclaim it. They form the ideal image of an early English manor-house, one of the few genuine examples of a style which dominated English building for three hundred years.

We can safely begin in the early fourteenth century. The manor then belonged to a Sir Thomas Cawne, and it was he who erected the buildings on the east or inner side of the court-yard. They comprised a Great Hall, a chapel, a crypt below it (which is possibly a survival from a yet earlier house), a kitchen, a solar and one or two bedrooms. In its essentials the whole of this house survives. It was extremely uncomfortable. The stone and timber roof of the hall, although a splendid piece of en-gineering, was designed not so much for effect as to collect the smoke from the central hearth and release it through gaps in the upper beams, but its great height made the fire almost ineffec-tive as a means of warming the hall. There was no dais to separ-ate the master's table from the servants', no oriel window to

The main entrance with its original fifteenth-century doors, looking into the central courtyard round which the house is built. Immediately opposite the gate is the great window of the hall

opposite The east side of the house, which is surrounded by a moat on all four sides. This is the earliest part and dates back to the mid-fourteenth century

The courtyard with the Tudor chapel and belfry on the left, and on the right the oriel window of the solar, or main withdrawing room, with finely carved barge-boards above

A bird's eye view of Ightham Mote from the south-west, drawn in 1901, since when the house has been little changed externally

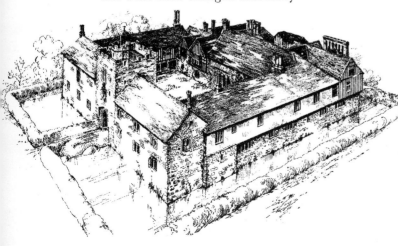

grace its walls, no decorated screen at the servants' end, no musicians' gallery. The hall was the centre of the household's life, rush-strewn and squalid, and its magnificence can be enjoyed better today than at any period when it was serving its original purpose. At a later date, during the fifteenth century, a fireplace and chimney were substituted for the open hearth, and a broad window of five tall lights was inserted in the west wall overlooking the courtyard. The old chapel and the crypt are even more massively austere, rooms that you might find in a Sicilian monastery, almost Norman in the grouping of their rounded stone, and even the kitchen has the same character of quasi-ecclesiastical architecture. One room only begins to foreshadow later standards of gentility. The solar on the upper floor, ancestor of the Saloon and modern drawing-room, ensured at least some privacy for the women of the house.

This was the house that served the Cawnes and their successors, the De Hauts, for about a hundred and forty years, say from 1340 to 1480. Then two other sides of the quadrangle were built, the west and the south. On the west or entrance side a central tower of three storeys was erected at the inner end of the bridge, and it was flanked by a large room on each side with bedrooms and another drawing-room above. A similar wing, possibly built on the lower courses of an earlier building, was added on the south side. At the same time improvements were made to the original house. One can visualise from the existing

buildings the De Hauts' tussle with mediaeval inconvenience and their resistance to the temptation to pull the whole thing down and start afresh.

The last major addition was the work of Sir Richard Clement in about 1520. He closed the north side of the quadrangle by a new chapel in the form of a timber framework overhanging the moat, with an open cloister beneath it. This chapel, together with the hall, is the chief glory of Ightham. In inspiration it is still Gothic. Its barrel-vaulted roof, richly ornamented with the Tudor rose and portcullis, its six windows inset with Dutch sixteenth-century stained glass, its pews, the tracery of its lovely screen, its hooded pulpit and linenfold panelling round the walls, all illustrate superbly the transitional style which the Continental Renaissance had barely begun to influence. In this way the courtyard was squared off as we see it today, and externally the house dropped its walls clean into the water of the moat on all four sides.

It had taken three centuries, the fourteenth, fifteenth and sixteenth, to create this delightful compactness. There was no more space to build, and when the Elizabethan owners, the Allens, needed more room for staff and stables, they were obliged to build a second quadrangle outside. Part of this survives. In any other place, these buildings would themselves be worthy of a pilgrimage, but at Ightham they can pass almost unnoticed. It is the water around the main house that first catches and holds

The half-timbered Tudor stables built on the west side of the house outside the moat. The wings on either side were originally much longer

The north-east corner of the house showing the characteristic mixture of fourteenth-century half-timbering and stone. The moat is crossed by bridges on three of its four sides and is fed by springs so that the water remains constantly clear

IGHTHAM MOTE

The entrance tower seen from across the moat. This dates from about 1480 and was originally approached by a drawbridge. The upper room of the tower is one of several which is reputedly haunted

above right The Great Hall, built by Sir Thomas Cawne in about 1340, and one of the best preserved fourteenth-century halls in existence. It still has its original oak-timbered ceiling, but the window on the left is a fifteenth-century insertion and the panelling is modern

your attention: the moat, the pool below it, the waterfall above it. And then the texture of the buildings: cobbles underfoot, walls of weathered native materials, patched unselfconsciously and each bearing some mark of its originator – a moulding, a chamfering, a pattern of leaded diamond panes, a carved head grimacing under the weight of a beam or peering cockney-like from the corner of a door.

But inevitably, and not to its disadvantage, the house bears evidence that it has been in almost continuous occupation since it was completed. There are Jacobean fireplaces, friezes and staircases; a Venetian window of the late seventeenth century and hand-painted wallpaper of the same period; windows of Walpole Gothic in the courtyard; some pretty Victorian bedrooms and an imitation of Tudor linenfold in the corridors. All these are due to the Selby family who owned the Mote between 1598 and 1889 – three centuries reduced to a mere incident in its history. In the early twentieth century the Colyer-Fergussons added some heavy oak embellishments to its interior. They obliterated nothing of significance, and they saved the house from falling to pieces.

Apart from the De Hauts and the Selbys, no family has long been in occupation of the Mote. It seemed destined to a constant change of owner, which explains the absence of any written records of its history and of any furniture dating back to its earlier periods. But the latest phase in the story is not the least remarkable. Ightham Mote belongs today to an American, C. H. Robinson. He first fell in love with the Mote when he saw a picture of it in an art-dealer's shop in London, and a few years later, on a bicycling-tour of England, he visited it. The idea began to take root in his mind that one day, perhaps, he might make it his own. The chance came thirty years later, in 1953. The Colyer-Fergussons could no longer afford to maintain a house that can quickly drain a fortune, and put it up for sale. They did not know of Mr Robinson's secret wish, nor he of their intention. The house found no buyer able to live in it, and it was again in danger of demolition. At the last moment Mr Robinson discovered the threat, and the house discovered Mr Robinson. He bought it. He repaired it. He refurnished it. He remade its lovely eighteenth-century garden. For several months in the year, as his commitments in the United States allow, he lives there. It is now his intention to make arrangements that the house shall survive his death, for he believes rightly that such a place, hidden though it is from its nearest neighbours in the Weald, has an enduring significance for the whole English-speaking world and should not be allowed to perish.

The drawing room with hand-painted wallpaper from the Restoration period and a hand-carved oak frieze. The Venetian window dates from *c* 1680

The 'squint' from the solar to the old chapel, which enabled sick members of the family to follow the services

The interior of the chapel, built in 1520. The barrel-vaulted roof is decorated with the Tudor rose, but the pulpit and stalls are Jacobean

HADDON HALL

DERBYSHIRE

A fine example of the transition between castle and house

In this part of Derbyshire scarcely a rock breaks the smoothness of the countryside, which swings, like the roads, in easy rounded gradients. The setting of Haddon is not therefore precipitous, although nineteenth-century water-colourists did their best to make it appear so. The house lies on a spur of a gentle hill above the River Wye which loops round its foot like a casually dropped ribbon. But the approach to the main gate certainly does give a first impression of strength and fortification. The path slopes steeply upwards for the last fifty yards towards a battlemented tower, and to the left of it are climbing turrets and knobbly projections that might have formed the sole inspiration of the romantic revival. This pageantry is not contrived. Not one of these buildings is less than four hundred years old, and the oldest dates back to the thirteenth century. They have grown together from necessity or convenience. The authenticity of Haddon is what makes it so endearing. Its simplicity, its sheer age, its fusion of styles, periods and needs, give it unity. The same grey gritstone, limestone and home-grown oak are used in every part of its construction. There is not a brick, not an ornamental piece of marble, in the whole building.

Haddon has worn well. It was solidly built, and although the Dukes of Rutland did not inhabit it during the eighteenth and nineteenth centuries, they kept its roof and main timbers in repair. Where its materials are roughened by time or use, they are still serviceable because they were originally as sound as simple craftsmanship could make them. A huge block of stone on the threshold of a gate or doorway may be worn into a deep groove by the tread of innumerable feet guided into exactly the same place century after century, but there is no need to replace it. A thick baulk of elm forming a table-top is scarred by knife-cuts, stained with wine and pitted by beetle-holes; after three hundred years you turn it over, and it is good for another three hundred. The entrance courtyard was so well paved that for all its unevenness and irregularity it can look little different today than it did in the thirteenth century. But perhaps the timelessness of Haddon is best sensed in the old kitchen, where can be seen the root of a huge oak which served generations of scullions as a chopping-block, and great vats and troughs which bear

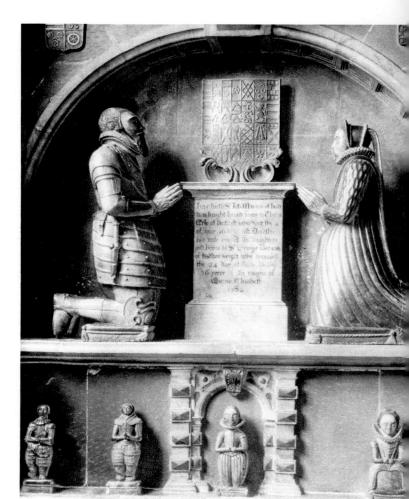

The tomb of Sir John Manners and his wife Dorothy Vernon in Bakewell Church, with the figures of their children beneath. It was through this marriage that Haddon passed from the Vernons into the family of the Dukes of Rutland

opposite The lower courtyard of Haddon from just inside the main entrance. In the centre is the archway leading to the Great Hall. The whole of this range of buildings dates from the fourteenth century, apart from the Tudor windows

The entrance tower, completed in about 1530 by Sir George Vernon

opposite top Haddon Hall by Rex Whistler, painted in 1933. The two figures in the foreground are those of the ninth Duke of Rutland and the present Duke, his son

opposite bottom The south front looking west from one of the terraces. The upper windows are those of the Long Gallery and at the far end is the fourteenth-century chapel

traces of the pounding, stirring and scouring to which they were daily subjected. Even the grand apartments are formed by the same combination of sturdiness and makeshift. Haddon can never have been a luxurious place, although it was the scene of much revelry and display; and even its Elizabethan owners never advanced much beyond carved panels and doorways, journeymen's paintings on the chapel walls and modest family crests in the dining-room. The mediaeval hall suited the Vernons and Manners of the Renaissance, and while they might add a parlour here, a gallery there, the house retained its old ground-plan and character. Without conscious antiquarianism, their restraint was a tribute to the building of their predecessors.

Thus, although Haddon achieved its greatest splendour in the last years of the sixteenth century, it is still the finest example of an English manor-house surviving from the Middle Ages. A house, let it be stressed, not a castle – a house struggling out of the chrysalis of mediaevalism. The original licence to surround it by a wall in the 1190's specified that the wall was not to be more than twelve feet high and was not to be crenellated (*muro exaltato xij pedibus sine kernello*, reads the document preserved at Belvoir), and throughout its history Haddon was never to withstand a siege. Most of its surviving walls and many of its rooms date from the fourteenth century, and one can be certain that the mediaeval extent of the house was not very different from that which we see today.

It was formed around two courtyards, an upper and a lower, each approached by a separate archway, the first for wheeled vehicles, the second for visitors on foot or horseback. The Vernons seem to have strained to the limit the ban on fortification. Although there was originally no crenellation, there were certainly watch-towers rising above the roof-line, and the builders were careful to see that the outer walls were stout and not weakened by too many external windows. But within the courtyards one finds evidence that comfort and feudal dignity were beginning to assume as much importance as defence.

The hall with its attendant kitchens and buttery divides one court from the other. It is approached by a wide flight of steps which lead to an arched opening. Immediately inside is a passage behind the screens, through which one glimpses a large, but not immodestly large, banqueting hall, with a dais for the family's table at the far end, a fireplace on one side and windows on both. This was the normal mediaeval arrangement of the heart of a house, which in essentials was to last until the beginning of the seventeenth century. At Haddon other rooms straggle round the two courts, neater individually than their haphazard arrangement would suggest, and they illustrate that the design of great manor-houses was already being influenced by the need for rooms of several purposes. The whole complex culminates in the Long Gallery, now known as the ball-room, a beautiful room 110 feet long, panelled throughout in oak and carved walnut. It is almost the only room in the house which reflects the

full spirit of the Renaissance. It was built over the existing walls by John Manners and his wife, Dorothy Vernon, daughter and heiress of Sir George Vernon, in the last years of the sixteenth century. Their marriage, following an elopement to which legend has attached details that belong more properly to romantic fiction, took Haddon to the Manners, later Earls and Dukes of Rutland, from whose hands the property has never since passed.

Early in the present century the ninth Duke of Rutland restored the house as nearly as possible to its condition when his ancestors left Haddon for Belvoir in 1701. As quite a young boy he had determined to make this his life's major interest, and set himself to study the architecture of its many periods, so that in converting Haddon into a summer home for his family he would not be guilty of solecisms. Even before his succession to the Dukedom, he embarked on his immense task. Haddon was not a ruin, but its roof was in danger of collapse, the stonework of the windows was perishing, it was almost empty of furniture and its lighting, heating, sanitary and cooking arrangements were as they had been left two hundred years before. The only running water in the house, for instance, entered the old kitchen by one conduit and left it by another. The work was sufficiently advanced by 1927 for the Duke to move in, but the restoration continued for several years afterwards. Let not the reader be dismayed by the word 'restoration'. Nothing was faked. The Duke merely replaced what had decayed by materials cut or quarried on the estates from which the original materials had come. Where the restoration required new work so extensive that it involved an almost complete rebuilding, as, for instance, in the roofing of the hall, new timbers were cut at Haddon or Belvoir and erected in such a manner that nobody could possibly mistake the new work for the old.

This latest phase in the history of Haddon is by no means its least glorious. The devotion of this nobleman, the present Duke's father, saved for the nation a house of much more than antiquarian interest. Haddon is the loveliest of the transitional houses of the Middle Ages. The terraced gardens, descending by flower-strewn grey walls to the river beneath, support a rambling building that immediately entrances every visitor. The first impression is not a fleeting one. The charm of Haddon increases with knowledge of its history and exploration of its hidden corners. Its theatrical appearance is due simply to its length of life. We must beware of tingeing our admiration with sentimentality, for its builders would not have known the meaning of the word.

Medallions which probably represent Henry VII
and his wife Elizabeth of York carved in the
panelling of the window recess in the dining room

top The Long Gallery or ballroom, reconstructed by Sir John Manners before his death in 1611. The square panels in the ceiling contain the Vernon and Manners arms

bottom The Banqueting Hall, dating from the early fourteenth century, looking towards the Minstrels' Gallery. The antlers have been there since the reign of Charles II

The main entrance on the north side of the house.
The tower block has remained unchanged since it
was built in 1482, but the windows in the buildings
on either side are nineteenth-century additions to
the original Tudor façade

An air view of Oxburgh Hall from the west,
showing the moat which encircles the house on all
four sides crossed by the bridge under the tower
on the left

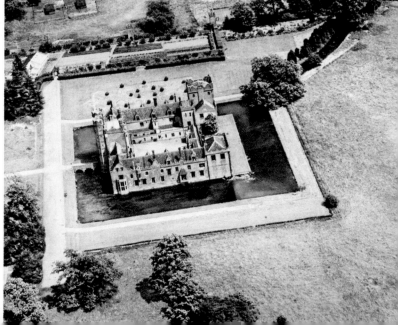

OXBURGH HALL

An early Tudor fortified house

The first sight of Oxburgh from the road could raise the question whether it should have a place in this book at all: it is apparently a castle, not a house, with all the outward apparatus of fortification – a moat, battlements, arrow-slits and a vast turreted, machicolated gatehouse. A closer look makes clear that all these features, while certainly deriving from mediaeval castles, have undergone subtle changes. The moat is now crossed by a fixed bridge, not a drawbridge. The majority of the arrow-slits are found to be in the rearward-facing turret tops, and are so sited that no bowman could possibly have let fly from them at an enemy below. Nothing can ever have been dropped from the machicolations on the south side, for they are sealed by the original stone. The gatehouse does not frown, for it is a work of architecture, not primarily a work of defence: it is built of brick, not stone, and it is pierced on its most exposed side by two large and delicate windows.

Thus the whole building forms an extremely interesting illustration of how a great county family, itself adept at war and experienced in the treacherous ways of the fifteenth century, was feeling its way towards greater comfort and architectural elegance even at the cost of increased vulnerability to attack. Oxburgh was started by Sir Edmund Bedingfeld in 1482, three years before the Wars of the Roses came to an end. The defences would have kept marauding beggars out of the courtyard, but little more; they could not have resisted an organized attack for a single day. The military embellishments were largely decorative and the layout was designed for display, entertainment on a lavish scale, and the raising of large families. The proof of its domesticity is that the house has been occupied as the home of the Bedingfelds for nearly five hundred years with scarcely a break and no basic change to its structure. Its claim to be a superb work of architecture has been endorsed by one critic after another. 'One of the noblest specimens of the domestic architecture of the fifteenth century,' wrote the elder Pugin. 'The finest building of its generation,' said Avray Tipping. And in his *Pattern of English Building* Clifton-Taylor calls it 'one of England's most enchanting pieces of architectural pageantry'.

Attention is first focused on the great tower, not only because

Sir Henry Bedingfeld, a staunch Catholic, who was entrusted by Mary Tudor with the custody of the future Queen Elizabeth. Oxburgh has belonged to the Bedingfeld family ever since it was built

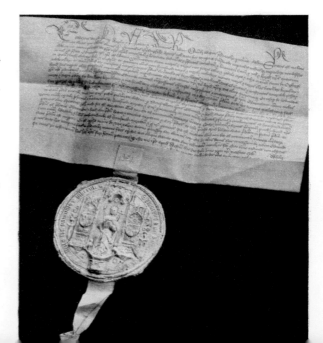

The original licence from Edward IV to Edmund Bedingfeld, dated 3rd July 1482, permitting him to build and fortify a manor house at Oxburgh

The interior of the courtyard looking towards the north-west corner. On this side the octagonal turrets do not extend to the whole height of the tower. The Bedingfeld arms are carved above the archway, with a square sundial above them

Oxburgh seen from the south-east showing the buildings which have replaced the Tudor Hall demolished by Sir Richard Bedingfeld in 1775. The tower is a nineteenth-century addition

it almost monopolizes the view from the entrance gates, but because it is by far the most striking feature of the house and the least altered. This splendid building rises from the moat like a cliff from the sea. It is formed by two octagonal turrets joined by a curtain wall. The turrets are placed close together to emphasize the height of the tower, and they are topped by doubly serrated battlements which have the majesty of tiaras. At intervals horizontal brick mouldings are slung like lace round the shafts, and the turret windows, thrown into deep shadow by their depth, are black caverns compared to the sparkle of the central lights. The tower is not quite symmetrical, for the windows are larger and more widely spaced in the left-hand turret than in the right, and a projection for the garderobes is attached to one side. But it gives the impression of symmetry because the skyline is perfectly balanced. Who could doubt, after examining this façade in reality or in a photograph, that its builders were acutely aware of the dramatic effect of what they were doing?

The reverse side of the gatehouse is remarkable because it is treated quite differently from the other. Here the turrets stop short of the parapet, and two watch-towers, corbelled outwards at the angles, carry the eye upwards. There is no main window on this side, only a large square sundial set in the wall between the turret tops and a stone achievement of the Bedingfeld arms below. You are now within the square central courtyard. The great hall originally stood opposite the gatehouse, and two-storeyed apartments ran round the other three sides. It is a place for the family, not the stranger; for stamping hooves, not the soft pad of motor tyres: but as you drive across the bridge, under the tower and into the courtyard, it is impossible not to sense something of the exhilaration with which generations of Bedingfelds have arrived home. One might expect to feel shut in by these great walls, towers and moat. But Oxburgh is an outward-looking house, for all its remoteness and seclusion. Its brick is so mellow, its external windows so numerous and large, its garden and surrounding countryside so friendly, that even the moat appears from within as nothing more formidable than an encircling lake.

The same impression is given by the interior of the tower, usually the grimmest part of a castellated mansion. There are only two main rooms within it, each occupying the full breadth and width of the first and second storeys, and known respectively as the King's Room and the Queen's Room ever since Henry VII's visit to Oxburgh in 1497. The word 'room' seems inadequate: one calls them instinctively 'chambers', for they have great dignity achieved by apparently artless means – plain whitewashed or mottle-brick walls, fireplaces with four-centred arches, window embrasures as large as small oratories formed from the turrets on both sides, high timber ceilings and floors covered most appropriately with mats of woven rush. The Queen's Room contains little furniture besides the bed, but the play of light on the walls and ribbed roofs of the octagonal chambers makes it an enchanting room just to stand in. The King's Room below is slightly more elaborate, and it holds Oxburgh's greatest single possession, the bed-hangings and coverlet embroidered by Mary Queen of Scots and Bess of Hardwick during the Queen's imprisonment. In these two rooms there is a lesson for the architect or decorator of any age. Their simple structural shapes, receding and advancing in three dimensions, now curved, now rectilinear, create a feeling of liveliness and welcome which could scarcely be bettered.

The staircase which links the two tower-rooms and rises to the leads is an astonishing feat of virtuosity. It is a tight spiral based on a geometrical design of such ingenuity that it is as difficult to discover exactly how it was done as it is for a shrimp inside a Nautilus shell to make out the secret of its convolutions. The only part of the staircase which is at rest are the flat treads: the soffit (underside) of the steps swings upwards, sweeping from concave to convex and back again with a smooth rolling motion that stands the bricks virtually on their heads and seems to presage imminent collapse: but it has stood the passage of five centuries. This is true of all the brickwork at Oxburgh. It has worn marvellously, even when exposed eighty foot up on the turret tops. The Norfolk bricklayers of 1480 have had no rivals since. To take a single example, the bricks forming the corners of the turrets have been cut by hand in five separate planes, none of them at right-angles, and the whole building must contain many hundreds of thousands of bricks shaped in this fashion.

Oxburgh retains its original ground-plan and main structure. But there have been many internal changes and one act of vandalism. In 1775 Sir Richard Bedingfeld pulled down the Tudor hall and Great Chamber opposite the gateway, and left the south side of the courtyard open to the moat. The gap was closed again in the nineteenth century by a passageway, and two low towers were raised at the south-west and south-east angles in the eighteenth and nineteenth centuries respectively. In about 1880 external corridors were added round the inside of the courtyard. These additions have not done as much damage to the appearance of the house as the loss of the Great Hall – though one would wish the corridors away – because the restorations of the last two centuries were usually carried out in a brick which fairly matched the Tudor originals. The dreadful consequences of using machine-made, mutton-red brick can be seen in the Victorian surrounds of some of the windows, and the design of them suggests that the Bedingfeld of the day threw at the west front every Tudor device that he could find in the architectural encyclopaedia. But nothing can dim the splendour of the old walls in which they are set, and nothing in the whole of architecture could be crisper than the fall of the angle-buttresses into the clear water of the moat.

Oxburgh survived, but only just. The staunch Catholic faith of the Bedingfelds led them into acts of desperate courage and acute distress. Three times the house was nearly abandoned for

The spiral staircase in the north-west turret of the great tower. The brickwork, which has remained untouched since the late fifteenth century, is an outstanding example of skilful construction

The Queen's Room on the upper floor of the tower. The simplicity of its construction and decoration has remained unaltered since the fifteenth century

scrap: once after the Civil War when it was left by Cromwell's soldiers ransacked and partly burning; again in the eighteenth century, when the family fortunes were drained to keep it in repair; and finally in our own times. In 1951 the heir to the property was forced by financial difficulties to sell the estate to a development company. It was the first time that Oxburgh had passed out of the hands of the Bedingfelds for five hundred years. Three months later the company put up the house for auction, and the only prospective buyer was a demolition firm that intended to pull it down. On the very morning of the sale, Lady Bedingfeld, who has lived here for sixty years, found the necessary money to buy it back. When the name of the purchaser was announced, the audience burst into spontaneous applause.

The King's Room on the central floor of the tower. According to tradition this was the room occupied by Henry VII when he visited Oxburgh in 1497. The four-poster bed is of seventeenth-century craftsmanship

opposite The main entrance to Oxburgh seen from the road between the piers of the gate, each surmounted by the Bedingfeld eagle

COMPTON WYNYATES

WARWICKSHIRE

A romantic manor-house of pink brick

The first and lasting impression of the house is its colour. An absence of twelve hours, or even a night spent within its walls, is enough to blur the memory of its startling appearance from outside, so that on returning the next morning it comes as a renewed surprise to find that something so old can glow so richly. It does not even need the sun to bring out the mottled raspberry of the brick. The bricks contain it. But not only the brick, for the stone tiles of the roof and the two half-timbered gables on the entrance side add a dash of grey and black which together with the surrounding trees and lawns turn the whole composition into a scattering of rose-petals in a glade. The second impression is of its situation. Cupped on all but one side in a tight circle of wooded hills, no great house is more deliberately lost in the flounces of the countryside. You only see it for the first time when you have approached within two or three hundred yards and a stab of colour suddenly pierces the canopy of leaves. But, though secluded, the house does not feel hemmed in. The water of the moat leads the eye northwards to the only gap in the hills (the 'wind-gate', which is one possible derivation of the name) over which stands, appropriately, a windmill; and the slopes of the valley have been flattened and terraced to form yew-filled gardens and grass walks which upholster the house on all sides.

The third impression is of its irregularity. This is not to say that the house is shapeless, for it is tightly knit on a roughly square plan, and there are no excrescences to spoil its compactness, vertically or horizontally. But it is not 'architected'. It grew new limbs as convenience demanded and the site made possible, and in no part of the house is there any attempt at symmetry. The gables are of unequal height and pitch, more than forty twisted chimneys settle inconsequently all over the roofs, turrets of different shapes and a curtain-wing were added on available ledges on the inner side of the former moat, and even the main east and west roofs were stepped higher behind than in front so that from a short distance one appears to extend the slope of the other. Compton Wynyates is in fact the most glorious of Tudor jumbles. It is as if little models of different parts of different buildings from all over the country had been assembled in this one place and blocked together to form a house. A knowledge

The deed made by Henry VIII in 1512 granting Sir William Compton the right to add the royal lion to the Compton arms

Sir William Compton, his wife and three children, from William Dugdale's *The Antiquities of Warwickshire*, 1765. This drawing was made from a window at Balliol College, Oxford, which was itself a copy of a window in the chapel at Compton Wynyates destroyed in the Civil War

Willielmus Compton miles, cum pia consorte sua, hanc fenestram vitari fecit, A. Dni. 1520.

opposite The north side of the house seen from across the surviving part of the moat. This part of Compton Wynyates has remained almost unchanged since Henry VII's time

The south front from a drawing made in 1771.
The farm buildings on the left were
demolished in 1855

The courtyard round which the house is built, with
the great bay window of the hall in the corner.
This window almost certainly came from Fulbroke
Castle near Warwick, material from which was
used in the embellishment of Compton Wynyates

of how it came to look like this, and of the events that happened
there, immeasurably increases its interest, but the immediate
impact made by the house is that here, obviously, is an expression of a native English style that had taken many hundreds of
years to mature and was as yet uninfected by the neo-classical
germ that was soon to sweep the country from Italy and France.

The Comptons, who climbed the social scale through knight-
hood, barony and earldom to the present Marquisate of Northampton, have lived on this site since the early thirteenth century.
The only certain trace of their first manor-house is the moat,
which encircled the present house until the mid-seventeenth
century. The position of the moat raises a problem. Today three
of its stunted arms lie round the garden to the north of the house,
and lawns fill the wide fosses by which it was once continued
round the entire rectangle in which Compton Wynyates lies.
Either the mediaeval house must have been almost double in
size to that which we see today; or the moat was extended to
include its garden; or the manor stood within the three existing
arms and the new house was built alongside it, the moat being
prolonged to include both the old site and the new; or the
original entrance was on the north side and outbuildings occupied the area of the present garden. Of the four possibilities the
last seems the most likely. But if the mediaeval entrance was on
the north front, this was one of the fundamental changes of plan
which Edmund Compton made when he decided to rebuild the

A view across the roof showing the stone tiles and dormer windows from the earliest period of the house. The fine octagonal chimneys were probably added by William Compton

below The entrance porch in the west front. Over the arch are the royal arms of England surmounted by a crown inscribed DOM REX HENRICUS OCTAV. Sir William Compton, son of Edmund Compton, the builder of the earliest part of the house, was a close friend of Henry VIII

manor during his ownership between 1481 and 1493. He switched the entrance and the outbuildings to the west, and enclosed the latter by another moat, perhaps dry, crossed by a second drawbridge. His home was therefore still patently a castle, and its fortification is the main argument for a late fifteenth-century date, of which no documentary evidence survives. The core of the present house, including the four wings around the internal courtyard and the Big Hall, was his; and we owe to him the extravagant choice of brick in a stone-country, and the grey roofs and the ceilings of carved timber which run round the north and west wings.

That it was a beautiful house as well as a strong one there can be no doubt. But Edmund's son, Sir William Compton, invested it with its present pageantry. It was he who built the chapel, the entrance porch and the towers at the four angles, and he who embellished the interior with bay-windows, stained glass and the roofing of the hall. He took some of his materials from Fulbroke Castle near Warwick, a decayed mansion dating from 1435, so that in effect he added an extra half-century to the date of his father's house. Later generations were equally solicitous of its Tudor character. In about 1730 the fifth Earl of Northampton added in the same general style a wing between the two corner towers on the east front, and over a hundred years later Sir Digby Wyatt was commissioned to Gothicise the Georgian windows and to build a new staircase. None of these

The south front seen from the hill above the late Victorian topiary garden, still known as the Best Garden. The large window in the centre is that of the chapel built in about 1515. Above the house stands the windmill, associated with the name 'wind-gate' or Wynyates

improvements have spoiled the Tudor work, while greatly adding to the convenience of the house. It remains in essentials the house which the two Comptons, father and son, built in thirty years of the reigns of Henry VII and Henry VIII.

They were a remarkable family. On Edmund's death in 1493 he left his eleven-year-old son a ward of the Crown, and the boy was appointed page to Prince Henry, aged two, later Henry VIII. The friendship between King and courtier was to last until William's early death in 1528. As companions-in-arms in war and tourneys, as master and emissary in diplomacy and politics, as constant partners in the hunting-field and banqueting-hall, their relationship is all the more remarkable for having been deepened by the passage of years instead of poisoned by it. King Henry knighted William Compton for gallantry in the Battle of Tournai (1512) and granted him the exceptional privilege of adding to his coat-of-arms the Royal Lion of England. The King stayed at Compton Wynyates on more than one occasion, as did Queen Elizabeth I, James I and Charles I, and it is next to certain that they all slept in the room still known as Henry VIII's Room, which includes their four monograms in the plasterwork of the ceiling. There is no place where the visitor can better savour the atmosphere of Compton Wynyates than in this room. For not only is this simple chamber in a comparatively modest house enriched by the memory of the four monarchs, but from its windows the inner courtyard is seen to its greatest advantage, ruddy with ageing brick, glinting with diamond panes and as peaceful as a college quadrangle.

But Compton was also the scene of battle. In the Civil War the second Earl of Northampton and his family were undivided in their loyalty to the Crown. The father and his three eldest sons (the fourth, aged thirteen, crying in indignation that he was not allowed to share the dangers with his brothers) fought in the Battle of Edgehill, six miles from the house, and the three youths were all knighted on the battlefield. The Earl was killed in the Battle of Hopton Heath in 1643 in the moment of victory, and when offered his life by the Roundheads, 'scorned to take quarter from such base rogues and rebels'. The six sons survived constant fighting until the Royalist cause was lost, but the house itself suffered. In 1644 Compton Wynyates was captured by the Roundheads after a two-day siege, and an attempt to recapture

Henry VIII's room, in which Elizabeth I, James I and Charles I also slept when they stayed at Compton Wynyates. The ceiling, dating from 1625, incorporates the monograms of all four monarchs

The Priest's Room, which owes its name to the five crosses roughly carved on the window-sill. The three staircases leading to it would have provided a choice of escape routes to a fugitive priest

it six months later was unsuccessful, perhaps because the Comptons, sallying out from Royalist Banbury, did not want to press home the attack to the point of utterly destroying the house which they loved so well. At the end of the war the family went into exile, and the moat was filled in by order of Parliament. The house was kept in sufficiently good repair during the two succeeding centuries for its main structure to have survived almost unimpaired. That the Northamptons lived mainly in their other house, Castle Ashby, saved Compton Wynyates, like Haddon Hall, from excessive modernization. When the sixth Marquess came to write the history of his family in 1929, he dated it from Castle Ashby, but entitled his book *History of the Comptons of Compton Wynyates*. As the Germans would say, it is Compton that they regard as their *Stammsitz*.

Nobody visiting the house could remain for long unaware of its strong sense of continuity. It is not only the scars of use and misuse which remind one of its past, the wearing of steps, paving-stones and banister-rails to which the present-day visitor innocently contributes by placing his foot and hand in exactly the same positions as came naturally to the occupants and soldiery of nearly five centuries; but the very structure of the place, which combined sturdiness with pride and elegance in a manner which we can admire but cannot imitate; and the peace which has descended on the house, a peace which its earlier owners neither sought nor found.

opposite The Big Hall looking across to the Minstrels' Gallery. The roof is fifteenth-century, imported from Fulbroke Castle in 1512. The linen-fold panelling of the screen dates from the time of Henry VIII

THE VYNE

HAMPSHIRE

A Tudor house transformed over three centuries

The name is of great antiquity. It occurs in a deed as early as 1268, and anyone who dares can take it further back to the *Vindomis* of the second-century Antonine Itinerary. This 'house-of-wine' could have been a private villa or an inn on the route from Winchester to Reading, and relics found in the garden support the theory of a Roman origin. The Vyne, however, does not need to draw on archaeology to confirm its reputation. It is a composition of the sixteenth, seventeenth and eighteenth centuries, of which each has contributed something of startling novelty for its time. That a house so gentle and apparently so traditional should have been the scene of architectural experiment comes as a surprise. That each period should blend so happily with the next is a tribute to the taste of the two families with which it will always be associated – the families of Sandys and Chute.

The house is basically Tudor. Its walls of rose-coloured brick, patterned unobtrusively with diamond diapering, proclaim it at once as a building of the early sixteenth century. It was built between 1500 and 1520 by the first Lord Sandys, Lord Chamberlain to Henry VIII, and he entertained his King there on three separate occasions. On the site, according to Leland, there had been a 'no very great or sumptuous manor place . . . and [Sandys] so translated it and augmented it that it became one of the most princely houses in goodly building in all Hampshire'. Nothing of the mediaeval house remains, unless Sandys used some of its materials, and when he came to build his own he adopted a style which owed little to any predecessor, except perhaps to the earliest period of Hampton Court. Because the Vyne was later associated with more famous men, Sandys has not always been given his due share of credit for this lovely building. But it was, for its age, revolutionary. The moat, which Leland mentions as surrounding the earlier house, was discarded. Tall windows were symmetrically arranged across both main fronts. The house faced outwards, with no internal courtyard. The hall did not occupy the whole width of the house, but only half of it, and it did not rise to the full height of the roof (though the point is still in dispute) but appears to have been ceilinged at first-floor level. At each corner, as eighteenth-century pictures show, stood a sturdy tower, rising an extra storey to give the

The north front seen from across the lake. The central portico, designed in 1654 by John Webb, was the first classical portico on an English country house

opposite One of a pair of stone eagles, given to John Chute by Horace Walpole, which flank the entrance. The brickwork is Tudor but the doorway was re-fashioned in 1654

The Tudor north front, dominated by the portico. On the left is the chapel with two blind windows added in the nineteenth century

building a rigidity and balance that one can describe without anachronism as architectural. Sandys extended its area by a 'faire base-court' (again Leland's phrase) which reached within a few yards of the present lake, and on the entrance front there was a forecourt, presumably with a gatehouse in its centre. Thus Sandys' inventiveness anticipated by fifty years or more an arrangement which became normal in the early years of Queen Elizabeth. The catalogue is still not concluded. He constructed one of the very first long galleries to be found in any English country-house. He broke up his main fronts and wings into small parlours and bedrooms, which on one Elizabethan occasion were able to accommodate the French ambassador and four hundred members of his suite. His only omissions were those for which he cannot be blamed: there were no sanitary arrangements except some primitive water channels; and there were no corridors. The first deficiency has been remedied, but so well was the house planned for convenience and comfort that none of his successors have found it necessary to make good the second.

That is still not all. Although Shakespeare in his *Henry VIII* puts into Sandys' mouth the self-deprecatory words 'I am an honest country Lord', he displayed in his house a quite remarkable flair for the work of contemporary foreign artists. One can attribute it partly to his proximity to the King, than whom few English monarchs have been less insular in their tastes, and partly to his long sojourns abroad in the King's service. At the Vyne there are four outstanding examples of such work, executed either by foreigners directly or by Englishmen working under Continental influence. Three of them are in the chapel: the stained glass is Flemish, probably imported direct from Liége; the lovely choir-stalls, Gothic in conception, incorporate lively Renaissance motifs; and the encaustic tiles are attributed by Bernard Rackham to the Antwerp workshop of Guido de Savino from Urbino. The fourth example is in the Oak Gallery. As a room it can be rather disappointing for one of the most

A detail of the panelling in the Oak Gallery dating from about 1520, with the royal arms over the door. The ragged cross, the badge of the Sandys family, and other devices are repeated frequently in the linen-fold panelling

opposite The Further Drawing Room, the first of a series of rooms on the north side of the house, decorated by John Chute and hung with red damask bought in Italy in 1760

47

The head of the classical effigy of Speaker Chaloner Chute, commissioned by John Chute for the neo-Gothic tomb chamber

A corner of the chapel parlour dating back to the original Tudor house. The linen-fold panelling is hung with Tudor portraits

famous rooms in Britain, since its great length is not balanced by window-bays of compensating depth and its single fireplace is not enough to break the monotony of the opposite wall. But one's attention is immediately caught by the four rows of linenfold panelling, extending from floor to ceiling along each side, making some four hundred panels in all. They are ornamented with the badges, crests or initials of the King, Sandys himself, his relations and his friends, with a joyful fecundity of invention unparalleled in any other wainscoting in the country. Unfortunately the panels were overpainted at some period in a warm chocolate-brown, and it has been found too dangerous to the woodwork and too expensive to remove it. The crispness of the carving is only slightly smudged by this outrage. It is English work and English in feeling: but one panel above a side-door departs from the general style of the remainder to illustrate two *putti* supporting the Royal Arms – a device so free and enchanting, so remarkable a break with Gothic tradition, that one begins to wonder whether one has strayed into the wrong country in the wrong half of the century.

William Sandys died in 1540, leaving behind him a beautiful house that none of his descendants wished to alter. It was sold by the sixth Lord Sandys in 1653 to Chaloner Chute, Speaker of the House of Commons during the Commonwealth. Chute's name has suffered an undeserved eclipse. The tributes paid to him on his early death in 1659 leave no doubt that he was regarded by contemporaries as one of the most outstanding men of his age, and that his personal charm and integrity acted as political stabilisers in a period of exceptional unrest. He made several important alterations to the Vyne. He swept away the courtyards, back and front. He replaced the mullioned windows by others in rectangular stone frames. And he commissioned John Webb, the disciple of Inigo Jones, to erect a Corinthian portico against the north front. It was a bold innovation, the first portico of its kind to be added to a private house. Seen from across the lake, it seems to stamp the house as Palladian, but it was erected nearly fifty years before Lord Burlington was born. Its cleanliness of line is slightly spoiled by abrupt side-openings, which are rectangular and bricked instead of arched and plastered, and it is tempting to suppose that the portico was never quite finished as Webb intended. In contrast, the lovely little garden-house or pigeon-loft in the form of a Greek cross with a central dome, also by Webb, is a perfect seventeenth-century pavilion that links the Tudor phase of the house to its second transformation a hundred years later.

The Speaker's descendant was John Chute, the friend of Horace Walpole. That he should be thus remembered, and not Walpole as Chute's friend, is due to the richness of Walpole's literary testament and the fact that he was born the son of a Prime Minister. For, of the two, Chute was the greater innovator. Walpole himself admitted it. He wrote to Horace Mann in 1747, 'If I were to say all I think of Chute's immense honesty, his sense, his worth, his knowledge and his humanity, you would think that I was writing a dedication.' For thirty-two years Chute had lived abroad, mostly in Italy, and only inherited the Vyne unexpectedly in 1754, when the last of his many brothers died childless. The house could not have fallen into more fitting hands. He respected the work of Sandys, but only on second or third thoughts, for he was an architect of the Strawberry Hill school – indeed, after Walpole, its leader – and he chose to have himself painted with an elevation in his hand for the Gothicising of the entire exterior. As it was, Chute and Walpole between them (with what irreverent jocularity their correspondence reveals) Strawberried only one room, the Ante-Chapel, and with its tawdry fretwork and dull colouring it cannot be counted a success. But for his major alteration Chute switched to a style of classical purity. He constructed an ice-cool staircase rising from just inside the front door in a series of columned galleries. The whole is evident at a glance, but the ingenuity of its different levels and openings, all contrived within a minimal space, make it, as Walpole himself observed, 'theatrical' and almost playful. Never was simplicity developed with so dramatic a touch. It would make an ideal setting for a children's charade, but at the same time it has grace and importance, and from no angle – and every angle was carefully considered – do its rosettes and pretty columns degenerate into frivolity.

In the series of living-rooms on the ground floor Chute was content with a more reposeful habitableness. His red damask, bought in Italy in about 1760, created a neutral background to the Strawberry Committee's endless conversations, and fortunately they did not tamper with Sandys' Chapel Parlour with its soothing linenfold and Tudor portraits, which is still the most pleasant room in the house. But Chute did add to the chapel itself a 'Tomb Chamber' to the memory of his ancestor, the Speaker. In it he placed a recumbent effigy of such indolent grace that the Speaker might be reclining in a hayfield instead of on a cenotaph constructed a hundred years after his death. That the sculptor of this superb figure is still in doubt – Thomas Bankes, say some; Thomas Carter, say others – is not untypical of the Vyne, but whichever it turns out to be will have established an undying reputation by this single work.

There is no need to go beyond John Chute's death in 1776 to describe the Vyne as it appears today. All that was most worthwhile had been done by then, and nothing that was still to come did much damage. The Chutes were not as progenitive as they were imaginative, and the house slipped sideways through cousins and nephews to keep the Chute name alive until 1956, when Sir Charles Chute bequeathed the house, its contents and the estate to the National Trust. It is still one of the most perfect of English houses. In spite of its size and richness it has a certain modesty of character, which is the product of linenfold, tapestry, coloured glass, Chippendale, portraits, flowers and a sound roof on wide brick walls.

The classical staircase and hall built by John Chute to replace the Tudor stone hall. The series of galleries flanked by Corinthian columns are an amazing achievement in the confined space available

The ante-chapel, redecorated in the Strawberry Hill style under the influence of Horace Walpole. The door leads through into the chapel

SPEKE HALL

LANCASHIRE

An Elizabethan black-and-white manor house

Lancashire, on the whole, has been unkind to its old buildings. It therefore comes as an agreeable surprise to discover within the boundaries of Liverpool one of the finest of half-timbered Elizabethan manor-houses. Speke Hall lies on the outskirts of the city in sound, if not in sight, of the airport, but its privacy is protected on one side by a vast elbow of the River Mersey and on the others by gardens and the remains of a park. It is a house without a view, even of the river. The same flatness of its site prevents it from being seen from more than a couple of hundred yards away. It could have been completely forgotten except by antiquarians were it not for the chance that it passed into the ownership of the National Trust in 1942 and the guardianship of Liverpool Corporation. Forty thousand people visit it in a year, among them parties of school-children who could not wish for a better window into the life of the Elizabethan age.

Speke is a 'black-and-white' house. The black is formed by its external timbers, the white by the plaster panels between them. The black is very black indeed, being darkened by pitch to protect the oak from damp, and the white is heightened by contrast with it. If this were all, if Speke were nothing more than a checkerboard, it would appear strident. But the closer you look at its eight façades (for it has an internal courtyard to double the number of exposed fronts), the greater variety of treatment you find. Structurally Speke's framework consists in uprights and horizontals, and the rectangles so formed are subdivided by sloping timbers and fretted panels into zebra patterns, diamonds and four-leaf clovers (quatrefoils). Scarcely two adjoining segments are quite the same, and none is quite balanced by another in symmetrical relationship to it. The effect stops short of jazziness; it is more like the camouflage applied to battleships in the first world war. Apart from the variety of the patterning, there is also a constant change of outline – gables big and small, windows hanging by their eyebrows from the eaves or in long wavy lines of mullioned lights, chimneys all over the place, queer finials like the swords of sword-fish, and suddenly a grinning face under an intricately carved bargeboard. The only consistent lines are the moat, now dry, which contains the house in a firmly defined square; and the roof,

Looking outwards from the passage behind the Great Hall into the garden. The archway bears the date 1605 and was one of the last structures to be added to the house

opposite The north-east corner of the courtyard round which the hall is built, illustrating the intricate patterns of black timbering and white quatrefoil panels

SPEKE HALL

The north or entrance front approached by the sixteenth-century bridge over the moat, which has now been drained. An inscription under the window over the entrance records that this wing was built by Edward Norreys in 1598

sitting solidly on its soft body like the shell on a turtle.

The other feature which gives it shape is the internal courtyard. This is by no means so regular as it first appears, but it provides a cool, still centre for the motley buildings around it. The two yews, which are said to have been planted contemporaneously with the earliest surviving parts of the house, have grown to a size that puts the courtyard literally in the shade. Their very antiquity excuses their selfish theft of light, and some visitors even welcome it, feeling the need for a dark mass to tone down the kaleidoscopic pattern of the walls. Any courtyard of this dimension, open or shaded, adds to the seclusion of a house, providing intimate vistas across it from the upper windows and

removing the main rooms one stage further from the outside world. Speke Hall is not a fortified house – its moat was intended for privacy, not defence – and its inward-looking character is more like that of a monastery, college or inn than of a castle. A modern draught-excluding screen divides the entrance from the court, but until quite recent times you could drive a carriage directly across the bridge into the heart of the house. To descend in a courtyard rather than in a simple forecourt is a pleasure which architects seldom have the opportunity to afford us today, but though the intention was probably not hospitable, the effect certainly is. Without its courtyard Speke Hall would lose half its charm.

The present plan of the house looks so inevitable and its building so much of a piece that one could be forgiven for imagining that a single man built it within the space of a few years. In fact it grew over a period of more than a century. First came the late-mediaeval hall on the side furthest from the entrance, built by Sir William Norreys in about 1490 on the site of his family's manor-house, now represented only by the moat and a deep window in the kitchen. In the middle of the sixteenth century his grandson, another Sir William, added the Great Parlour at one end of the hall, and then the east and west wings to accommodate his family of nineteen children. On William's death in 1568 the house was therefore open on the north side to the entrance bridge, and his son, Edward Norreys, closed it by building the north wing. Above the archway he set his inscription: 'This worke, 25 yds long, was wholly built by Edw:N:Esq: ano 1598.' Apart from two big bay-windows in the hall and parlour, no later additions were made to Speke Hall.

It is an astonishing record of fidelity to a single theme. For although the first Sir William may not even have imagined his manor-house to be capable of such expansion, he would not have been dismayed by the finished result. In deference to his taste if not his expressed will, his successors built as he would have built himself. The later parts of the house reveal a conscious imitation of the earlier – the quatrefoils, for example, which were a Tudor, not Renaissance, device, and the refusal to adopt a symmetrical arrangement of doors and windows which had become the mark of a gentleman in the second half of the sixteenth century. It is only here and there that one can observe signs that times had changed. There is a grouping of Ionic pillars in the hall, and chunky ornaments like those on the garden-wall at Hardwick deck the parapet of the bridge. But even here there are Gothic jokes: a stone ball on the bridge has been roughly carved with the features of a smirking publican or friar; and an extraordinary device with mirrors was built into the wall of one of the bedrooms, so that the occupant could watch from his bed the approach of friends or strangers to the front door.

If the exterior was consistent, even anachronistic in parts, the interior was designed for comfort. The old hall was equipped with two splendid fireplaces and with a screen, while the Great

The fireplace in the Great Hall with its huge oak mantelbeam decorated with vine and cable carving

The northern bay of the Great Hall, added in about 1530, with windows containing ancient heraldic and ecclesiastical stained glass. The portrait is of a local giant nine foot six inches tall

left The seventeenth-century four-poster bed in the state bedroom. The tradition is that Charles I slept in this room in 1630

The centre panel of the overmantel in the Great Parlour showing Sir William Norreys (1524–68) with his two wives and below them his children

The garden front, built between 1490 and 1550, with the Great Hall in its centre. The irregularity of the elevations, with no two gables alike, contrasts with the firm squareness of the ground-plan

Parlour is a room that could be used as the main reception room of any house. Upstairs there are bedrooms of considerable refinement, and, like the downstairs rooms on two sides of the courtyard, they are linked by lovely corridors, a remarkable innovation for the period. Speke lacks a long gallery, although one could easily have been fitted in at roof level, and, instead, there are all sorts of annexes approached by secret doors in the wainscoting – an eavesdropping chamber, for example, from which every word spoken in the hall can be overheard, and hideaways with escape routes through the roof and walls, which may have been intended for serious use in time of trouble, for the Norreys family was Catholic, but might equally have been due to nothing but playfulness. The character of the Norreys family speaks through their buildings. They had a great sense of tradition combined with inventive audacity and complete indifference to fashion. The house cannot be described as a work of architecture since it is almost shapeless: but to deny it quality would be as absurd as to call Chaucer clumsy because he was sometimes ungrammatical.

The story of the house does not end with the last period of its construction in the 1620's. The Norreys family died out a hundred years later, and the estate passed by marriage to Sir Sidney Beauclerk. He and his worthless son, a friend of Johnson and Reynolds, treated the place abominably. They rented it to a series of farmers, who stabled their cattle in the hall, cut up the tapestries for horsecloths and burned the floor-boards for firewood. A rescuer came from the most unexpected quarter. In 1797 the Beauclerks sold the property to Richard Watt, a Liverpool merchant who had made a fortune in the West Indies. He spent much of it on repairing the havoc done to the house, and by the time of his death in 1812, it was not only habitable but refurnished by Watt with heavy oak furniture that is not at all ill-suited to the rooms. A curious catalogue is preserved in the Liverpool Public Library announcing the sale of the furniture on Watt's death: 'It is quite new and but just finished in very good taste, and never has been used.' It seems to have found no purchasers, for Watt's descendants continued to live at Speke Hall until 1921, and the house still contains what he collected.

CRATHES CASTLE

KINCARDINESHIRE

A sturdy Scottish tower set in a beautiful garden

This type of domesticated tower, of which Crathes is a splendid example, occurs nowhere else but in Scotland. You find them hidden in a belt of trees, at a junction between river and loch, or standing bluntly in an open field. They are grey or whitish in colour, roughly plastered in a manner that the Scots call 'harled', and often later buildings have been added to them, just as the northern English would extend their pele-towers by a Jacobean mansion once the border troubles had died down. But originally the Scottish towers were self-contained little fortresses, not designed to resist serious siege, but strong enough to deter marauding Highland bands. There were no fortified outworks, except perhaps a stockade for the cattle, and never a moat. The towers rose as squat as pillars, with a heavily barred door on the ground floor and nothing but slit windows as high up as any assailants could reach.

On the upper floors, like a captain's cabin on the higher decks of a man-of-war, the house proper began. Here more light could safely be let in, and the rooms became bigger. Externally, the almost blank walls sprouted turrets and dormer windows, corbels and weird decorative features, so that the finished tower resembled a stout post that has unexpectedly broken into leaf. They are not very beautiful, since their builders did not think in aesthetic terms and when they added their upper works they built as fancy or convenience dictated, and knew or cared nothing of symmetry. But they have an undoubted grandeur and even nobility. They are honest buildings. They reflect a harsh way of life. They are relics of one of the most difficult periods of history for us to visualise, since nobody can quite know to what extent the toughness of Scotland before the union of its crown with England's dominated its people's lives. Crathes is one clue. It illustrates better than any comparable building the way in which a laird of the sixteenth century chose to live.

Crathes, though not a large house, took over forty years to build, 1553 to 1595. It was begun by an Alexander Burnett and finished by another of the same name, his great-grandson. The family had been established in that part of Deeside since the fourteenth century, when Robert Bruce gave them rights in the royal forest and a jewelled ivory horn, still preserved in the castle

Looking towards the castle from the garden. Towers, turrets, dormers and machicolations make the skyline of Crathes intensely dramatic. The 'cannon' below some of the windows are made from solid stone and are purely decorative

opposite The figures of Alexander Burnett, twelfth Laird, and his wife Katherine Gordon, together with their intertwined monogram, carved on the head of the late sixteenth-century four-poster bed in the laird's bedroom

Crathes seen from its famous garden. On the
right is the Queen Anne wing added during the
early eighteenth century

as a family talisman, which was the symbol of their tenure. Their
first home had been a gaunt castle on a neighbouring loch-
island, for which almost any exchange would have been an improvement. When they began to build Crathes, they were a
family well-known in the district but of minor distinction, and
they built big enough to assert their status, but modestly enough
not to attract undue attention. When the tower was finished,
the Burnetts abandoned their island home and moved in. For
over a hundred years virtually no changes were made to the
house, and when the Burnetts of the early eighteenth century at
last decided that slightly more elegant and comfortable apartments were required, they added a wing without tampering with
the sixteenth-century tower. The wing is a pleasant enough
Queen Anne building adapted to the Scottish vernacular style,
but it has no special pretensions. What matters is the tower.

This sturdy pile has lost some of its exterior austerity from
being surrounded by a lovely park above the Dee, and graced by
a garden on the south side which has been developed gradually
since the eighteenth century into one of the horticultural wonders of the north. The entrance is as formidable as one would
expect. The outer door is a nail-studded bastion of timber; the
inner a trellis of interwoven ironwork that a tank could not
wrench from its hinges. Stone machicolations are poised high
above to deluge the unwelcome visitor in molten lead. Around
the door are coats-of-arms embedded in the stonework as hap-
hazardly as an incomplete page in a stamp-album. Once inside
the door, you are confronted by a spiral stone staircase which
winds upwards without any preliminary hallway. To the right
there is access to vaulted kitchens and a windowless dungeon.
Then, gradually, as you mount inside the house, the grimness
lessens. You find that this is a family's home, not a garrison's
quarters. The room on the first floor, filling almost its entire
extent, is a baronial hall with a vaulted ceiling of roughly mor-
tared granite blocks, and deep windows pierced slitwise through
six-foot-thick walls. The hall has been made more comfortable
by the addition of a large eighteenth-century window at one
end, further widened in the nineteenth, and an Elizabethan
fireplace; but it has been rendered bleaker by the loss of its
original plaster ceiling, painted in gaudy colours. It is possible
to imagine oneself passing a pleasant evening in this room, but
one would need to be of a romantic disposition and well fortified
against the draughts and ghosts. A Green Lady, with a baby in
her arms, is supposed to haunt a neighbouring room.

On the top floor is the pride of Crathes, and indeed the finest
room of its age and type in the whole of Scotland. This is the long
gallery, running the full width of the house like a suspended ark.
Judged by contemporary English standards it is a simple room,
and the oak panelling of its ceiling is more ingenious than elegant; but it is remarkable that it should have been attempted at
all in a house that still put most of its emphasis on defence. But
elsewhere, too, a native awkwardness in design is balanced by a

The Great Hall on the first floor of the tower.
The vaulted ceiling was once plastered and
painted, but is now bare to the granite. In the
case over the mantelpiece hangs the Horn of Leys,
a horn of tenure, given to Alexander Burnett in
1323 by Robert Bruce with the lands of Crathes

quite deliberate effort at adornment. The ceilings of some of the
lesser rooms are painted with bold representations of Virtues
and heroic immortals, accompanied by appropriate verses, part
patriotic, part moral, painted along the ceiling joists. Charlemagne, for instance, is honoured in these lines:

> A league wit Scottis of mutual amitie,
> This Charlis maid to last eternalie
> Whais successors obseruis the same alway,
> Inuiolat untio this present day.

This distortion of history, inscribed in 1602, the year before
James VI of Scotland became James I of England, strikes a
delightfully archaic note. In fact, the Burnetts were ready to

The heavy entrance door and the inner iron
grating door, recently transferred to the outside

The Green Lady's Room with its fine ceiling painted in tempera.

below A detail of the painted ceiling (1602) in the Chamber of the Nine Nobles, showing the figures of Joshua, David and Charlemagne

Photo 'Country Life'

take full advantage of the union of the two Crowns. Within a few years, the laird of Crathes was to become a Baronet: his younger brother became Lord Crimond; the latter's son was Gilbert Burnett, the celebrated Bishop of Salisbury; and Gilbert's son William emigrated to America and became in turn Governor of New York and New Jersey, Governor of Massachusetts and Governor of New Hampshire.

The house, like the family, blossomed unexpectedly. At one moment you find yourself peering down sinister slits in the masonry or entering small shapeless chambers that boded no good for their occupants; at the next you find dignity and even comfort in the well-tooled furniture or wide window-seats. It is a house in transition, a family on the eve of greatness. What is more surprising is that they were willing to inhabit it unchanged for another hundred years. How did their smart ladies descend those spiral stairs in full skirts? How did they tolerate the inconvenience of a house built in a tower, or endure for so long the darkness of the rooms? That they did so out of family pride or mere habit is our gain. Crathes remains one of the most spectacular architectural conceptions in Scotland, and one of the least spoiled.

opposite The Long Gallery which runs the whole length of the top of the castle from east to west. The oak panelled ceiling is unique in Scotland

Photo 'Country Life'

LONGLEAT HOUSE

WILTSHIRE

The most classical house of the English Renaissance

Sir John Thynne, builder of Longleat, a portrait painted in 1560. A man of domineering disposition, he had the taste, knowledge and audacity to build the first classical house in England

opposite The south drive leading directly to the entrance front, seen through Wyatville's gateway constructed in 1810

The first sight of the house is from a mile away and several hundred feet above it. The approach drive from the Warminster road swings through parkland to the crest of a wooded hill, and then suddenly, through columns of grey trees, you see the house standing on a plateau of closely cropped grass, and below it, a chain of lakes formed from the long *leat* or watercourse which gave the house its name. The park surrounds it in silence. On all but one side the hills create a bowl in which the house rests, but the undulations of the countryside are so harmonious, so artfully furnished with trees, bridges and avenues, with no walls or hedges to divide road from grass, grass from woods, that one can be forgiven for describing Longleat first in terms of its setting.

It comes as no surprise to learn that we owe it to Lancelot Brown, whose reputation had reached its zenith when Lord Weymouth commissioned him in 1757 to remodel the park. Brown swept away the elaborate gardens seen in the Kip engravings, and created the woodlands, lakes and vistas over the apparently natural countryside. Already by 1760 Mrs Delaney could write ecstatically: 'We got to Longleat! There is not much alteration in the house, but the gardens are no more! They are succeeded by a fine lawn, a serpentine river, wooded hills, gravel paths meandering round a shrubbery, all modernized by the ingenious and much sought-after Mr Brown!' Not everyone shared Mrs Delaney's enthusiasm. Lord Weymouth was criticised for doing away with the *parterres* and clipped alleys of his ancestors, and Longleat was often quoted as the most glaring example of Brown's 'vandalism'. But in its present maturity, the landscaping of the park is seen as a work of art complementary to the house itself.

The builder of Longleat was Sir John Thynne, a faithful adjutant in war and peace of the Lord Protector, Duke of Somerset, by whom he was knighted on the battlefield of Pinkie (1547) while his wounds were still bleeding. Somerset was executed in 1552, and Thynne shared in his master's disgrace to the extent of spending two years in the Tower of London and paying a £6,000 fine. On his release he returned to his Wiltshire estates and until his death in 1580 applied himself almost exclusively to the building of his house. A contemporary portrait of him at the

age of fifty-one leaves only one aspect of his character unexplained. Hand on sword-hilt, his stance proud and aggressive, his glance betraying the hot temper with which he ruled his army of workmen, one would scarcely have guessed that this was the man who created the most perfectly classical house of the early English Renaissance. From whom did he obtain his knowledge, his taste, his eye for foreign detail? Part of it could have come from the Lord Protector, who reconstructed Syon and built Somerset House, which incorporated much French ornamentation. Two Frenchmen, Allen Maynard and Adrian Gaunt, and the Englishmen Robert Smythson and William Spicer, later Surveyor of the Queen's Works, are known to have been employed at Longleat for long periods at a time, and they must have contributed their own ideas. But the records still preserved in the house make it quite clear that Sir John Thynne was not only the driving force, but was capable of conceiving startling architectural innovations. For instance, he wrote to Spicer in 1557, 'All stairs are to ryse above the house and are to be tiped [? given tops]; four to have little stairs wonne from the roof so they may serve as banketting houses.' What he meant by the last phrase is not at all clear, for there is scarcely room in these domed turrets for a dolls' tea-party, let alone a banquet, but in this brief note there is sufficient evidence to attribute to Sir John himself one of the most original and effective features of the house, and he carried it through to completion with typical audacity and persistence.

The huge cube of Longleat, like so many other houses of this date including Syon, was raised on the site of an earlier priory. One of the two inner courts may rest upon the foundations of the monastic cloister, for several coffins of the Black Canons were discovered here during reconstructions of the early nineteenth century. But if one excepts the Great Hall, there is nothing mediaeval about the house itself. The exterior was composed of symmetrical units of Elizabethan windows forming bold bays and recesses on a scale that only Lord Burghley was attempting elsewhere. The proportions of the façades would be strong rather than graceful were it not for the incorporation of Italianate motifs of astonishing maturity for so early a period. The three classical orders, Doric below, Ionic in the middle and Corinthian at the level of the top storey, were superimposed between the windows across the whole width of each façade. Below the windows were set circular recesses for busts of Roman emperors. Thick cornices were sandwiched between the floors, and a balustrade runs the whole length of the flat roof, crowned most effectively since 1685 by four baroque statues. In 1575 the house had been erected as far as the top of the second storey, by which time construction had been in progress for at least twelve years, interrupted by a fire in 1567 which was not brought under control for four hours. The top storey may have been added after 1580 by Sir John's son, for there is no mention of a Corinthian order in the records, only of 'Dorrick and Yonk', the

A view through some of the ornamental stonework on the roof, typical of Thynne's daring originality

A sketch by Sir John Thynne of the plan of the ground floor of Longleat which he sent to Lord Burghley for his comments. It is still preserved at Hatfield

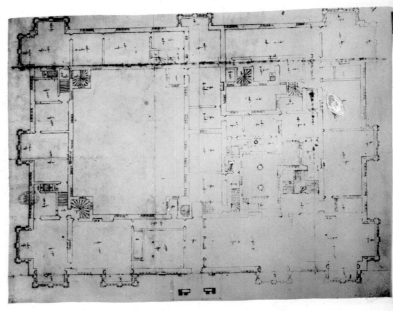

opposite Longleat in 1676, a painting by Jan Siberechts. The entrance front has remained virtually unchanged, but the forecourt has been destroyed and the stables to the left were replaced by Wyatville's huge block behind *below* Approximately the same view photographed today

65

master-mason's approximation to Doric and Ionic, which he described in stone better than in his spelling.

The second great innovation of Longleat was its plan. Hitherto, houses had been built either to the E-plan, the two wings and the porch forming the horizontal strokes of the E, or to the courtyard plan, with the main rooms facing inwards. Sir John Thynne's house has two inner courtyards, but they are light-wells more than architectural features in their own right, and every main room looks outwards to the park. The original floor-plans, which Sir John sent to Lord Burghley for his comments, show that the north side of the house was closed only by a wall. Conceivably this wing was destroyed by the 1567 fire before it was completed, or its building was prevented by Sir John's death. But in the early nineteenth century Wyatville added on the fourth side a careful imitation of the other three fronts, thus completing what was probably Thynne's original intention.

Unfortunately it is not possible to visualise the appearance of the interior in the sixteenth century, since in three separate bursts of energy and affluence, the successive Lords Weymouth (the Thynnes acquired the title in the reign of Charles II) totally transformed the internal structure of the house and the decoration of the rooms. Apart from the hall and cellars none of them contain any original Elizabethan features. Even in the maids' bedrooms the old fireplaces were ripped out and replaced. It is almost equally sad that the seventeenth and eighteenth-century renovations should have gone the same way as the Elizabethan. Only one great room survives from that period – Bishop Ken's library on the top floor. Thomas Ken (1637–1711), Bishop of Bath and Wells, was befriended by the first Viscount Weymouth after falling foul of James II and William and Mary, and was given this room in which to house his fine collection of books and live a life of study and contemplation. Bishop Ken's Library, as it is still called, runs the whole length of the east front. It is shaped like a long Elizabethan gallery, but beautifully modified by projecting bays filled with leather-bound books, globes, pictures and early scientific instruments.

Between 1801 and 1811, Thomas Thynne, second Marquess of Bath, employed Sir Jeffrey Wyatville to remodel the interior once again. At exactly the same time his uncle James Wyatt was performing the same service for Wilton, and both nephew and uncle made use of the identical technique of attaching corridors to all four sides of the inner courtyard to provide better access from room to room. At Wilton it was more skilfully done than at Longleat, for Wyatt made charming cloisters of his corridors, while Wyatville seems to have been quite unconcerned by their bleak appearance seen across the courtyard. He further added a huge central staircase to replace an earlier one attributed to Wren. But in compensation, he was responsible for two excellent features at Longleat, the north wing already mentioned, and the stable block which reproduces the spirit of the Elizabethan building so faithfully.

One of the domed turrets containing the top of a spiral staircase, set among the decorated round chimneys and sculptured figures on the roof

opposite top An engraving by Kip of Longleat in 1690 showing the formal gardens demolished by Capability Brown in the mid-eighteenth century, when the gardens were re-landscaped

opposite bottom An air view of Longleat looking towards the entrance front. The orangery and formal garden are behind and Wyatville's stable block on the left. On the right is the site of the great parterre swept away by Capability Brown

Finally, in 1860, the fourth Marquess, on his return from the Grand Tour, imported to Longleat a team of Italian craftsmen who italianised the state-rooms beyond recognition. The workmanship is of superb quality, but its richness in no way compensates for the loss of the gentler native idiom which it replaced. When one recalls that Sir John Tynne employed at Longleat a 'connynge plasterer' whose work was so excellent that Sir William Cavendish enquired whether he might borrow him for Chatsworth (a request that was probably granted), one snaps one's fingers in irritation at the careful ceiling panels ('after Veronese') and gilded cornices of the Italians. Nevertheless, nobody could deny these rooms magnificence, and they are filled with works of art and family portraits of high quality. In several of them, particularly the Saloon, the proportions are the same as those of Sir John Thynne's original house, and for that reason alone they can give the visitor great pleasure.

Longleat under the care of the present Lord Bath has become one of the most visited houses in the country. Even if it were closed and empty, its incomparable setting and the beauty of its four palatial façades would still place it among the chief architectural glories of England. But Longleat is not a shell. Part of it is still lived in by Lord Weymouth, Lord Bath's son, and the grandest rooms are open daily to the public. In other corners there are hidden reserves, among them Bishop Ken's library, in which this description of the house was written.

The saloon, once the Elizabethan long gallery, which was completely re-designed in the 1860s. The tapestries are sixteenth-century Flemish

opposite A detail of the mantelpiece in the Great Hall. This probably dates from the late sixteenth century, and its vigorous English sculpture contrasts strongly with the Italianate decoration of the exterior of the house

The Great Hall, the least changed part of the Elizabethan house, looking towards the Minstrels' Gallery. The original hammer beam roof was closed in about 1700 by the present flat ceiling, and the hunting scenes were painted by Wootton

The gable of the south front, built by
Lawrence Washington in 1560. The arms of
Queen Elizabeth I are supported by a lion
crowned and a dragon, with the initials ER
above them

SULGRAVE MANOR

NORTHAMPTONSHIRE

The Elizabethan home of the Washington family

This manor-house was already much dilapidated by the end of the eighteenth century, and it was only because of the sturdiness of its construction that it was still standing as a common farm-house a hundred years later. Why then does it merit inclusion in a book about the great houses of Britain? There are three reasons. It is an excellent example of the smaller houses of the sixteenth century, extended in the eighteenth; it has been restored and furnished since 1914 with more taste and skill than can have been applied to any comparable building in the country; and it was built and inhabited by the direct ancestors of George Washington, the first President of the United States.

Sulgrave, moreover, is a very charming house. It is separated from the surrounding farmlands and village by a garden which is partly based on Elizabethan patterns but is planted with many shrubs and flowers that the Elizabethans never knew. The grey limestone of its walls and stone-tiled roof set it apart from the humbler thatched cottages of its estate without saddling it with an arrogance to which its builders never aspired. Its rooms reflect in miniature the best of two centuries of the English domestic arts. To the student of architecture it is a text-book of early methods of house-construction. To the historian it is a symbol of the past which the English share with the Americans. And, as if this were not enough, Sulgrave is a perfect illustration of how a house should be shown to the public. Scarcely a guard-rope, a notice or a drugget carpet mars the interior, and in their place we have bowls of beautifully-arranged flowers, chairs that could be sat upon and beds that could be slept in but are not, a kitchen fit to serve a banquet, and an absence of fuss that is a standing lesson to every decorator and housewife.

General George Washington was not particularly interested in his English ancestry, and he had never heard of Sulgrave. But he recorded a family tradition that 'they came from the north of England'. He was right. The Washingtons stemmed from Washington, originally Wessington, a village in County Durham, where they were to be found at the end of the twelfth century, and it is this village that ultimately gave its name to the capital of the western world. From there they moved to Lancashire in the early fourteenth century. The builder of

The arms of the Washington family in the right-hand spandrel of the doorway of the south porch. This theme of stars and stripes is supposed to have been the inspiration of the national flag of the United States

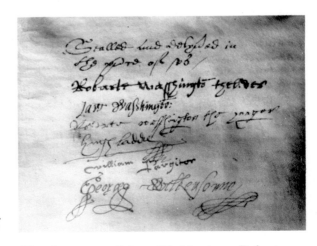

The signatures of three Washingtons: Robert Washington the Elder, Lawrence Washington, and Robert Washington the Younger, on a deed of 1606

The south front. The porch and the wing to the right of it are all that remain of Lawrence Washington's original house. They contain the Great Hall on the ground floor and the Great Chamber above it. The left-hand wing was rebuilt in the 1920s when Sulgrave had been acquired as an Anglo-American memorial to the Washington family

Sulgrave Manor, Lawrence Washington, migrated to North-amptonshire in about 1530 and made a small fortune as a wool-merchant in London and Northampton (of which he was twice Mayor) and later as a member of a sheep-raising partnership in the neighbourhood of Sulgrave. He was wealthy enough to buy the manor from the Crown in 1539 on the dissolution of the Priory of St Andrew at Northampton, to which it had belonged from at least the time of Henry I. He built the present house soon afterwards and completed it in about 1560. His son Robert added to it sufficient rooms to house his fifteen children by two successive wives. The house was sold to Robert's nephew, Lawrence Makepeace in 1610, and it again passed by sale from the Makepeaces to the Plants in 1659, and from the Plants to the Hodges in 1673.

top right The east front. The wing to the right was added in 1700, but the outlines of a fireplace and the beams visible on the gable-end prove that the original Elizabethan house once extended over the rose-garden in the foreground

bottom right The north front, with the Queen Anne wing on the left, forming a small courtyard. The central door leads to the Great Hall

The descent of the house is complicated, and need not concern us in detail; but the Washington line is quite clear. Colonel John Washington, a great-great-grandson of Lawrence, the builder of Sulgrave, emigrated to Virginia for business reasons in 1656, and he was the great-grandfather of the President, who was born in 1732. Thus George Washington was the direct descendant in the seventh generation of the Lawrence who built the house. In the late nineteenth century the tenant-farmer of Sulgrave would point out a Victorian bedstead in the Great Chamber as the bed in which the President was born. His pocket may have benefited more from the fiction than his reputation. But the connection is there all the same.

Compact though the manor is in its setting and general style, it is only partly the house which Lawrence built, but the part

73

The Great Hall on the ground floor of the Elizabethan house. It has now been restored to much the same appearance as it would have had in Lawrence Washington's day. Over the fireplace is a portrait of George Washington by Stuart

that has survived is the heart of the house, with its original entrance porch, great hall and great chamber. An east wing which extended over the present rose-garden has disappeared, and a west wing by which it was further lengthened on the other side was also demolished at some period in the eighteenth century. This curtailment of the house was to some extent compensated by the addition of a north wing at right-angles to the main house by John Hodges in about 1700 and the partial rebuilding of the west wing by Sir Reginald Blomfield in 1930. In 1914 Sulgrave had been acquired and was later refurnished by Anglo-American subscriptions 'as a centre from which sentiments of friendship and goodwill between the British and American peoples will forever radiate'. Thus, if falsely sentimental associations are to be avoided, it is as important to understand the growth of the house as the descent of the family. Sulgrave is of three periods, Elizabethan, Queen Anne and the twentieth century, and only the first has any connection with the Washington family itself.

But the house was never grand. The display of Queen Elizabeth's arms over the porch, their supporters repeated in plaster within it, was a loyal convention, not an assumption of a greater dignity than its builder ever earned or claimed. The hall is a lovely room, which owes more to its fine proportions and solid masonry and woodwork than to any elaboration of its detail. With its carefully chosen furniture of the period it must look very like the room in which Lawrence and his wife Amee entertained their guests and amused their eleven children. Even more satisfying is the Great Chamber above it, which contains a splendid Elizabethan bed from Battle Abbey in Sussex and is roofed by a double-frame of oak beams as clean, strong and simple as the

The Great Chamber which lies immediately above the Great Hall. The Elizabethan four-poster bed comes from Battle Abbey in Sussex

structure of a ship's hull. There are more splendid rooms in other houses of this date, but there is none so satisfying and none which makes more immediate an impression of what it felt like to be caged in oak, bedded in oak and surrounded by oak furniture that was passed devotedly from father to son.

After seeing these two main rooms of Lawrence Washington's house, one could expect the Queen Anne wing to be out of harmony with the memory of the family whose name is invariably linked with Sulgrave. If only the Hodges family had inhabited it, the manor might not now even exist. In fact John Hodges' north wing is in itself a period-piece of great charm, by which he contrived, consciously or not, to extend the Elizabethan building in the style of his own age without destroying the unity of the house. The Queen Anne addition is only slightly more stylish than the better type of contemporary farm-house, and the kitchen, now splendescent in the copper and polished steel of an early eighteenth-century range imported from Hampshire, was the main room of the later part of the house.

Sulgrave lies on the outskirts of its manorial village, surrounded by the cornfields and sheep-walks out of which the village grew and by which it still lives. Before the days of the railway and bus it was so isolated that it and three neighbouring hamlets were known as 'the lost villages'. Now it is known to most Englishmen and many Americans as the place where the Washingtons settled and from which they carried to America the greatest name in its history. But would Sulgrave be a place of pilgrimage instead of Washington in County Durham, were it not for the manor-house, so faithfully restored by the two nations, which so well preserves the spirit of Christian neighbourliness with which the Washington family were endowed?

The kitchen in the Queen Anne wing. The collection of eighteenth-century kitchen equipment comes from Weston Corbett in Hampshire

The inscription on the floor of Sulgrave Parish Church over the graves of Lawrence Washington and his wife Amee. The date of his death (1584) was never filled in on the tablet

MONTACUTE HOUSE

SOMERSET

One of the most perfect of sixteenth-century houses

It is fortunate that one of the very finest houses to survive from the late Elizabethan period should also be one of the least altered. Changes were made to Montacute, notably to the west front towards the end of the eighteenth century and to the interior by Lord Curzon at the beginning of the twentieth, but they were made with taste and tact. Its convenience was thereby improved, but its Elizabethan character has remained un-affected. What we see today is substantially the house which Sir Edward Phelips, a Somerset landowner and lawyer who rose to be Speaker of the House of Commons and Master of the Rolls, began to build in the last decade of the sixteenth century. The date 1601, carved above the east doorway, probably marks the year of its completion.

Sir Edward collaborated with a local master-mason of near-genius named William Arnold. The latter was a little less than the 'architect' of Montacute, in the sense that we would employ the term today, for the difference in social standing between himself and his employer, and the energy with which a great man of the times applied himself to the building of a house designed to display and heighten his status, would have made such a relationship impossible. But Arnold was also much more than clerk-of-works. Probably he had a freer hand than Lyminge had at Hatfield, or than Arnold himself was given by Robert Cecil, first Earl of Salisbury, at Cranborne a few years later, for we are told that he spent 'every day a whole hour in private' with the Lord Treasurer, and their conversation is unlikely to have been one-sided. There is no question, however, that Arnold's influence at Montacute was dominant, and that the chief credit for this remarkable house belongs to him.

The Arnold-Phelips, or Phelips-Arnold, conception of domes-tic grandeur is best illustrated by the east front, originally the entrance front. From this direction the house at first appears rather flat – three superimposed tiers of enormous mullioned windows extending across a façade nearly two hundred feet in width and ninety high. But if it were nothing more than a suc-cession of grids let in to a stone cliff, Montacute would be a disappointment; and the first sight of Montacute never disap-points. The front, though perfectly symmetrical, is full of vitality.

opposite One of the statues of the Nine Worthies set in niches between the mullioned windows of the second floor of the east front

The oriel window in the north front at the end of the long gallery overlooking the Elizabethan garden

77

The east front in 1787 just before the entrance was moved to the west side. On the left is the *Mons Acutus* from which Montacute takes its name

An aerial photograph of Montacute taken from the north-west

The changes in the building-line occur effortlessly, sometimes by simple projections, as in the porch and wings, sometimes by subtle curvature, as in the accentuated lines of the Flemish-type gables, sometimes by a line deliberately angled, as in the shallow bay-windows at the ends of the wings.

The east front is abundantly decorated, but one has to search for the decorative elements that the eye has unconsciously taken in. At ground level there are six steps down from the terrace to the gravel path, not meanly centred on the porch, but spread across the full width between the wings. On the terrace itself are six free-standing columns, matching the columnar structure of the chimneys high above. There are curved cornices to some of the windows, niches with scalloped canopies, curious circular indentations in the walls like impressions left by cannon balls which failed to penetrate, but probably intended for terra-cotta medallions; there are three classical entablatures marking the ceiling-levels within, the centre one plain, the uppermost enlivened by stone dentils and the bottom one by a primitive triglyph frieze. There is a handsome cornice and a balustrade with obelisks at roof-level, and below it, between the windows of the top storey, the most daring and pleasing device of all – the statues of the Nine Worthies (Joshua, David, Judas Maccabeus, Hector, Alexander, Julius Caesar, Arthur, Charlemagne and Godfrey of Bouillon), all dressed as Roman soldiers and gesturing with apparent unconcern in the security of their lofty niches.

One reason why this amount of detail, much of it Italian in inspiration, is not only acceptable in a very English house but passes almost unnoticed by a superficial glance, is that every part of it, even the row of statues, is made of the same stone. Montacute is built of stone from the local quarry of Ham Hill, which has so greatly enriched southern Somerset and the adjacent parts of Dorset. It is a tawny ochre stone which absorbs rather than reflects the sun, and is particularly attractive to lichens which give it a mottled appearance and spread the colour unevenly as if on a painter's palette. It exudes colour like honey, in much the same way as long-weathered Pentelic marble. Equally effective is the use of the same stone inside the house, where it appears creamier, richer and skin-smooth in texture. But the outer walls of Montacute in a setting sun are of such loveliness that if it were the face of a quarry instead of the face of a house, one's pleasure at the sight of it would scarcely be diminished.

Below the east front extends a forecourt. The centre of it is grassed, and it is closed on three sides by a balustrade exactly matching that on the roof, raised above the flower-beds on low walls. Along the top are spaced slender obelisks, with stone lanterns at the central points and identical domed pavilions at each end where the garden is divided from the park. These pavilions are Arnold's masterpiece. Nobody having once seen them could ever again say that Elizabethan builders were incapable of delicacy. They are, and apparently always have been,

The east front, which has remained unaltered since it was completed in 1601. It was originally the entrance front

quite empty, without even an internal floor to divide them into the two storeys which the windows suggest from outside. They are follies, architectural doll's houses, Elizabethan editions, as Avray Tipping first suggested, of the towers flanking a fortified mediaeval forecourt. On each of them, the ogee roof curves upwards with the grace of a swan's neck to a pinnacle topped by a sort of stone astrolabe. The oriel windows swing outwards from all four sides with a certainty of line and proportion that is amazing in something so miniature. On arriving, on leaving, and throughout a prolonged visit to Montacute, one's eye wanders back to them again and again.

The other side of the house, the west side, has been the entrance front since the late eighteenth century. In 1786-7, Edward Phelips, who inherited Montacute at the age of nine and lived there for sixty-three years, did away with the old frontal approach, removed a lake from the park and the bridge which crossed it (both can be seen in the Collinson drawing, made in the year of the change) and seems to have re-used the balustrade of the latter to construct the low wall which closes the fore-court between the two pavilions. But he did much more than this. He bought the porch and other ornamental features of a late-Tudor house six miles away in Dorset called Clifton May-bank, and fitted them boldly between the two wings of the west front of Montacute. The Clifton Maybank façade formed the centre of the new entrance front, and although it was some fifty years earlier in date, it was made of the same Ham Hill stone and anticipated the Renaissance detail of Montacute so brilliantly that it would be difficult for anybody but an expert to tell them apart. Indeed, the reliefs and finials around and over the porch are among the most vigorous and pleasing work to be seen here. It was a splendid adaptation, and incidentally a noble feat of rescue work, for Clifton Maybank was then being pulled

A detail of the stonework over the porch on the west front. This dates from 1550 and was brought to Montacute from Clifton Maybank in 1787, when the arms of the Horsey family were replaced by those of Edward Phelips

The north-east pavilion, one of two flanking the original Elizabethan forecourt on the east side. These are purely decorative and contain no upper floors

Looking into the library, formerly the Great Chamber. The fireplace of Portland stone is the finest of the original Elizabethan fireplaces at Montacute

down and these parts of its structure were acquired at the sale of the materials. But it also served a functional purpose. It supplied the first and second storeys of Montacute with internal corridors, which added greatly to the convenience of a house where even a bedroom could only be entered by passing through another.

To the north and south there are ornamental gardens, which form, together with the forecourt, three large panels of green from which the ochre house stands up magnificently. The only flower-borders are those down each side of the forecourt, planted from designs made by V. Sackville-West in the 1950's. The other two gardens rely for their effect on large lawns, gravel walks, sentinel rows of clipped yews and a serpentine balustrade around a central pond. The north garden follows in essentials the Elizabethan plan. It is confined by paths raised on broad parapets around the whole circuit of the lawn and with a vista at the far end over the Somerset countryside. From this point, too, one can see the north front of the house to perfection. This façade is plain compared to the main fronts, but is relieved by the great oriel window of the Long Gallery, its corbels supporting the light framework of the window with the strength and flexibility of an elephant's trunk.

The interior of the house remains almost unaltered from the day it was built. Montacute is therefore the *locus classicus* in which to study the transition between Tudor clumsiness of plan to an arrangement of rooms which falls little short of modern conceptions of convenience. Of course, there are deficiencies. The original absence of corridors has already been mentioned, and the distance between the kitchens in the south wing and the family's main dining-room on the first floor of the north wing involved a walk – or rather a procession of dish-bearing footmen – of over seventy yards. All the rooms are large and very light. The huge windows not only enliven the exterior by their patterns of mullions and transoms and diamond panes catching the light from slightly different angles, but turn the rooms into boxes as airy as bird-cages. The finest of them is the library, previously the dining-room and before that the Great Chamber where the Phelips may have held their manorial courts. It has four windows, two of them of twelve lights, one of eighteen and the fourth of twenty-one. The upper two rows of lights are in each case filled with armorial bearings of coloured glass. An inner porch of richly carved wood leads into the room, and the chimneypiece of Portland stone, the panelling and plasterwork frieze are all original. The bookshelves are nineteenth-century, but excellent of their kind.

If no other room quite approaches the Great Chamber in restrained magnificence, the whole interior of Montacute repays the most careful study. In every part of the house one finds evidence of Arnold's skill. He was happier when improvising on the traditional English forms than when adapting half-understood Continental models, and much of the interior work of the latter type contrasts crudely and unexpectedly with his use of classical motifs on the façades. An instance is to be found in the hall, where the screen, apart from its two lovely arches, is a fantastic jumble of styles and different coloured stone, while the plaster panel filling the upper part of the opposite wall is a spontaneous expression of native humour. In other places, Arnold relied on the simplest grouping of his excellent materials. The north staircase could not be plainer in its construction, with great blocks of Ham Hill stone forming the short flights of steps, punctuated by quarter and half-landings, and a massive core of the same stone. In its own way, it is more successful than the open timber staircases which were to become fashionable only a few years later in great houses like Knole and Hatfield.

The north staircase, which runs in broad flights of stone steps from the ground floor to the Great Chamber and the Long Gallery

The stone screen at the south end of the Great Hall. The curious Ionic columns betray the uncertainty with which William Arnold handled classical themes, contrasting with his sure treatment of traditional English motifs

HARDWICK HALL

DERBYSHIRE

Bess of Hardwick's last and finest building

'Can you imagine yourself building a house like that?' said the tripper for want of any better comment on her first sight of Hardwick. Looking at her companion, one could only assume the answer to be No. But she did not mean it like that. She thought the house eccentric, weird, uncomfortable and a fantastic waste of money. The immediate impulse to take her by the shoulders and shake her was followed by the reflection that she might, after all, be right. Hardwick is all these things. But it also happens to be one of the most beautiful buildings ever created. Nobody who has ever wandered round its rooms and gardens can ever again be in doubt whether he is by nature a romantic or a classicist. If the house appeals to you through and through, if you find yourself lowering your voice in instinctive response to the quietness of the rooms, if you enjoy the feel of rush matting and stone steps beneath your feet, if the crookedness of a door does not irritate you and you have no desire to paper an expanse of whitewashed wall, if you hate the guard-ropes and the electric blueness of the Blue Room, then Hardwick is for you: you are an incurable romantic.

Hardwick is probably the finest surviving house of the late Elizabethan period. One does not associate that quarrelsome age with muted tones or an attitude of reserve, and even less its builder, Elizabeth Shrewsbury, known throughout history as 'Bess of Hardwick'. But here she managed to balance overstatement outside by understatement inside. The exterior of the house is splendidly arrogant and adventurous; the interior is as cool and sedate as a convent. It seems almost impossible that those vast windows should let in so little glare.

The story of Bess of Hardwick must be briefly retold, for the romance of the place is inextricably bound up with it. She was born in the old manor-house at Hardwick in 1520, the third daughter of a country squire of little importance and less wealth. The house, which stood within a stone's throw of the present Hardwick, was a one-storey, half-timbered building, little more than a farm-house. At the age of twelve Elizabeth was married to a near-neighbour's son, Master Robert Barlow, aged fourteen, who died a few months after the wedding, leaving considerable property to his young widow. She was twenty-seven when she

A portrait of Elizabeth, Countess of Shrewsbury – Bess of Hardwick – which hangs in the gallery at Hardwick

opposite The staircase which winds inconsequently through the house like a long passage. It is built of stone in its lower flights and of wood higher up

overleaf The west front, which has little surface decoration and relies for its effect on the huge expanses of glass. The Tuscan colonnade was originally intended to extend the whole width of the façade

HARDWICK

opposite The 'old' hall from a window of the 'new' hall. Embedded in this ruin is the original farmhouse where Elizabeth Shrewsbury was born

opposite bottom The wall of the Elizabethan garden surmounted by stone fleurs-de-lys

married her second husband, Sir William Cavendish from Suffolk, who held an important position at Court and made a fortune from it. Elizabeth persuaded him to sell the Suffolk properties and buy the manor of Chatsworth, which she immediately began to rebuild. The work went on for the next twenty-five years, but at intervals she built three other large houses, Worksop, Bolsover and Oldcotes. Sir William, dying in 1557, left her all his possessions, despite the claims of his children by two former wives. Three years afterwards she hooked Sir William St Loe, Captain of the Queen's Guard and Grand Butler of England. The sequel can by this time be foreseen: Sir William died only a year or two later, and once again Bess netted the whole of his property. Finally, in 1568, she found a fourth and even richer and more distinguished husband, the sixth Earl of Shrewsbury. A condition of their marriage, imposed by Bess, was that two of her Cavendish children should marry two of the Earl's on the same day as she married the father. Lord Shrewsbury had seven houses of his own (Sheffield Castle, Sheffield Manor, Worksop Manor, Buxton Hall, Rufford Abbey, South Wingfield Manor and Shrewsbury House in London), and Bess at least four. By then she was the richest and most formidable woman in England, with one exception: the Queen. Not bad going for the third daughter of an insignificant squire.

The strangest part of this extraordinary story was still to come. Lord Shrewsbury was appointed jailer to Mary Queen of Scots,

Hardwick Hall seen from across the lake at the foot of the park. The ruins of the old hall stand against the skyline on the right

if by that term one can understand a man of great courtesy, undeniably susceptible to his prisoner's charms, who entertained her for fifteen years in the protective custody of his many mansions. Bess became acutely jealous of her, and for the last few years of his life she was not on speaking terms with her husband. However, she was quite well enough off to indulge still further her passion for building. She rebuilt her ancestral home at Hardwick to such vast dimensions that her father's little hall was quite lost within it. No sooner was Lord Shrewsbury in his grave – for even she had not quite the face to do it during his lifetime – than she began at the age of seventy to construct her last and greatest house. This was Hardwick Hall, not a hundred yards away from the 'old' hall which she continued to enlarge simultaneously with the erection of the 'new' hall, striding imperiously between the workmen from one to the other. The two buildings stand virtually side by side, the old hall now a ruin, the new hall a lasting memorial to her energy and taste.

Elizabeth Shrewsbury signed the house with her initials in fretted stone against the skyline. She had every claim to do so, for not only was she its begetter, but the full building accounts which have happily survived, show that she checked every detail of expenditure and supervised every phase of the work. Possibly Robert Smythson, who had played a big part in the design of Longleat and Wollaton, gave her professional help, but it is difficult to withold from Bess herself the credit for the novelty and swagger of Hardwick. The whole building bears the impress of her character. She was a task-mistress who would stand no incompetence from others, but allowed herself the privilege of frequent changes of mind. Thus an item in the accounts would be crossed out, and against it, in the Countess' bold hand, is written, 'pott out by me'; or, 'because the walls ryse and be not well nor all of one colore, the most [they must] be wheyted [whitened] at the plasterers charge.' On another occasion she ordered that the turret-windows be heightened by an extra row of lights after they had been finished. One can imagine her standing between her buildings and deciding that there was still more wall than glass, and that the proportions must be reversed, whatever the expense.

In October 1593, only two-and-a-half years after the foundations were laid, the core of the house was finished. From the garden forecourt the west front rises tier upon tier of sparkling glass, the windows increasing in magnificence, like her marriages, as they mount upwards. There is not much surface decoration. The Tuscan colonnade between the two wings and the roof balustrade above it are the only external concessions to classical fashion. The windows need no borders to enhance the splendour of their glass, the mullions and transoms forming ladders between the rows of diamond panes. It is basically a three-storey building, but without the turrets it would be little more than a smaller Longleat. The turrets were the master-stroke. They are purely decorative: five of them can only be approached

from the leads of the roof, with a staircase in the sixth. One feels nothing but sympathy for the men-servants who were forced to sleep in them as late as the nineteenth century, but they not only give Hardwick its romantic skyline, which seems from a distance more like a castle than a house, but break up the four façades with bays and recesses making the whole building glitter.

There are three particular architectural features within the house which no visitor should miss: the staircase, the High Great Chamber and the Gallery. The staircase is built of stone in its lower flights, of wood in the upper, and it is quite bare of decoration. It has no mouldings, no carpet and the mere pretence of a banister. It is exceptionally wide, and owing to the slight movement of its structure, part of it tilts at odd angles. It does not mount within a continuous rectangular stair-well, but wanders lengthwise through the house like a passage. At intervals the broad straight steps turn into spirals where shortage of space demanded it, radiating from the newel like the ribs of a fan. The most beautiful effects of line and shadow are thereby achieved. It is hard to say whether Bess deliberately contrived them. They look accidental, but there is no knowing to what extent her eye for dramatic effect could reach.

But the High Chamber is no accident. Sacheverell Sitwell has called it 'the most beautiful room, not in England alone, but in the whole of Europe'. It is extremely difficult to illustrate this claim photographically, for the faded *pot-pourri* of the tapestries and moulded frieze merge into a monochrome blur, and the effect of the room depends upon seeing it in all its subtle colouring and dimensions. The proportions are extremely simple, a rectangular box extended on one side by a window embrasure, itself as big as a normal parlour, which occupies the whole space within one of the turrets. The immensely tall windows of the third storey throw diamond patterns across the rush-matted floor. The ceiling is quite plain, without even the simplest cornice. The walls are hung with eight Brussels tapestries purchased by Bess in 1587, in time to design the room to contain them exactly. Above them runs a plaster frieze of Diana and her hunters, sometimes as crude in detail as cave-paintings, but wonderfully beautiful in their overall effect. They illustrate to

Venus chastising Cupid, a detail of the plaster frieze by Abraham Smith in the bay window of the High Great Chamber

opposite The south front seen from the garden, showing clearly the initials ES (Elizabeth Shrewsbury) worked in the fretted stonework of the parapet

perfection a particular quality of Hardwick, that while it owes much of its inspiration to classical sources, the execution is entirely English. Among the 375 names of workmen recorded in the accounts, there is scarcely one recognizable as foreign.

The Gallery opens off the High Great Chamber. Here the dominant colour is the lavender of the tapestries, woven in Brussels in 1578 and bought by Bess in 1592. Once again they determined the dimensions of the room. It runs the length of the east front and is lit by twenty of the tallest windows. Its immense length, second only to the gallery at Montacute and of infinitely greater subtlety, turns the far end into a pool of hazy colour. Standing in this stupendous room one feels overwhelmed, not by the size of it, but by the creative energy of the woman who devoted the last years of her life to realising the dream of her old age. The portrait of Bess of Hardwick hangs against the gallery tapestries, surrounded by three of the four husbands whose wealth she ransacked to such glorious effect.

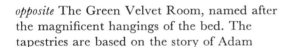

opposite The Green Velvet Room, named after the magnificent hangings of the bed. The tapestries are based on the story of Adam

The Gallery, which runs the whole length of the east front. This immense room is hung with tapestries acquired by Bess of Hardwick shortly before the house was built and the Gallery was designed to fit them

The entrance door to the High Great Chamber. Over the door, stags support the Shrewsbury arms

KNOLE

KENT

An archbishop's palace transformed into a sumptuous private house

'I, who am a lover of all antiquities,' wrote Edmund Burke to John Frederick Sackville, third Duke of Dorset, 'must be a very great admirer of Knole. I think it is the most interesting thing in England.' That was two hundred years ago. What then must it mean to us, who can see the same buildings, decoration and contents which Burke saw, virtually unchanged since his time? Set us down there a further century back, in 1660: still no change. A further century, in 1560; then one would see considerable differences in the interior, but few outside. In 1460: then the greater part of the house was being built. Five centuries of continuous occupation is no great rarity among English houses, but if the last three-and-a-half have left almost no mark upon the house, it becomes something remarkable. If, further, it happens to be one of the largest houses in the country – containing 365 rooms, it is said, but nobody has ever counted them – and has belonged to a noble family who were wealthy at a time when wealth was used to greatest advantage, it becomes a phenomenon. Choose your century, from the fifteenth to the seventeenth, and you can find corners or whole suites of rooms at Knole which will evoke its atmosphere exactly. Ask to see the eighteenth, and you will be shown only the clock-tower, a few pieces of furniture and a single fireplace. The nineteenth? A row of windows in the orangery on the garden front. The twentieth? You left it outside.

This does not mean that Knole is an uninhabitable museum, for a condensation of its history must disregard the constant process of repair and modernisation which today enables nearly forty people to make the house their home and its care their main concern. Nor does it mean that because Knole is old it must be melancholy. V. Sackville-West, who was born there and wrote its history, said that Knole 'has the deep inward gaiety of some very old woman who has always been beautiful, who has had many lovers and seen many generations come and go, smiled wisely over their sorrows and their joys and learnt an imperishable secret of tolerance and humour'. To endow a house with human perceptions of this kind is a romantic way of saying that those who built it, enlarged it, furnished it and embellished it did so in the hope that later generations would approve their

Thomas Sackville, first Earl of Dorset, who received Knole as a gift from his cousin, Queen Elizabeth I, in 1566. The house had been largely built by Thomas Bourchier, Archbishop of Canterbury between 1456 and 1486

opposite A Gorgon's head from the Jacobean screen, added to the Great Hall by the first Earl of Dorset

Knole from the north, showing the vast extent of the house, which resembles a small town

Inside the Green Court, the first and largest of the seven courts round which the house is built. The clock tower was added in the early eighteenth century, but the main structure is fifteenth century

motives and share their tastes, and that their hopes were not disappointed. A house, being more durable than its owners, is a record of their passage. Stone, brick and timber cannot smile on them: but they have smiled on it. In time their affection for it becomes, by legitimate analogy, its affection for them.

Certainly Knole is a very agreeable place to live in. It has a cellular or collegiate layout, court leading into court through arches in the cross-wings, and it increases in intimacy as the womb of the house is reached. The courts both divide and link. They break up the great grey mass into detached units, so that the house has very many external façades, each different, each a surprise: but at the same time they are courts to cross, treading on grass or gravel or paving-stones or cobbles, and courts to look into from upstairs windows, secluded and differently shadowed, but remaining part of the house although open to the sky. There are seven of them in all. Two are little more than light-wells; one is an open, irregular passageway from the kitchen to the hall; two are large service courts for the stables and the kitchen area; but the other two, the Green Court and the Stone Court, are noble in proportions and form the main entrance, one behind the other, giving Knole its chief architectural distinction. From inside, the house does not appear so very large, or it may be that familiarity reduces its scale, since one comes to take for granted the distances to be covered in passing from one corner to another, and much of the house consists in outbuildings or 'show-

94

opposite The west or entrance front. The central tower and wings were probably built by Archbishop Bourchier, but the Flemish-style gables were added in about 1605 by Thomas Sackville

An aerial view from the north-west showing how the house is formed round courtyards like a college

The Stone Court, the second of the two great courtyards in the middle of the house, looking across to the windows of the Great Hall and the Tuscan colonnade added by Thomas Sackville in about 1605

rooms' where one only penetrates for special purposes. But from outside, particularly the north-east, where the park rises to one of the loveliest cricket-grounds in England, you look over a cataract of roofs and towers and the courts are lost between them, trebling the area covered by actual buildings. It seems more like a small town such as Urbino or Vézelay than a house. Nor is it easy from this distance to disentangle the splendid parts from the merely functional, or one date of construction from another. The plainest stone-facing or gable-ends can conceal the finest rooms; the sturdiest battlements surmount a garage and a slaughter-house. All is built of the same material, Kentish ragstone capped by brown tiles, and the house seems to resist dissection into historical periods, for it is all very much of one character if not all of one piece. The attempt, however, must be made, and except for the very earliest period it is found to be surprisingly simple.

It is simple because Knole is really the creation of two men:

96

Thomas Bourchier, Archbishop of Canterbury, between 1456 and 1486; and Thomas Sackville, first Earl of Dorset, between 1603 and 1608. Other Archbishops and other Dorsets completed or extended what these two men began, but they did so in the same style and with the same purpose, and their individual contributions were in a comparatively minor key. Nobody knows for certain whether any part of an earlier mediaeval manor-house survives, nor indeed whether it ever existed. Knole was a manor in the thirteenth century, but a manor does not necessarily imply a manor-house, since its owners had other houses nearby, and on this site there could have been nothing but farm-buildings. On the north side, however, there is a jumble of towers, gables and entrances among which archaeologists may one day decipher early mediaeval work. If so, it was probably modest, for Bourchier paid no more than £266.1.4 for the whole manor in 1456. The written evidence is contradictory. Richard Kilburne, in his *Survey of Kent*, published in 1659, says that 'there Bourchier built a faire house', which was enlarged by his successors in the See of Canterbury. But Philipott, whose history of the county was published in the same year, says that Bourchier 'added much of Pompe and Magnificence by a new Supplement or Superstructure *to the ancient Pile or Fabrick*'; and the Lambeth Palace accounts of 1467–8 refer to 'repairs' at Knole and to 'a new tower' and 'a new solar', which suggest that something fairly substantial was there before. The point is important, because if Bourchier built the whole house on a virtually virgin site, Knole would be by far the largest private house surviving from the fifteenth century; but if he merely added to 'an ancient Pile', his work, while certainly on a princely scale, becomes an adaptation and not a wholly original enterprise. Without entering into further detail, it can be said that Knole was for eighty years the palace of five successive Archbishops of Canterbury, from Bourchier to Cranmer, and that each of them, but particularly Bourchier, contributed to the building which we see today. Nothing of any size except the clock-tower was added to it at a later date.

Henry VIII acquired Knole from Cranmer in 1538, and for nearly twenty years it was a royal palace. Queen Elizabeth gave it to her cousin, Thomas Sackville, later her Lord Treasurer and first Earl of Dorset, but the gift was subject to a lease which did not expire till the year of the Queen's death in 1603, and it was only in the last five years of his life that Lord Dorset was able to call it truly his own. He used those five years to transform it.

Dorset's work fuses beautifully with the Archbishops', although the whole of the early English Renaissance lay in between. There is nothing at Knole that can be for certain identified as Elizabethan, for its royal period left no structural mark. What we see is a Jacobean rendering of a Perpendicular shell. Dorset achieved this feat by adding at significant points ornamentations which gave the house a more elegant and symmetrical appearance and greatly increased its commodiousness. Externally, he

The south and east fronts from the rose garden. To the right is the row of gables added by Thomas Sackville to the fifteenth-century building, and on the left the chapel

The Great Staircase, built between 1604 and 1608, and the first timber staircase in Britain to be designed as a main architectural feature. The newel posts are surmounted by the Sackville leopard

The Great Hall, built about 1460. The oak panelling, the screen, and the plasterwork ceiling were added by Thomas Sackville, first Earl of Dorset. Above the screen is the Minstrels' Gallery, pierced by wooden lattices

The richly carved frieze of mermaids and gryphons below the Jacobean plaster ceiling of the Ballroom

left intact the tall double-arches of the windows and the crenellations of the walls and towers; but he imposed on them the swirling Dutch gables and the sentinel leopards of his family crest, a Tuscan colonnade at the inner side of the Stone Court and a row of friendly gables above the eastern state-rooms. Internally, he lowered the high Gothic roof of the hall by a plastered ceiling and replaced Bourchier's screen by a Jacobean screen of barbaric sumptuousness; he remodelled the interior wall-facings, ceilings and fireplaces in almost every part of the house; he built a beautiful timber staircase, set leopards on its newel posts and painted its walls in *grisaille*; and he employed foreign craftsmen to embellish his window-reveals and to add decorative devices in plaster, wood-carving or paint to almost every internal surface that would take them. In all this work one traces a consistent taste: a feeling for the excellence of the Archbishops' work, and, except for the hall screen, a delicacy of touch which conforms well with what is known of his non-belligerent, reserved character. It should be remembered that before he took to politics Thomas Sackville was a poet who occupies a respectable place in the history of English literature.

This double origin of Knole explains the puzzling appearance of the house from outside. How can so severe a house contrive to look so charming? How can the entrance front, apparently only one step removed from a castle, convey so hospitable a welcome? The answer lies in the addition of the gables and their leopard-finials, an embellishment that grows out of the earlier work without unbalancing it, a stroke of architectural inventiveness and tact which could not have been bettered. Within the Green Court one discerns exactly the same motive. Here there was not even a basic symmetry for Dorset to work upon: the flanking towers were not of equal width and Bourchier's gatehouse was not central. Dorset destroyed nothing, but he pulled the façade together by two more gables ingeniously placed to disguise the lack of symmetry, and one likes to imagine that he was also responsible for turfing the courtyard with its two great squares of grass. He added further gables to the centre of the south, or garden, front. It was a process of softening and rounding. He found an edifice and turned it into a house.

The long galleries must also have been of his making, since no gallery of this size is known earlier than that at Hampton Court, which dates from the reign of Henry VIII. In Bourchier's day these rooms would have been divided for the great retinue that surrounded an Archbishop into a warren of chambers, alternately large and small. As Dorset's internal reconstruction barely tampered with the main fabric, it is remarkable how easily the rooms run together, gallery to bedroom, bedroom to dressing-room, Great Chamber (now called the Ballroom) to staircase, staircase to Hall, when the original disposition of rooms must have been quite different and the Archbishops' ground-plan is beyond recovery in the ingenuity of its reconstruction. Most Jacobean houses have one gallery: Knole has five, if one counts,

98

opposite The Ballroom, originally the Great Chamber of the Tudor house. The walls are hung with portraits of the Sackville family

The Brown Gallery, lined with Jacobean panelling
and hung with sixteenth and seventeenth-century
English portraits. It contains some fine pieces
from the collection of early English furniture

as one should, the huge Retainers' Galleries running along the
top of the house. They are rooms of controlled magnificence,
which until the middle of the eighteenth century were the main
living-quarters of the Sackville family together with the set of
less grandiose apartments on the ground floor of the garden
front. The latter were the only ones which the family permitted
themselves to touch: here you will find that isolated eighteenth-
century fireplace in a drawing-room adjoining the library, and
grisaille paintings of the same date in the Colonnade. But the
show-rooms, which have been open to the public for at least
two hundred years, were regarded as sacrosanct, and the very
thought of William Kent or Robert Adam or Wyatt daring to
add their own version of refinement is an impertinence.

The Sackvilles deliberately cultivated the antique. Their
furniture was often as much as a century old when it was first
installed. We find, for instance, that in the little rooms allotted
to Lady Betty Germain between 1720 and 1750, the carpet is late
sixteenth-century, the chairs are Charles II, the stools Queen
Anne, and her four-poster bed is mid-seventeenth-century, and
nobody has touched a single object since she was there. The
Brown Gallery and the Leicester Gallery contain Elizabethan
and early seventeenth-century furniture in their original cover-
ings that have no equal in any other collection: many of them
were brought there from Hampton Court and Whitehall by
the sixth Earl of Dorset, who died in 1705. When the furniture
was beyond use, the rooms were maintained intact and the
family moved to others, where the process was repeated. There
is no written proof that this was their policy, in spite of the considerable documentation of Knole throughout the whole of
this period, but the evidence is there for all to see.

Knole is undoubtedly one of the half-dozen greatest houses in
Britain, whatever criterions of greatness are adopted. It is very
large; it has a distinguished history; its two main periods blend
with remarkable sympathy; its contents are unique; it remains
in the occupation of the Sackvilles. It is, above all, as V. Sackville-West said, a very English house. 'It has the tone of England,' she wrote. 'It melts into the green of the garden turf,
into the tawnier green of the park beyond, into the blue of the
pale English sky. . . . The brown-red of these roofs is the brown-
red of the roofs of humble farms and pointed oast-houses, such
as stain over a wide landscape of England the quilt-like pattern
of the fields.' Those words were written by one who never pretended to a scholar's knowledge of the history of architecture but
loved the house as she might love a grandmother, sensing that it
once had a youth but finding in it something much more identi-
fiable and appealing, the serenity of a fine old age.

The Cartoon Gallery, so-called from the set of
copies of Raphael cartoons by Daniel Mytens
brought to Knole in 1701

opposite The richly carved and gilded bed in the
Venetian Ambassador's Bedroom. This bed came
from Whitehall Palace and according to tradition
was the one in which the Old Pretender was born

FOUNTAINS HALL

YORKSHIRE

An elegant manor built from the stones of Fountains Abbey

In the hidden valley of the River Skell in the West Riding of Yorkshire is to be found an astonishing combination of three centuries: the twelfth-century Fountains Abbey; the sixteenth-century Fountains Hall; and the eighteenth-century pleasure-gardens of Studley Royal. All three are superb examples of their kind. They are linked together scenically and historically, and as they passed into the ownership of the same family two hundred years ago, it is possible to speak of all three as if they had always been a single artistic concept.

The ruins of the Cistercian Abbey are among the most famous in Europe, rivalled only by those of the Abbey of Jumièges in France. Apart from the great tower, which was erected in the early sixteenth century, nearly all the buildings date from between 1170 and 1250. They form the most complete surviving record of the layout of an important English monastery in the centuries before the Dissolution, and an architectural achievement of staggering size and beauty. The Cistercian Order was dedicated to a monastic existence only slightly less austere than the Trappist, and the monks lavished on their Abbey all the magnificence that they denied themselves in their communal life. There was little decoration even in the church, and elsewhere only the minimum comforts to keep the Brothers alive, but the structure of the nave, choir, cloister, refectory, chapter-house and other buildings, in their vast scale and the splendour of their proportions, was as important an expression of their spiritual values as the discipline which ruled their lives. Today the ruins are roofed only by the flight of birds and their floors are paved in turf, while the great windows frame only the sky, but to see the Abbey in ruin is paradoxically to understand more clearly the faith that inspired such Cyclopean skill and effort. The exposure and desolation of this soaring grey stone give it a quality which even the greatest cathedrals lack.

Fountains Hall is a direct descendant of Fountains Abbey. It was the inheritor of the monastic lands; it was built of its stone; and it lies within its outer precincts. When the Abbey was dissolved by Henry VIII in 1539, the estate was sold by the Crown to Sir Richard Gresham, father of Sir Thomas Gresham, the great Elizabethan merchant and builder of the Royal

Fountains Abbey, looking along the south aisle of the church. It was dissolved in 1539 and the estate sold. Stones from the Abbey were used in the construction of Fountains Hall

opposite The south front seen through the entrance gate. The fine oriel window over the porch and the stone figures of knights decorating the porch and balcony are distinctive features of the house

Exchange in London. Sir Richard profited from the Abbey by selling the lead from its roof, and his grandson resold the property in 1597 to a local iron-master, Sir Stephen Proctor. It is to him that the building of Fountains Hall is usually attributed. The date 1611 has been accepted as the year of its completion on the strength of a weathered inscription on one of the entrance piers. But the date, seen in strong slanting sunlight, is clearly not 1611, but 1577. It seems unlikely that so simple a stone would have been removed from another house into its present position. If one accepts it as original, the question then arises whether the house could be Gresham's, not Proctor's; Elizabethan, not Jacobean. At first sight the porch seems to confirm the later date: it bears Stephen Proctor's initials and family motto RIEN TROVANT, GAINERAY TOUT. But the porch could structurally have been Proctor's addition to an earlier house, and the crispness of its carving and lettering contrasts strongly with the yokel crudity of the statuary around it. The plan and elevations of the house do not preclude a mid-Elizabethan date, and the shape of the fireplaces suggests it. But in the absence of further evidence, all that can safely be said is that here we have a fine example of a medium-sized house of the late sixteenth or early seventeenth century.

Fountains has only one true façade, the south, for the house is built so close against the steep hillside that there is another entrance at the back on the level of the third storey. Consequently

The full extent of the south front. The windows are delicately proportioned and the whole design is typically late Elizabethan

opposite top The west end of the house illustrating the steepness of the hill against which it is built. Flights of steps lead up the hill to provide a back-entrance at third-storey level

opposite bottom An aerial view showing the relationship between the Abbey and Fountains Hall in the top left-hand corner

left The entrance porch built by Sir Stephen Proctor in about 1610 and carrying his family motto *Rien Trovant Gaineray Tout*

The oriel window of the Great Chamber on the third floor. It is inset with the arms of Sir Stephen Proctor and the families to which he was allied

The pleasure gardens of Studley Royal designed in the eighteenth century as an approach to Fountains Abbey and the Hall. An engraving made in 1758

it is unusually tall for its depth, rising to five storeys including the gables and basement. From the front its narrowness is not apparent. We see a highly decorative arrangement of bays and recesses, gables and battlements, balcony and statues, stringcourses and windows of different shapes and sizes. All except the castellation on the roof line is original. Its friendly little entrance gate, flanked by the oddest version of Corinthian columns that can ever have been thought up by a country mason, leads to a small forecourt and the steps up to the entrance floor of the house. Proctor's porch, with its confident Ionic columns, seems to reprove the homespun manner of the remainder. But nobody could wish away the stone figures of knights, now almost as shapeless as melting snowmen, which stand in niches or on pedestals, two in front of the Ionic columns, two above them and a further five on guard along the balustrade of the third-floor balcony. A square sundial with the unhelpful motto SIC TRANSIT GLORIA MUNDI (*sic* what?) is immediately above the front door. These inspirations culminate in the best feature of all: a semicircular bay window opening onto the balcony. From whatever viewpoint or distance you look at the south front, the eye picks up this detail instantly. Apart from the columns and archway of the front door, it is the only curved line in the entire façade. It is immensely delicate in conception and construction, and looks equally attractive from inside looking outwards as from the garden. On each side of it are the tallest windows in the house, a clear signal that behind them must lie the most important room.

So it proves. The room is called the Chapel Room, but only because the bases of two holy-water stoups, probably re-used as lamp brackets, have found their way into it from the old Abbey, and not because Sir Stephen Proctor, an ardent Protestant, could have used it or them for worship. It was clearly the Great Chamber of the house, sited, like Hardwick's, at its central and almost highest point. Besides the three lovely windows, it contains a contemporary fireplace of surpassing vulgarity and a modern copy of a Jacobean ceiling at Canonbury Tower in London. Fountains is not however an ugly house within. Its splendidly varied frontage give it well-lit rooms of pleasant outlook and excellent proportions. It lacks a long gallery, but possibly this was included at roof-level, as at Montacute, and was removed in a subsequent rebuilding of the top floor. Its two staircases, one enclosed in a square well and the other of spiralling stone lifted bodily from part of the Abbey, are an agreeable reminder of its dual origin. The hall, with a black and white floor and pretty minstrels' gallery, could with the minimum alteration serve as a hall in our present sense. But the use of the conditional reveals the tragedy of Fountains. Its only inhabitants are estate employees for whom flats have been constructed in the corner wings. The Vyners, to whom the house has come by descent, have kept it in good repair, but only for five years (1940–5) in the last two hundred has it been a family home.

The Vyners and their predecessors, the Aislabies, lived at Studley Royal, an early-Georgian house just over a mile away, now destroyed by fire. It was the eighteenth-century Aislabies, John and his son William, who linked Fountains Hall and Abbey to Studley Royal by a triumph of landscaping. Along the deep valley of the River Skell they created a half-garden, half-park, by damming the river at intervals to form weirs, lakes, straight stretches of canal and ornamental ponds. Around them they planted trees in profusion, and little temples, belvederes and fishing pavilions. At the west end of this paradisical approach was the Surprise View. It was, of course, the first view of the ruined Abbey, for which not only the Aislabies' park but the whole of eighteenth-century romantic landscaping might have been specially created. Here was the folly to outshine all follies, ready-made and, incidentally, genuine. The park has now grown to its perfect maturity, and the first view of the Abbey from it is still among the wonders of Britain. But further on, when the visitor thinks that he has seen everything that he could reasonably hope to see, comes a second surprise view: the gem-like Fountains Hall, hidden around a corner from the Abbey of which it was the child.

The 'Surprise View' of Fountains Abbey from halfway across the park. In the foreground is the 'Half-Moon', an artificial enlargement of the River Skell

HATFIELD HOUSE

The magnificent Jacobean house of the Salisbury family

Robert Cecil, first Earl of Salisbury, who built
Hatfield House between 1607 and 1611.
A portrait by Gheeraerts.

opposite The Marble Hall, looking towards the
Minstrels' Gallery at the east end. On the right
is Nicholas Hilliard's portrait of Queen Elizabeth
and at the far end a portrait of Mary Queen of
Scots by Oudry. The floor and the ceiling paintings
are Victorian additions

Robert Cecil, first Earl of Salisbury, the builder of Hatfield
House, was the second of the three members of his family who
have become chief ministers of the Crown. The first was his
father, Lord Burghley; the third, the Marquess of Salisbury
who was three times Prime Minister to Queen Victoria. Robert
Cecil remains the most enigmatic figure of the three. Although
he was forceful and occasionally ruthless in his public life, his
great office rendered him aloof, even friendless. The tension at
which he lived in the later years of Queen Elizabeth and the
early part of the reign of James I, when he was the butt of
intrigue and slander by less brilliant men, was increased by his
physical disabilities. Not much more than five foot three inches
in height, he was partly crippled by a curvature of the spine
which aroused the ridicule even of his cousin, Sir Francis Bacon.
More affectionately, Queen Elizabeth would call him her 'little
elf', and James I 'my little beagle', 'my pigmy'.

Of the two largest houses which his father built, Burghley,
from which he took his title, descended to the Earl of Essex, and
Theobalds so entranced James I that he suggested to his chief
minister that he should exchange it for the royal palace at Hatfield, a suggestion which Robert Cecil found difficult to refuse.
The old palace at Hatfield, built by Bishop Morton of Ely
towards the end of the fifteenth century, had been the home, at
times virtually the prison, of Henry VIII's children. While
seated under an oak tree in the park (which, wired and pitifully
battered, is still shown to visitors), Princess Elizabeth received
the news that her sister Mary was dead and that she was now
Queen of England.

As soon as the exchange of Theobalds for Hatfield had been
completed in 1607, Robert Cecil began to build a vast new
house for himself, a hundred yards south east of the old palace.
He was in a sense his own architect, for not only did he define
its main floor-plans and elevations, but the men whom he
employed on the actual construction – a factotum named
Thomas Wilson, the head carpenter Robert Lyminge, the
master-mason Conn, and a host of joiners, plasterers, inlayers,
carvers, glass-painters and gardeners from England, France,
Italy and Flanders – were required to submit their designs for

his approval. The house was completed in five years, 1607–11. It was an extraordinary achievement of planning and organisation. The stone was brought from Caen, where a special quarry was opened by licence of the French king; marble from Carrara; bricks from the old palace; timber from the estate. Even before the house was half-built, the terraces were laid out around it, and John Tradescant, the first of the great English botanists, was scouring the Continent for unusual trees and plants.

Those same five years were Cecil's busiest. As the ablest administrator of his age he was running the country almost single-handed, and simultaneously was building Salisbury House in London, making extensive alterations to Cranborne in Dorset and managing distant estates like St Michael's Mount in Cornwall. As one walks through the immensely elaborate house to-day fresh from studying the manuscript records of its building, one can conceive something of the anxious urgency with which the different elements, often prefabricated in widely separated workshops, were fitted together with shipwright's precision. Anyone who has had the satisfaction of building or adapting a far more modest house can imagine the solace which Robert Cecil must have derived from the knowledge that his house was growing in his absence, and that one day soon he would sleep there. But his health broke under the strain of office. He stayed no more than eight nights at Hatfield before it was barely habitable, and died at Marlborough on 24 May 1612 at the age of

All that remains of the old palace at Hatfield, a hundred yards north-west of the present house. A large part of the building was demolished in 1607 and the brick used for the new house

opposite The east window of the chapel at Hatfield painted with scenes from the Old Testament in 1609–10 by English, French and Flemish glass painters.

The north front, now the entrance front. Originally the two corner towers were topped by cupolas

opposite top The south front. The forecourt and the elegant Renaissance loggias contrast with the austerity of the north front

opposite The centre of the south front, possibly designed by Inigo Jones. The date of 1611 set in huge stone numerals over the porch marks the completion of the house

forty-nine. It was left to his son to add the finishing touches.

Like Blickling, another great Jacobean house of which Robert Lyminge was part-architect, Hatfield illustrates perfectly what a nobleman of the early seventeenth century conceived to be the essentials of a private house fit to receive his Sovereign. The approach to it must be impressive, but not forbidding; the plan must allow for great state receptions as well as for privacy; the interior must incorporate works of art built into the fabric as fireplaces, ceilings, doorways, panelling and staircases to compensate for the comparative sparseness of contemporary furnishing; the house must be lit by great windows and warmed by capacious fires; and from the windows there must be views of formal gardens abruptly separated from the surrounding park.

In carrying out his ideas, Robert Cecil was part traditionalist, part innovator. Nowhere is the contrast better shown than by the two main fronts. The north front presents a façade which differs little from the accepted style of the late sixteenth century, a cliff of warm brick ridged by shallow bays and recesses and broken by tall wide windows symmetrically disposed. Its rather overpowering, sawn-off appearance today is partly due to the substitution in the nineteenth century of plate-glass for the original small leaded panes and the removal of the ogee-shaped domes to the angle turrets, just visible in Knyff's and other eighteenth-century views of the house. But the south front represents a quite different conception of grandeur. Here the projecting east

and west wings form a forecourt of great dignity, varied but not muddled, to which the central 'Italian' arcade, the Flemish-type gables and the white timber tower behind add a note of such elegance that it has been attributed to Inigo Jones, an attribution that the heavy Jacobean porch makes unlikely.

The house is in the shape of the Greek letter *pi*, or flattened U, the wings forming the two uprights. Cecil followed the Elizabethan style to the extent that he placed a great hall in the centre of his house, a long gallery and three or four great chambers on the first storey, and a chapel at the side. But in the west wing, which he intended for himself, and in the east wing for his guests, he inserted many smaller rooms, sometimes two or three in the width of the wing, which foreshadow the arrangements which we still accept as inevitable and right. Thus Hatfield is really three houses: the two wings, and the central block. Already the Great Hall and the Long Gallery were becoming anachronisms, although Hatfield would lose much of its splendour and interest without them. The Marble Hall, as it is called today, is the Jacobean elaboration of the hub of a mediaeval and Tudor house, retaining all the old features of screen, minstrels' gallery, bay-window and a huge fireplace, but functionally it was neither a hall in the old sense nor a room in the new sense. The convenience of the Long Gallery as a place for gentle exercise in cold or wet weather and in which to display furniture and pictures was not to compensate much longer for

A reception for Queen Victoria held in the Long
Gallery at Hatfield in 1846. The gallery runs the
whole length of the first floor and apart from the
gilding of the ceiling has remained unchanged
since the building of the house

its awkwardness as a room for conversation nor for proportions that appeared increasingly clumsy to fastidious eyes. The gallery at Hatfield is 180 feet long by only twenty wide, and although its decoration is superb of its kind, it is basically a long wooden box unrelieved by window-bays and relying on the two splendid fireplaces to break the monotony of its great length. The illustration of the crowded reception for Queen Victoria in 1846 shows its unsuitability for even the grandest occasions.

Hatfield owes as much to its fitted woodwork, marble and painted glass as to the works of art that were added subsequently. The hall screens, the Grand Staircase, the east window of the chapel and the ubiquitous Jacobean fireplaces produce an effect of Mannerist splendour. Jacobean ornamentation can be crisp and even playful, but it can suddenly degenerate into grossness and vulgarity. Strapwork on the ceilings and below the stairs, and stern caryatids thrusting their torsoes outwards from the walls or from below a balcony, contrast oddly at Hatfield with the lovely panels in the gallery and the balustrade of the staircase. The latter is the showpiece of the house, and rightly so, for not only is it the second staircase (after Knole's) to be treated as an architectural feature in itself, but it climbs from the level of the Marble Hall to the King James Drawing Room in short wide flights of steps, surmounted by snarling lions and laughing boys, that make it as free and vigorous as the ascent to the poop of a galleon.

In later centuries Hatfield was cared for by successive Lords Salisbury with skill and devotion. The house suffered one major disaster: in 1835 the central part of the west wing was burnt to the ground, and with it perished the aged Lady Salisbury, whose charming portrait as a young woman by Sir Joshua Reynolds makes so dreadful a death even harder to contemplate. Her son rebuilt the gaping hole, and glassed in the open loggia of the south front to form the Armoury, one of the most effective nineteenth-century transformations to be seen in Britain. His son, the third Marquess, Queen Victoria's Prime Minister, renewed every part of the house that showed the defects of its age. Something of the many-sided character of the family is revealed in Lord David Cecil's casual account of the way in which the Prime Minister, a scientist as well as statesman, installed electricity at Hatfield in 1881: 'It was one of the first houses to be so lighted. The installation was very dangerous. Apart from the risks of shocks, the naked wires on the Gallery ceiling were apt to break into flame. The family sitting beneath nonchalantly threw up cushions to put the fire out and then went on with their conversation.'

below The North Gallery, opening off the Long Gallery. In the foreground is the cradle used by the infant Charles I

The Grand Staircase. The elaborately carved woodwork shows the influence of the Italian Renaissance on English ornament

The Armoury, originally the open loggia on the south front. The fretted and glazed screens were added in 1830. Much of the armour was captured from the Spanish and presented to Lord Burghley by Queen Elizabeth

BLICKLING HALL

NORFOLK

A Jacobean house set in an eighteenth-century garden

To begin a description of Blickling in a corner of its garden from which the house is not even visible may be thought eccentric. The first sight of the entrance front from the public road is so famous and breathtaking that every passing motorist brakes instinctively to have a longer look. But the secret of the place is only discovered late in the day among the trees and flowering shrubs that stretch upwards from the east side of the house. Never has there been a garden quite like it, not at least since the eighteenth century, which created the idea of long avenues crossing each other at bosky *rond-points* and culminating in a white pavilion.

Memories of Versailles, Knyff's famous series of views and the legacies of Brown and Repton have prejudiced the English against the idea of the formal avenue. But an avenue is formal only if it is undeveloped or kept too trim. The garden at Blickling is neither. It remains decade after decade – and this is no paradox – at its prime. Elsewhere it might be called a wilderness, but here the term is quite inapt for something so leafy, so sunlit, so well-ordered and fulfilling so perfectly the intention which its creators never lived to see. Great arches of beech and oak form choirs and aisles, and under them grow azaleas, rhododendron, magnolias and the wild bluebell. At the end of each avenue is a stone urn or a glimpse from different angles of a Tuscan temple perfectly sited for the presiding deity of this glorious profusion, but more likely to have been used in the eighteenth century for tea-parties. Beyond stretches the park. At first the trees seem to continue the idea of the garden outside its encircling ha-ha, but then they thin out: grazing animals take the place of shrubs, and the silver crescent of a lake curves out of sight behind a natural hill.

That the eighteenth century should so strongly permeate the surroundings of a Jacobean house is not accidental. Much of its interior was refashioned at that time and the house recovered its former glory as a centre of arts and politics, as it did again in our own century when Lord Lothian was the owner. When Blickling was built, between 1616 and 1625, the arrangement and interior decoration of the rooms achieved standards of convenience and elegance which did not put later and more fastidious

Sir Henry Hobart, Lord Chief Justice to James I and the builder of Blickling Hall. A portrait by Daniel Mytens

opposite Two drawings of Blickling Hall made in about 1735 by Edmond Prideaux, who sketched a number of English country houses. The top picture shows the entrance front, which has remained virtually unchanged, and below it is the west front before the rebuilding of 1769

above The south or entrance front. The front is capped by an ogival cupola similar to those at Hatfield and is one of several features the houses, both built by Robert Lyminge, have in common

opposite The east front from a corner of the formal garden created in the 1930s

generations to discomfort or shame. It is true that they rebuilt
one-and-a-half wings, but the one was reconstructed in 1769
because it was falling down, while the half was rebuilt by the
second Earl of Buckinghamshire a few years later, with the
apparent purpose of making room to hang a large and very
beautiful tapestry which he had acquired as Ambassador to
Catherine the Great. But when they rebuilt, they scarcely
altered the original appearance of the house, using the same
brick, respecting the old proportions and retaining the south and
east fronts exactly as Robert Lyminge had erected them a
century-and-a-half before.

Lyminge had been chief surveyor during the building of Hatfield, which was completed five years before Blicking was begun.
His new master, Sir Henry Hobart, the Lord Chief Justice, seems
to have given him a rather freer hand than he had been allowed
by Robert Cecil. Lyminge had by then developed his skill and
self-assurance to the point where his patron could trust him
implicitly and give him the credit that was his due. He was
permitted to incorporate his cypher RL among the stone
decorations above the south entrance porch at Blickling, a
privilege which the Lord Treasurer would never have counten-
anced at Hatfield; and the parish register of burials described
him without qualification as 'the architect and builder of

Blickling Hall'. It is perhaps not too fanciful to find further evidence of his greater independence in the more relaxed lines of Blickling compared to the earlier house. Hatfield's north front verges on the severe and its Long Gallery is gaunt. Blickling gained no advantage from its site – it is low-lying and hemmed in by the fosses of an earlier moat, while Hatfield was built on virgin and rising ground – but one senses immediately that its architect's intention was hospitable.

The forecourt is formed by two detached buildings enlivened by Flemish gables that roll like breakers towards the entrance front, and their curves are taken up by vast yew hedges that extend down to the road. This is the view that takes the visitor by surprise and makes him gasp. For, closing the fourth side of the rectangle, is a façade that combines colour, dignity, excitement and pageantry to a degree that was to become impossible only a few years later, when Inigo Jones rendered such indigenous creations out of date. The second Earl could refer to part of it, not unkindly, as 'Gothic'. Though Blickling owes something to Dutch and Franco-Italian influences, it is as English as a Constable. If Montacute proves that the Elizabethans could be graceful, Blickling's two untouched fronts prove that the Jacobeans could be light-hearted. All the elements of Hatfield are present here – the ogival cupolas to the corner turrets, the

The Peter the Great Room, reconstructed by the second Earl of Buckinghamshire in about 1700 to accommodate the tapestry of Peter the Great at the Battle of Poltava seen on the far wall

dominating clock-tower, the heavily decorated porch, the strap-work, the pierced balconies – but they lift the spirits in a manner which Hatfield never quite succeeds in doing.

Blickling has one major fault in its design, the meanness of its two inner courts. The second hides its clutter so shamefacedly that it can only be seen from a few upper windows. They are forgotten or ignored as soon as one goes indoors. Facing the front door is a monumental staircase. It does not occupy its original position, for considerable internal rebuilding in the eighteenth century, not yet quite clarified, did away with the Great Hall and substituted for it a hall in the more modern sense of the term, extending across the whole inner width of the house between the east and west wings. It is from this hall that the staircase rises in two branching flights linked at their upper ends by a landing that continues the balustrade round the fourth side. Lyminge's staircase was of one branch only, and it probably led to the present ante-room. The existing stair-case incorporates much of his original timbers and carving, but the doubling of it, the adaptation of its style and its reconstruction in a far more spectacular position, were due to Thomas Ivory, a Norfolk architect, in 1760. This was the very year when Robert Adam launched his great innovations in design which left not even Blickling untouched, and it is amazing to find that

The shape of one of the oak newels of the original Jacobean staircase preserved in the plaster wall of the ante-room

left The grand staircase, which divides into two flights at the first landing. It is a partial reconstruction of the original Jacobean staircase which consisted of a single flight

Thomas Ivory's original drawing, dated 1760, for the reconstructed staircase

a craftsman and patrician patron of that contemptuous period could create together so proud an anachronism instead of sweeping Lyminge's work away. To mount this staircase is more impressive to the touch and tread than the ascent of the most gorgeous *treppenhaus* in a German baroque palace. The very creaking of the oak reminds one of the ingenuity of its construction; one clings to the banister-rail like a child. On each newel-post stands a lovely wooden statuette, not two the same – a musketeer, a soldier in a cocked hat, a Highlander, a bearded courtier – some Lyminge's originals, some eighteenth-century improvisations on the same theme, which form an ascending sculpture gallery so romantic that the ages of Lyminge and Ivory (did the second know even the name of the first?) seem bridged by it across a hundred and fifty years.

The state-rooms on the first floor are no anticlimax to this splendid approach. They are tall, well-lit chambers which illustrate once more how happy a marriage was arranged at Blickling between the early seventeenth and late eighteenth centuries. The ceilings, doors and windows were for the most part left untouched; the Jacobean fireplaces sometimes remain, and there is a magnificent specimen in the south drawing-room, stripped to its parent oak. The walls surrendered their panelling to Gainsboroughs and Flemish tapestries, and the floors their exposed planks to Axminster and Moorfields.

There is one room, however, which remained almost unaltered till the nineteenth century and still has the bearing of one of the noblest rooms in Britain. This is the Long Gallery, which extends a hundred and twenty feet along the greater part of the east front. Its immense plaster ceiling is renowned, its library is comparable to Longleat's, but its proportions are what make it so immediately acceptable as a great work of art. Few long galleries are later in date than that at Blickling, and at the moment when the awkward tradition was about to die, it at last found its justification in this room. Its unusual width makes its great length not merely tolerable but superb. Its window embrasures are large enough to accommodate a sofa. It is a room in which one can converse or work, and yet it clamours for a state ball. From its windows you look across the garden and the park towards that little white temple among the trees where this inadequately short journey began.

opposite The Long Gallery with its elaborate plaster ceiling incorporating coats of arms and allegorical figures. The bookcases and the painted frieze above are nineteenth-century additions, but most of the room has remained unchanged since its construction in 1620–30

One of the panels in the ceiling of the Long Gallery representing a virgin astride a dragon

The original engraving on which the ceiling panel was based, taken from Henry Peacham's *Minerva Britanna*, 1612, a series of symbolic representations of the major virtues

Pulchritudo fœminea. 58

A VIRGIN naked, on a Dragon sits,
One hand out-stretch'd, a chriftall glaffe doth fhow:
The other beares a dart, that deadly hits;
Vpon her head, a garland white as fnow,
Of * print and Lillies. Beautie moft defir'd,
Were I her painter, fhould be thus attir'd.

WILTON HOUSE

WILTSHIRE

A Tudor house transformed by Inigo Jones

It would be rash to name any one of the great English houses still in private hands as the greatest, but Wilton must come close to it if one does not require that it be of enormous size, that it be built all of one piece and all at one time, and that the exterior be grandiloquent. Wilton demonstrates that greatness can be composed of the opposite qualities. Large it is, but not so enormous that parts of it must now be shut up, curtainless and cold. It is a unity, retaining through the centuries its four-square compactness, an almost keep-like sturdiness of plan, but each addition, reconstruction and amendment was an initiative, daring for its age. Wilton is the product of a succession of experiments and accidents which taste and time have blended into a whole.

One cannot visit Wilton without becoming aware of the firm continuity of the family, generation to generation. The Herberts, Earls of Pembroke and Montgomery, are as closely linked as any noble family in Britain, brother to brother, father to son, and it is the house which links them, for since the time of Henry VIII until today none but the Herberts have owned it. The evident pleasure which they take in each other's company, a pleasure that can reach back four centuries without affectation, has never frozen into ancestor-worship. On the contrary, one of the most endearing characteristics of the Herberts, which has left a significant mark on the house, is their refusal to be satisfied with the way in which things were decided and done in their childhood. There was not only a strong streak of adventurousness in their character, carried to the point of political and military audacity, but a feeling for the arts and sciences, and a delight in the company of innovators.

The house had its origins in the great Abbey of Wilton, and part of the Abbey's knobbly stone wall has recently been uncovered, reaching high into the core of the present house. On the dissolution of the Abbey in 1544, Henry VIII presented the lands to William Herbert (1507–70), son of a distinguished Welsh family, who served François I as a soldier of fortune and was recommended by him to the English king. William married the sister of Catherine Parr, Henry's sixth Queen, and in the reigns of Edward VI, Mary and Elizabeth he became one of the

A drawing of the east front of the Tudor house as it appeared in 1566, taken from a scroll of the first Earl's estates still preserved at Wilton

opposite The interior of the Palladian Bridge looking towards the south front

The south front constructed in about 1635–40 by Isaac de Caus under the direction of Inigo Jones. It was originally intended as one wing of a much larger house

opposite The Palladian bridge constructed over the river Nadder by the ninth Earl of Pembroke and Roger Morris in 1736–37. It was widely admired and the subject of many imitations

most powerful figures in the country. It was he, the first Earl of Pembroke, who built the original house at Wilton as soon as the property came into his hands.

Two parts of the Tudor house survive. One is the great tower in the centre of the east front, until the early nineteenth century the main entrance to the house. Flanked today by a mixture of mid-seventeenth-century building and Wyatt's Gothick, and itself touched at parapet level by Wyatt's hand, it still outshines them both. Tall and broad, proud in its proportions, particu-

126

larly of the central oriel window, it led the visitor to expect a superb house behind. He would not have been disappointed. He rode through the archway to the courtyard which still, in essentials, remains as the open centre of the house, and dismounted at an inner porch, the second of the Tudor survivals. Attributed to Holbein (but with scant authority, for Holbein died the year after the property was acquired), it stands today at the end of a long garden path, a beautiful example of the fusion between the English Gothic and Italian Renaissance styles of architecture.

It was in this house that Philip Sidney wrote his *Arcadia* and Ben Jonson and Donne were visitors. There is adequate reason to believe that Shakespeare's *As You Like It* was first performed there, whatever one may think of the claims of William Herbert to have been the Mr W. H. of the Sonnets. But splendid as the Tudor house undoubtedly was, it alone was not enough to satisfy Philip, the fourth Earl, who succeeded his brother William in 1630. When the house was barely eighty years old, Philip pulled down the south block and erected in its place a façade and a set of rooms that have no rival for their period in the whole of English domestic architecture.

Philip's architect, it can be proudly if loosely said, was Inigo Jones. Certainly Jones was consulted, and Henrietta Maria, for whom he was then (1635) finishing the Queen's House at Greenwich, pressed the Surveyor of the Royal Works upon Wilton, for which she and the King had a deep affection. But Jones was too busy to do more than sketch an outline, and passed on the detailed work to an assistant, a Frenchman from Dieppe named Isaac de Caus. A drawing bearing de Caus' name was recently discovered by Mr Howard Colvin in the library of Worcester College, Oxford, and it is here reproduced. It has created consternation in the world of architectural historians. For not only did it confirm beyond doubt Aubrey's hint that a Frenchman, and not the great English master Inigo Jones, was sufficiently responsible for the famous façade 'all *al Italiano*' for a contemporary elevation of it to bear his name, but it showed that the existing building is less than half that intended by its creator. There was to have been a central portico of six Corinthian columns, flanked on the far side by a wing of equivalent length. In front, aligned on this portico, extended a vast garden, a thousand feet in length by four hundred wide, with a broad central path carried over the River Nadder on a bridge as flat and unemphatic as a culvert on a modern by-pass. The garden was actually constructed and maintained by an army of gardeners for over a hundred years. But of the south front only the right-hand wing was built, possibly because the outbreak of the Civil War and Philip's quarrel with the King placed the family fortunes in jeopardy.

A comparison between the de Caus elevation and the photograph of the present south front shows that nothing was lost by the curtailment of the plan. Instead, it was adapted by a stroke

The 'Holbein' porch, which originally stood on the north side of the inner quadrangle, but was moved to the garden by Wyatt in about 1805. It dates from *c* 1545, but it is doubtful whether Holbein actually designed it.

opposite The chimney-piece in the Double Cube Room, which remains exactly as Inigo Jones designed it. The painting by Van Dyck is of the children of Charles I

129

opposite The west end of the Double Cube Room.
It retains all the original decorations by Inigo
Jones and John Webb, but some of the furniture
is later. The painting of the Herbert family
is Van Dyck's largest conversation piece

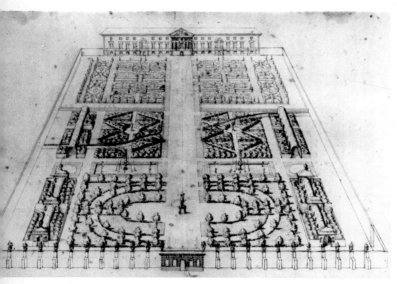

A drawing by de Caus at Worcester College,
Oxford, showing the original plan for the south
front. Only the right-hand wing of the building
was completed, but the garden, crossed diagonally
by the River Nadder, was actually constructed

The east front, which was the entrance front
until 1801. The central tower is all that survives
in situ of the original Tudor house

of genius which one feels tempted to attribute to Inigo Jones
himself. The great Venetian window, which was to have been
matched by another in the middle of the west wing, became the
central feature; and de Caus' rather weak roof line was lifted at
each end by towers topped by pedimented pavilions. A symmetrical and perfectly composed façade was created out of the
wreck of the original plan. Seldom can an architect have turned
disappointment to such advantage.

The south front shields on its first storey a magnificent set of
seven state-rooms, two of which, the Single and the Double
Cube rooms, rise to roof height. A fire destroyed part of this
block in 1647, only a few years after its completion, but Christopher Hussey has argued convincingly that it did not do as
much damage as was once supposed. If we accept his thesis that
the existing façade is the de Caus-Jones original (*c.*1635–40) and
that a Double Cube room was already part of the house before
the fire, we need only attribute to Inigo Jones and John Webb,
Jones' nephew-by-marriage, the repair and redecoration of the
suite in 1648–53, and not its total reconstruction. In any case,
the whole work, pre-fire and post-fire, occupied less than twenty
years, inspired by Inigo Jones throughout and executed in turn
by two of his ablest assistants, each of them an architect in his
own right.

These seven famous rooms make on every visitor an impression of restrained richness, to which scale, colour and furnishing
all contribute. To contemporaries, for whom a magnificent Jacobean house like Hatfield was barely thirty years old, Wilton
must have appeared an extraordinary novelty. Italian in in-

spiration outside, French within, it contrives to be essentially English. The series of smaller rooms leading to the Double Cube are caskets of subdued gold. One of them, the Corner Room, occupies the south-east angle of the house, where one would expect to find a large room taking advantage of the windows on the two sides. Instead, though not the smallest of the seven, it has a warmth and intimacy rare in great foreign houses of the period, and the same is true of the Hunting Room at the opposite end. Between them, the Double Cube and the Single Cube lift the scale to palatial proportions. The first is sixty feet long by thirty wide and thirty high; the second is half the length but of the same width and height. Both are decorated by great swags of fruit and flowers, carved in wood, gilded in different shades of gold and attached by screws to the walls of white-painted pine. The doorways, of which drawings annotated by Inigo Jones and Webb survive, the chimney-pieces of Italian marble and the coved ceilings are particularly ornate, but nowhere is there the same assault on the eye as is made by the interiors of near-contemporary French houses like Vaux-le-Vicomte, where scarcely a square inch was left unenriched.

The Single Cube Room, exactly thirty feet in each dimension. It is now thought that this room survived the 1647 fire and therefore remains as Inigo Jones and de Caus designed it.

The Hunting Room, the last of the seven State rooms on the south side of the house. The hunting scenes which give the room its name are by Edward Pierce, *c* 1653

Design for one of the State-room doors, annotated by Inigo Jones (*top left*)and John Webb

The Double Cube was redesigned after the fire to hold the magnificent series of family and royal portraits by Van Dyck, commissioned by the fourth Earl in 1632–4. They were brought down from Durham House in London, at what risk and labour one can imagine from their size, and form around the walls panels which owe almost as much to the dignity of the sitters as to the skill of the artist. How the room was otherwise furnished in the seventeenth century is not known, but the gilt and red velvet settees, the chairs and mirrors by Chippendale and William Kent, were clearly designed for the room, and although a century later in date, conform admirably to its tone and style.

By 1653 the house was complete. Still set on its square Tudor base, with carriages of increasing lightness and magnificence passing into the central courtyard through the arch of the great tower and leaving it by an equivalent arch on the opposite side, Wilton retained throughout the eighteenth century its national importance as a focus for politicians and artists and the hub of a remarkably enterprising family. There was one black sheep, the seventh Earl, a spendthrift and suspected murderer; but his brother Thomas, who succeeded him in 1683, was a man of great learning who held many high offices of state under five sovereigns and assembled the larger part of the art-collection which still enriches the house. It was his son Henry, the 'Architect Earl', who in 1736, with the help of his clerk-of-works Roger Morris, built the Palladian bridge.

James Lees-Milne rightly calls the Wilton bridge 'one of the most beautiful buildings in all England'. It crosses the little River Nadder on a level with the east front, so that the house is seen at an angle through its arches and columns, and the bridge at an angle from the southern windows, postponing the moment of delight and surprise when one walks across the lawn to view it from the side. Even if the ninth Earl had limited himself to constructing the five arches of the bridge and the balustrade, it would still have been a great achievement. But what gives it charm and originality (for it owed little to Palladio and nothing to anyone else) is the temple-portico which rises unnecessarily, extravagantly, but with the utmost grace, above it. There can be few better examples of heaviness of structure lightened by design. Mounting the mossy steps, you feel cradled in stone. The splash of the waterfall beneath, the dancing of shadows on the diamond-patterned ceiling, the enfolding arms of the balustrade, even the swan which floats obligingly below, create a mood of exhilaration and suspense. It is only afterwards that one considers in how many different variations the Palladian-bridge idea could have been carried out, and wonders at the ingenuity of the man who gave it this sublime form.

At the beginning of the nineteenth century Wilton suffered a transformation. Between 1801 and 1810, by which time relations between architect and patron had degenerated to the point of mutual insult, James Wyatt modernized the house. His work was completed by Sir Jeffrey Wyatville, his nephew. That Wyatt did not employ at Wilton the neo-classic style of which he was a greater master, but instead Gothicised it, has been much regretted. That he destroyed the hall, staircase and chapel, and displaced the 'Holbein' porch, is to our eyes unforgivable. The patently blind wall with fake doors and windows which he erected on the east side of his new approach court is one of the few architectural crimes of which Wilton remains a victim. But given all this, there is no doubt that Wyatt did the house a service by the two-storeyed cloister which he built round all four sides of the inner courtyard. Not only was it an added convenience to a house without corridors, but it is in itself a fine construction and a perfect setting for the Pembroke collection of classical sculpture and other works of art. Now that its walls and vaulting have been repainted by the present Earl in warm terra-cotta with grey ribs, it forms an adjunct to the house by which previous centuries would have been startled, but not, one likes to think, ashamed.

This account of Wilton has been traced chronologically. But such is the composure of the house that a description room by room, sliding the centuries in and out, would have served as well. It is a palimpsest of styles, and none except certain parts of Wyatt's contribution jars upon the rest. What blemishes it has, have been masked by the taste of the present owner, the sixteenth Earl. Its perfections, its superb contents, have never been shown to better advantage than they are today.

The Corner Room, one of the small anterooms leading to the Double Cube Room redecorated after the fire of 1647

GROOMBRIDGE PLACE

KENT

A small Restoration house surrounded by a mediaeval moat

Several of the houses described in this book are squared off by a moat. Where they are still water-filled it is usually a sign that the building has changed little since moats went out of fashion. But at Groombridge, when the house was totally rebuilt in 1660, the moat was kept as a decorative feature. It is wide enough to justify substantial bridges across three of its four sides, and its water is constantly on the move, filled from a mill-race and emptying into a long eighteenth-century canal that runs beside the approach drive. It creates a constant play of reflected, dancing sunlight on the inner sides of the window-frames; it is a reminder of distant history and forgotten men; and it is in itself a lovely adjunct which nobody would have invented had it not already been there.

A moat suggests grandeur, but Groombridge is reticent to the point of self-effacement. What house standing in the open countryside would present to the world only one effective façade, unless its builder was an exceptionally modest man? Even the garden front is an apologetic confusion of windows which do not add up to a pattern; only one of them is the window of a room, and that a servant's bedroom. At the back the outlook is on corn-stooks, agreeable enough but almost accidentally so; and the façade is split centrally by a chimney-stack. On the side of the stable-court, an almost windowless wall drops sheer into the moat, very prettily but again the effect has not been contrived by anything more than the right use of good materials. This leaves the entrance front, the façade that immediately attracts every eye and camera, and it places Groombridge among the most perfect of smaller Restoration houses. The effect is achieved by an almost bucolic adaptation of contemporary taste. There is a hipped roof with dormers, two projecting wings, early eighteenth-century sash-windows and a front door on each side, as if even this normally emphatic feature must be played down to avoid any charge of ostentation. But then something was added, perhaps as an afterthought, which suggests that after all some kind of simple flourish was considered appropriate. An Ionic portico extends between the two wings. It is not necessary to the design, but it greatly enhances it, and the wonder is that so classical a frontispiece fits in with so very English a composition.

Looking outwards from within the Ionic entrance porch towards the moat

opposite The entrance front from across the moat. Groombridge was totally rebuilt in about 1660 on the site of an earlier mediaeval house

135

136

above The stable block on the south side which drops directly into the moat

opposite top The back of the house. The same trouble has not been taken on this side to achieve a symmetrical arrangement of windows and chimneys

opposite A bird's eye view of the house and garden drawn by C. E. Kempe in 1884, but including a seventeenth-century coach

The north wall of the garden. These walls extend round three sides of the garden and are contemporary with the moat and the earlier fifteenth-century house

It must have been this loggia which justified John Evelyn's surprising description of Groombridge as 'a modern Italian villa'.

Evelyn was a friend of its builder, Philip Packer, and he visited the house soon after it was finished. He had also known and described the house which it replaced, the 'pretty, melancholy seat' of the fifteenth-century Waller family, and regretted that Packer had not rebuilt it higher up the slope of the valley instead of on its floor. Mr S. W. Mountain, the present owner, insists that the low-lying, mediaeval site is the best one. Groombridge is not shut in. It lies beside a stream that forms the boundary between Kent and Sussex, and although the house cannot be seen from any great distance, the views from its windows do not appear confined, and its lovely farm-buildings at the back form an extension of the house. Besides, without water for its moat it would have lost much of its attractiveness, and there is as much to be said for a garden climbing up from the house as for a house standing above its garden.

The garden at Groombridge is of great antiquity. It preserves its grey buttressed walls from the fifteenth century, against which there are concentrations of herbaceous colour, and between them, mounting in a series of terraces, there are yew hedges sheltering little orchards and lawns. It is a garden full of scent and bird-song. The water of the mill-stream coruscates soundlessly, and the main path ascends at right angles towards gates which add just the right touch of formality.

Not only the garden-walls and moat survive to remind one of the Wallers' house. Groombridge also contains much of its wainscoting. Whether Philip Packer incorporated it in his new house out of sentiment or economy is impossible to tell. Perhaps it was a combination of both, since the panelling and fireplaces had been in place for less than a hundred years when the old house was torn apart. Only one main room, the drawing-room, was entirely repanelled in the seventeenth-century taste to accommodate the series of Packer portraits which have remained with the house in spite of a fairly frequent change of ownership. The others – the dining-room, the Morning Room and the Hall Chamber – resemble Elizabethan rooms and presumably had their counterparts in the original house. It is consistent with this view that the house has a predominantly Elizabethan ground-plan, forming an H with the hall in the cross-bar and bedrooms in the upper floor of the wings. The dining-room, previously the hall, lies immediately below the Hall Chamber, and both occupy the whole thickness of the house. This should not suggest rooms of any great size or magnificence. They are companionable, with low ceilings, and scarcely large enough for more than two groups of people to sit down to separate conversations. Their windows look out along the valley on both sides, towards the lake and villages on the approach front, and to the untroubled fields on the east. The interior absorbs the calm of its surroundings, and the furniture, most of it collected by Mr Mountain's father, is an evocation of its period.

The drawing-room, decorated in Restoration style. The oak wainscoting was made to fit the series of seventeenth-century portraits of the Packer family, who rebuilt Groombridge in 1660

A detail of the panelling in the Hall Chamber showing the black and gold decoration painted on the wood in imitation of inlay

The Hall Chamber on the first floor, now used as the main living room. The panelling is sixteenth-century and comes from the old house

WESTON PARK

SHROPSHIRE

Lady Wilbraham's masterpiece in brick and stone

From the air, or from the middle of Capability Brown's park, one sees a long line of buildings, stone mixed with brick, grey with pink, and one would know it at once as the seat of a great English family who have enjoyed and improved their property over centuries. The different sections of this train of buildings identify themselves immediately. On the left is a small eighteenth-century church with an earlier tower, in which one would expect to find the memorials of the family. In front of it, clearly an addition of the nineteenth century in its best classical style, is an orangery linked to the house by a loggia. To the right of the house is a two-storey wing faced with stone, which again illustrates the tact with which the Victorian owners of Weston increased the size of an already considerable mansion without destroying its proportions. Beyond this wing, which connects the house to it, lies a stable-block of pink brick, a larger version of the stable attached to Mompesson House in Salisbury Close, and of almost exactly the same date, 1688. Behind rises a mass of subsidiary farm and horticultural buildings, of which one, an immense Georgian barn with flanking towers, is a reminder of the agricultural revolution of the 1780's. Still further to the right, embedded in the front edge of a wood, is a domed garden-temple which one discovers to be the creation of James Paine, one of the architects of Kedleston, in 1760–70.

But the eye is inevitably drawn back from these outriders to the house itself. It stands on a platform of terraces facing outwards to the park on three sides. From the south, one is looking at the original entrance front – a façade composed of alternate panels of brick wall and stone-framed windows, its centre emphasized by a broad band of stone rising to roof height. Arched gables at either end describe two faultless bows, each inset with an *oeil-de-boeuf*. They are joined by a pillared parapet along the flat roof, from which rise three chimney-stacks with shallow blind arches sunk into their nearer sides. The house, it could be said, owes its particular distinction to everything above the top windows. But much of its charm is also due to the colour of the brick, an orange pink, which has been accidentally enhanced by scoring it with diagonal grooves as a key for the stucco by which the house was faced in about 1825. Happily this stucco

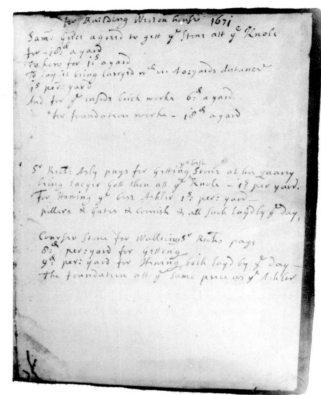

Notes on the cost of building work at Weston made by Lady Wilbraham in 1671 on the end-papers of a copy of Palladio's *First Book of Architecture*

opposite Looking between arches of the inner hall into a corner of the Tapestry Room

An aerial view of Weston taken from the south-east showing the whole range of buildings from the church on the left to the stables on the right. The park was laid out by Capability Brown, one of whose lakes can be seen behind the church

A detail of the brick and masonry on the east front showing how the brick was scratched with diagonal grooves to hold the stucco with which the façades were covered in 1825. The stucco was removed in 1939

was removed in 1939, restoring the variety of colour and pattern which was an essential part of the original design.

Weston was built by a woman in the 1670's. Lady Wilbraham, born Elizabeth Mytton, was heiress to the earlier house which stood upon the site, and after her marriage to a Cheshire baronet, Sir Thomas Wilbraham, in 1651, they appear to have lived here almost without a break. Twenty years later, she decided to rebuild the house completely. Preserved in the library at Weston is her copy of Godfrey Richard's translation of Palladio's *First Book of Architecture* (1663). On one end-paper at the back of the book there are notes in her own clear hand headed 'For building Weston House 1671'. Scrappy as they are, and with the date apparently added as an afterthought, the notes reveal the businesslike methods of a remarkably gifted woman. One wishes that her actual drawings could have survived, but to hold this small leather-bound volume in one's hand, with the single word PALLADIO blocked in gold on its spine, is to understand something of the architectural fervour that inspired the late seventeenth century.

The style of Weston is not, however, Italian: it is Dutch. Soon after 1660 Hugh May had introduced from Holland the fashion for combining brick with stone, rounded with classical pediments, and incorporating in the exterior of a building blind arches and giant Corinthian pilasters. All these features are present at Weston except the last, and of this there is a faint

The east front with the stone wing added in the nineteenth century on the right. The *porte cochère* was added in 1865 when the entrance was moved from the south to the east front

reminder in the curling stone leaves above the angle-quoins from which the rounded pediments spring. But Weston is far from being a slavish imitation of any other building. May's houses, for instance, were two-storeyed and had hipped roofs. Lady Wilbraham's inventiveness is further illustrated by the quite different treatment of the church and stables. The former is roofed by most attractive barrel-vaulting, while the latter demonstrates her confident handling of the now classic English style of Wren. Her epitaph is on a tablet in the church, but her true memorial lies in this group of three buildings upon which she lavished so much art and affection.

Apart from the building of the orangery and east wing, the chief alteration subsequently made to the house was the removal of the entrance from the south to the east side in 1865. Why this was done is not quite clear, unless it was to bring sunlight into all the main living-rooms, but retrospectively it is seen as a fortunate change, for the bulky *porte-cochère*, which the Victorians attached to their houses as much to impress their guests as to shelter them, was placed against the east front instead of the architecturally more important south front. It also left its mark on the inside of the house. The library became the hall, the hall the drawing-room, and the drawing-room and breakfast-room were combined to form the present library. The staircase was reconstructed in marble in about 1900, and the inner courtyard was covered in to form billiard and smoking

Elizabeth, Lady Wilbraham, a portrait by Sir Peter Lely. Despite her lack of architectural training, she designed Weston herself

The drawing room with the library beyond. Before the entrance was moved, this room was the hall, with the main door on the left

Looking through the front hall to the staircase with its delicate wrought-iron balustrade. This was reconstructed in 1900

rooms. The main reception rooms run along the south front, opening one into the other, each with separate access from the hall. These three rooms – tapestry-room, drawing-room and library – are in their different ways rooms of great charm. The first owes its name to beautiful rose-pink Gobelin tapestries which were made for a room on the upper floor but have been splendidly adapted to the walls of this corner room on the terrace level. The other two are long but intimate rooms, enlivened by internal pillars. The oval ceiling of the drawing-room and the rich bindings in the library create exactly that difference of texture and play of light needed to give them variety.

It was in these rooms that Disraeli, the ageing Prime Minister, consoled himself for the loss of his wife by the company of Selina, Countess of Bradford. In the last eight years of his life he daily sought her company and wrote her 1,100 letters, sometimes three on a single day when he was to see her that very evening. It was an innocent affair, although the style of the letters, romantic and sometimes desperate for her affection, could suggest otherwise until one remembers their ages: Disraeli was sixty-eight when he formed this new attachment, and Lady Bradford, though fifteen years younger, was already a grandmother. The relationship was accepted by the Earl of Bradford, then Master of the Horse, and one of the reasons could be that his wife was clearly a little bored by it after the compliment had lost its edge.

To the two remarkable women with whose names Weston will always be associated, should now be added a third, the present Countess of Bradford. She has transformed the centre of the house from what could have been a mausoleum of Victorian taste into inner halls and rooms as light-hearted as a conservatory. Weston has not only survived as a superb example of Restoration architecture: it is also a model of adaptation to our present needs and tastes.

opposite The south front seen from the Italian garden. The house is a remarkable adaptation of the Dutch style fashionable in the 1670s

BELTON HOUSE

LINCOLNSHIRE

A perfect house from the age of Wren

In the garden at Belton, drawing out the date of the house effortlessly at either end, are a Norman church and an early-Victorian orangery. The latter, with its slim vertical lines and well-proportioned statuary on the roof, does no discredit to the superb house across the lawn. But the church is even better, not so much for its pleasantly chunky exterior as for the memorials which it contains. A visit to Belton might well begin here. Family tombs have a way of becoming monotonous with their cold marble and unfailingly eulogistic inscriptions. But the Belton memorials are so continuous, generation to generation for nearly 350 years, that their cumulative message of mingled affection and pride is deeply impressive.

Here is the founder of the family fortunes, a Jacobean lawyer, Richard Brownlow (1555–1638), stiff in his niche and ruff; here his son and daughter-in-law, marble hands clasped everlastingly in mutual consolation for their childless marriage; here the lovely tablet to the memory of Sir John Brownlow (1660–97), to whom no statue was raised since it was enough to point to 'the testimony of his noble house which he built from the ground'; here Speaker Cust's memorial, the House of Commons mace peeping out discreetly from behind a shield; Lord Tyrconnel, the early eighteenth-century owner of Belton, comes next, surrounded by as delightful a canopy as ever framed a Georgian fireplace: and then succeeding Earls and Barons Brownlow attended by heavily draped ladies in attitudes of mourning or pointing the way to heaven, or more directly represented by recumbent effigies in crusader-like poses, one with a jowelled bulldog at his feet. Clearly they were proud of each other, and with reason, for each has contributed something to his country's and family's greater honour, and to the estate which binds them together across the centuries.

One meets the same people again inside the house, less solemn in their portraits than in their effigies, people with passions and prejudices as well as virtues and pedigrees, each with a taste for his or her contemporary furniture and decoration, and as prone to disappointment, enthusiasm, ambition and a desire for occasional solitude as the rest of us. But as so often, the impress of the builder on the house is the strongest of all. Not much is

One of the brass lock plates in the Saloon, engraved with the greyhound crest of the Brownlow family, who have owned Belton since it was built by Sir John Brownlow in 1684–7

opposite The Chinese Bedroom furnished according to fashionable eighteenth-century taste. The walls are hung with hand-painted paper and the bed hangings are of finely wrought Chinese silk

147

An aerial view of Belton from the south-east showing the relation of the main house to the stables on the left, and the orangery and church behind

opposite top The north or garden front, which is almost identical with the entrance front and has remained unaltered since the house was built

opposite The entrance front from the south-west. The pilasters and entablature to the front door were added by Wyatt in 1777

known of Sir John Brownlow's public life except that he was High Sheriff of Lincolnshire and twice Member of Parliament for Grantham, but his private life glows more strongly through the mist of time. He married his cousin when they were both aged sixteen, and died before he was forty. In that short interval he had created two great legacies: a family of five beautiful daughters (his only son died of smallpox in his infancy), and one of the loveliest houses to survive from the age of Wren.

Belton is not an original house in the sense that it introduced any new fashion in architecture. It is simply a summing-up of all that is best in the only truly vernacular style that England had produced since the late Tudors. Built with astonishing rapidity in three years (1684–7), it followed very closely the design of Clarendon House in Piccadilly, which was completed by Roger Pratt in 1647 and was demolished only the year before Belton was begun. 'Pratt's masterpiece,' says Sir John Summerson, 'was the most influential house of its time among those who aimed at the grand manner . . . Belton is much the finest surviving example of its class.' The contracting mason, William Stanton, is known, but the architect is not. The parallel with Clarendon House, however, is so close that any able draftsman could have drawn the plans of one from the other. The only difference between them is that the ends of the two wings have been narrowed at Belton from three windows' width to two, the main front has seven windows to Clarendon's nine, and there are equivalent changes to the number of dormers in the hipped roof. These changes make no difference to the proportions; if anything, they are even better at Belton.

The north side of the house which faces the garden is identical with the entrance front, but the former is slightly the more satisfying since it lacks the pilasters and entablature with which Wyatt framed the front door in the 1770's. If one were asked to show a stranger a single example of an English country-house at its proudest and most serene, one could not do better than lead him into the garden at Belton. Houses often have the same characteristics as different types of person of different ages. Belton exactly matches its builder's in the year of his death: a man of modest public distinction aged thirty-seven. Here is maturity without loss of vigour; no trace of pompousness, and little feminity; pride, certainly, in the display of arms in the pediments, but no attempt whatever to daunt the stranger – the deeply indented wings are as companionable as the arms of a chair. This effect is achieved with the minimum of fuss. Partly it is due to the beautifully weathered ashlar from the nearby Ancaster quarry, and on the south side to the lacy wrought-iron gates and railings attributed to Thomas Robinson, *c.* 1710; but mainly it is a lesson in balance and proportion, that indefinable quality, recognised when seen, that will be discussed later in the account of Antony, a Cornish house that shares many of Belton's merits. In the official guide to the house, the exterior is con-

trasted with the interior and called 'austere'. The description could not be less apt. Austerity implies that there has been no attempt to please. Belton has no other aim in view, and by the subtlest methods it succeeds brilliantly.

Within the house we find the same friendliness. Although the present Lord Brownlow lives in the west wing only and opens to visitors the remainder of the house and the whole garden from spring to autumn, the 'public' rooms still seem private. The ceilings are for the most part of only moderate height and the rooms are nowhere of dimensions that would make them unusable except on the grandest occasions. There are bedrooms so superbly furnished that their contents would be accepted gratefully by any museum tomorrow, but they look as if they could be slept in tonight. In the Saloon, the drawing-room and particularly the small tapestry-room, the richness of the furniture, walls, ceilings and works of art is subdued to the point where each demands examination in turn instead of competing against each other in a blaze of vainglory. One can still imagine them as they were in the early eighteenth century, occupied by Sir John's formidable widow and her five marriageable daughters. Once, it is said, the girls were giving an unsanctioned tea-party in an upper room at Belton when they heard their mother's footsteps approaching. There was only one thing to do. The whole tea-service – unfinished cups, tea-pot, table-cloth, cakes – was tossed out of the window just in time.

The impression which Belton makes today is not inconsistent with the spirit of these pretty, unmanageable girls. It is a light-hearted house. At the same time it is exquisite in its detail. From the resplendently gilded greyhound which flashes from the cupola above the house to its smaller companions on the brass door-plates in almost every downstairs room, it bears the stamp of family pride and care. There is nothing lavish about Grinling Gibbons' festoons and picture-surrounds in the hall, Saloon, chapel-gallery and elsewhere. They are simple, delicate works of art. That they should form the most important decorations at Belton is symptomatic of its whole character – gentle, undemonstrative, fanciful and yet supremely confident.

The Red Drawing Room, furnished in the Empire style and containing some of the finest paintings at Belton

opposite top A painting of the house soon after it was completed, said to have been made by Sir John Brownlow's butler. It shows the entrance front before the stable court was added

opposite bottom The Saloon, hung with portraits of the Brownlow family. On the table is displayed some of the fine collection of family silver

A detail of the wood carvings by Grinling Gibbons, set against the wainscoting of the chapel gallery

151

UPPARK

SUSSEX

A Restoration house on the edge of the South Downs

The word Uppark is pronounced with equal stress on both syllables, as if to distinguish it from Downpark which lies in the valley behind, and to proclaim, with no risk of misunderstanding, that this is a house in a park on top of a hill. The house is as straightforward as its name. It rises on the edge of an escarpment of the downs, looking southwards towards the sea over a huge landscape of sliding, dipping and crossing hills, which are so varied by their contours and woods that even Humphrey Repton conceded that any addition would be superfluous. But this stupendous view comes as a surprise. The visitor climbs the hill to approach the house from the north, where trees, outbuildings and the bulk of the house itself conceal the view and lead him to suppose that there will be a formal flattish garden on the far side. He comes round the corner of the house to discover the secret of its situation. There is no garden on this side. Instead, the open parkland, once cropped by deer and now by sheep and cattle, runs up to the very doorstep. Previously there was an oval pond in front of the house, and still earlier a small *parterre*, but later generations have tacitly agreed that the view should be as unimpeded as its approach is secret. Where one had expected to find at most a barn, thrust out by its lane into the middle of downland, one finds a palace. It could not be quieter nor seemingly more remote. It stands beautiful and compact, as if all civilization had led up to this point in space and time, and there was no object in going further.

Turning round to face the house from the park, one sees an impressive façade of brick and stone, simple in its proportions but boldly decorated. The arms of Fetherstonhaugh are thickly encrusted on the tympanum of the pediment, and festoons of stone flowers hang round the door and upper window. Most remarkably and effectively, the modillions (brackets) under the cornices of roof and pediment are richly ornamented. It is this combination of strong exterior decoration with the plain stone borders to the windows that gives the house its masculine character. For while it is immensely elegant, there is no fuss or sentimental delicacy in any part of it. It represents a style that is fully mature, owing something to the Netherlands, but immediately recognizable as English of the Restoration period.

Ford Lord Grey, later Earl of Tankerville, as a youth. He built the house in 1690, but his grandson sold it to the Fetherstonhaugh family

opposite top The south front seen from the park. The stable block is to the left behind the main house, and its twin, the kitchen block, is on the right

opposite bottom A drawing by Kip of Uppark in the early eighteenth century when the entrance was on the east side. It shows clearly the setting of the house in the Downs with the sea in the distance on the left

The dining room. The white and gilt pilasters are contemporary with the building, but the room was redesigned in the early nineteenth century. Emma Hart, later Lady Hamilton, is said to have danced on the table for the pleasure of Sir Harry Fetherstonhaugh

One of the marble sphinxes which flank the fireplace in the Stone Hall

The architect is not known. But we do know that Uppark was built about 1690 for Ford Lord Grey of Werke, later Earl of Tankerville. It is normal for English families to prefer their more disreputable ancestors to the respectable, but Lord Grey is an exception. He was a mean man, a seducer, a political turn-coat and a trickster. 'Cold Caleb,' Dryden called him, 'below the dignity of verse.' But he did build Uppark, and for that much can be forgiven him. An earlier family house had stood upon the site, of which some masonry survives in the basement, and the park was already mature when Celia Fiennes rode this way in 1694, soon after the house had been completed. 'I went to Chichester,' she wrote, 'through a very fine Parke of the Lord Tankervailes, stately woods and shady tall trees for at least 2 mile: in the middle stands his house which is new built, square, 9 windows in the front and seven in the sides, brickwork with freestone coynes and windows: its in the midst of fine gardens, gravell and green walks and bowling green.' When she saw it, and until the early nineteenth century, the entrance was on the east side. The first sight of the house and the view to the south was, therefore, originally obtained from a distance, along the downs from the east, and one can be forgiven for wishing that it was still so. But Repton considered that nobody would want to look out of his bedroom window onto a forecourt, and switched the entrance to the north front – the 'useful' front, as he called it – where a huddle of domestic buildings already existed and he could screen them with a new Doric portico. In his defence it can be said that the original architect had taken little trouble about this façade, and that Repton destroyed nothing. Indeed, the change of front has made possible a charming lawn on the east side, from which the brick and stone rise even more effectively than from the adjoining park.

One of the most endearing characteristics of Uppark is that each of its past owners has left his or her distinctive mark upon it. Only six generations have lived in it as their home since the time of its building. Lord Tankerville's grandson sold the estate in 1746 to Matthew Fetherstonhaugh, a youth from a Northumberland family, who inherited a vast fortune and bought a baronetcy to go with the place. It is to Sir Matthew and his wife Sarah Lethieullier that we owe the eighteenth-century decoration of the main rooms. The chief of them, the Saloon, is a double-cube room comparable to that at Wilton, although a century later in date and immeasurably lighter in style. For while in the Wilton room Inigo Jones and Webb had made use of heavy doorways and ornate swags against the walls, the decoration of the Uppark Saloon is of a gossamer fragility that anticipates Adam by more than a decade. Its colour is ivory, spangled with dull gold. The doorways, the reveals of the windows, the surrounds of the pictures and the ceiling coves are fondled by straying tendrils of gilded wood, in complete contrast to the virile decoration of the stonework on the wall outside. The Saloon is on the ground floor of the house, but its slight

opposite The Saloon, which lies in the centre of the south front on the ground floor. It was re-designed by Sir Matthew Fetherstonhaugh soon after 1760

elevation on the basement podium and the sharp drop of the parkland outside the windows give the impression of a first-storey room, like the Double Cube at Wilton. Through these windows the sun streams in upon a carpet patterned like a garden-bed, while the curtains, drawn up into thick flounces during the day-time, are of French brocade, carefully cleaned and reconditioned by the present owner.

Sir Matthew's only son, Sir Harry Fetherstonhaugh, was born in the house and succeeded to the estate in 1774 at the age of twenty. He lived there for ninety-two years. He was the buck of the family, the close friend of the Prince Regent, who often used to drive over from the Brighton Pavilion to enjoy Sir Harry's excellent table and string of race-horses. But Sir Harry's name will always be connected with two women, one his mistress, the other his wife. The mistress was none other than Emma Hart, later Lady Hamilton. When Sir Harry knew her, she was only sixteen years old. The daughter of a Cheshire blacksmith, she had come to London and found employment first as a maid-servant and then as a model in a 'Temple of Hymen' run by a quack doctor. She was a girl of startling physical attractions, and Sir Harry installed her for a year at Uppark (whether in the actual house or not is uncertain, for his mother was living there at the time), and then as abruptly rejected her.

Sir Harry's marriage was even more spectacular. In 1825, when he was over seventy, he walked one day along the terrace west of the house and heard a girl singing in the dairy. Her name was Mary Ann Bullock. Sir Harry made her acquaintance, and soon afterwards proposed. 'But do not answer me now,' he said. 'If you will have me, cut a slice out of the leg of mutton that is coming up for my dinner today.' When the mutton arrived, the slice was cut. The dairy still survives, a graceful little pavilion as light as buttermilk itself, at the end of the grass terrace. The dairymaid lived at Uppark as Lady Fetherstonhaugh until her death in 1875.

The remarkable history of Uppark had one further surprise in store. In the 1880's, a boy of fourteen, the son of the house-keeper, sat down at the kitchen table and began his first literary composition, a daily newspaper called *The Uppark Alarmist*. The boy was H. G. Wells. 'The place had a great effect on me,' he wrote in his autobiography. 'It retained a vitality that altogether overshadowed the insignificant ebbing trickle of upstairs life.' Today the whole house is revitalized. Admiral Sir Herbert and Lady Meade-Fetherstonhaugh have looked after the superb contents with a skill and care that have become proverbial. No other house in England is quite like it for the perfect condition of its eighteenth-century furnishings and hangings. The memories of all that has happened there are treasured as much as the works of art. An atmosphere of Elysian calm pervades its quiet rooms and downland park.

opposite The east front, originally the entrance front, before it was altered by Humphrey Repton in 1810

The dairy where Sir Harry Fetherstonhaugh found his bride. It forms a pavilion at the end of the west terrace

The kitchen in the basement. At this table H. G. Wells, son of the housekeeper, wrote his first literary compositions

CHATSWORTH

DERBYSHIRE

The magnificent palace of the Dukes of Devonshire

Chatsworth is the first name that comes to mind when one thinks of great English houses. 'Houses like Chatsworth, Blenheim, Hatfield, Knole . . .' we say, beginning to count the gems in a glittering necklace, but however much the order of the others may vary, it is always Chatsworth first. The reasons for this are various and cumulative, but it might be useful to begin by stating what Chatsworth is not, in order to emphasize later what it is. It is not the largest private house in England; its rooms are not as magnificent as Houghton's or Holkham's, nor is its exterior as great a work-of-art as Kedleston's, Wilton's or Longleat's; it has not been the scene of events as significant in history as those associated with Hatfield or Blenheim; it was not, until the motor-age, very accessible, and one might have expected this to have had some effect upon its fame; and it does not incorporate, at least visibly, the structure of any period earlier than that of William and Mary. That is quite a formidable list of negatives. Yet Chatsworth is still visited by hundreds of thousands of people annually, who rightly feel that to see this house at least once in a lifetime is an essential part of an Englishman's experience. Why?

The answer can be given by an equivalent list of positives. Its situation; its garden; its palatial appearance; its works-of-art; its ducal atmosphere. All these are incomparable. And for those who take the trouble to find it out, there is the strange story of its original construction and subsequent alterations.

A house had stood higher up Chatsworth's hill in the Middle Ages, but its true history begins with Elizabeth Cavendish, 'Bess of Hardwick', who in 1549 persuaded her husband to buy the manor and to erect on it a house even vaster in its main structure than that which we see today. It occupied the same levelled terrace above the River Derwent and contained the same internal courtyard, but it was four, in parts five, storeys high, instead of the present three, and attached to it on the river side were outbuildings proportionate to the state which the Cavendishes kept. No stone of this house can now be seen except by climbing into the roof, but at least one of its inner walls extends into the core of the present house. It was one of several houses where Mary Queen of Scots was kept in decorous confinement

An aerial view of Chatsworth from the west

The south front and the great Emperor fountain, the second highest in Europe

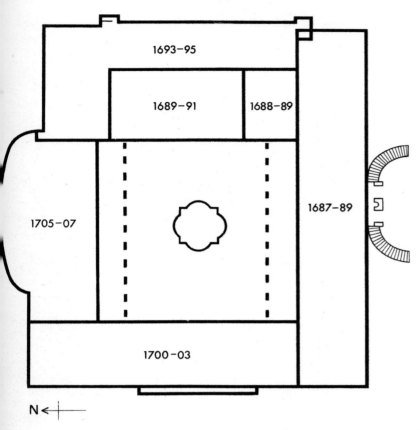

A plan of Chatsworth giving the dates when the various parts of the house were completed

opposite The west front, probably designed by Thomas Archer, aided by the first Duke. Over the pediment are the arms of the Devonshire family

overleaf left The Chapel, which has remained untouched since it was completed in 1694. The ceiling and wall paintings are by Louis Laguerre, and above the altar is *Doubting Thomas* by Antonio Verrio

overleaf right The Painted Hall. The walls are decorated with episodes from the life of Julius Caesar by Laguerre and the ceiling shows his reception among the Gods. The present staircase and galleries date from 1912 and replace two earlier versions

during the fifteen years when she was in the custody of the Earl of Shrewsbury, Bess's fourth and final husband. It stood entire for about a hundred and twenty years.

This was the house which the fourth Earl, later the first Duke, of Devonshire inherited in 1684. It was reported to him that the old building was 'decaying and weake', and he determined 'to pull down the same or great part thereof'. We owe the present Chatsworth very largely to him. At first his intention was to rebuild one front only, the south. 'When he had finisht this Part,' recorded his private chaplain after his death, 'he meant to go no farther.' But the building mania of his great-great-grand-mother had bitten deep into him, and one reconstruction was followed by another until the whole of her house had been replaced. One must therefore look upon Chatsworth as the product of a single man's energy, working by trial, error and fluctuating enthusiasm and fortune over a total period of twenty years, 1687–1707. As the Elizabethan house was built on a rectangular plan, the Duke was able to rebuild each front separately, shoring up the 'decaying and weake' parts until the new front was far enough advanced to lend them its own support. In speaking of 'new' fronts, one should not imagine simply a face-lift to bring the appearance of the house up to date, but the total destruction and reconstruction of the wing to its full depth and height, except where the old inner walls were sound enough to be made use of. But because two sides of a nearly square house, and all four sides of its interior courtyard, can be viewed simultaneously, no sooner was one finished than the Duke became dissatisfied by the contrast between the old style and the new. Thus he was led, front by front, like changes of scenery on a stage, to rebuild the entire house afresh. His piecemeal methods made necessary architectural devices which can still be seen on close scrutiny, and they were not always very happy. No doubt, if he could have foreseen the end of his work at the beginning, the Duke would have started by pulling down the whole of Bess's house to its foundations and built his own house from scratch. In that case he would certainly have reorganized its arrangement of rooms and entrances and might even have moved the house higher up the hill where it would have been clear of flood-water and dominated the landscape.

The Duke encountered other difficulties of his own making. The first was his inability to visualize the finished appearance of a façade or a room from architectural drawings. Once it was there before him, he would order the destruction of part of it so that it could be rebuilt a second time in a manner more in keeping with his new ideas. The second difficulty was financial. Hanging over him during the early period was a fine of £30,000, awarded against him for the ludicrous offence of tweaking the nose of Colonel Colepeper, one of his political opponents. The fine was waived in 1689, but for a man who was engaged on building a palace and was heavily addicted to horse-racing in addition, it was a limiting factor on his architectural ambitions.

Both failings led to constant quarrels between the Duke and his architect and builders. He could not, or would not, pay the bills. He claimed that his further rebuilding, when he changed his mind on seeing the finished work, was allowed for by the contract, and that the price should remain the same just as if the contractors had been engaged on the same terms as employees on his estate. A further obstacle was a shortage of coin of the realm: his agents could not supply the necessary amount of loose cash even when the Duke chose to pay. Clearly he was in a weak position, legally and financially, and the matter was eventually brought to court. No less a person than Sir Christopher Wren was sent down to Chatsworth to adjudicate on the costs incurred up till 1692, and he assessed them at £9,025.16.6¾, 'with very little or no proffitt to the Archt.', whose reward for his pains was left to the Duke's discretion.

The architect of the south and east wings was William Talman. He was not widely known when the Duke first employed him at Chatsworth, having previously completed only one major building, Thoresby House in Nottinghamshire, of which Hawksmoor later said, 'It was never good, and was burnt down as soon as finished.' After the Duke's squalid quarrel with him, Talman was not invited to submit designs for the other two fronts, and it remains in doubt who was responsible for them. It could have been Thomas Archer, to whom the Duke left £200 in his Will 'in acknowledgement of his favour and his care and trouble touching the building of my house'; it could conceivably have been Wren, who may have sketched a design while he was at Chatsworth; it could have been John Fitch, who signed and approved a version of the west front which is still preserved; or it could have been the Duke himself, by that time fed up with professional men, with the assistance of skilled master-masons in whom he was more successful in inspiring confidence and loyalty. It is to the Duke – or to the Duke-*cum*-Archer-*cum* Fitch – that we owe the most original external feature of the house, the bow-fronted north façade by which he contrived to mask a difference in plane between the flat wall-surfaces on either side, an awkward inheritance from the Elizabethan building. This was the last of the new works to be completed. In the same year, 1707, the Duke died.

The appearance of Chatsworth soon after his death can best be seen in the painting by Jan Siberechts now at Ombersley Court. It was made from above the cascade looking towards the south-east corner of the house. Nobody could by then have guessed that it incorporated part of the carcass of an Elizabethan building. It was an original and self-contained adaptation of the architectural style current in the reign of William III. 'It stands,' wrote Celia Fiennes, when she visited the still uncompleted house in 1797, 'on a little riseing ground from the River Derwent which runs all along the front of the house. . . . Before the gates there is a large Parke and several fine Gardens one without another with gravell walkes and squairs of grass with

opposite The State Drawing Room. The tapestries were woven at Mortlake *c* 1635 after cartoons by Raphael. The ceiling painting is by Laguerre

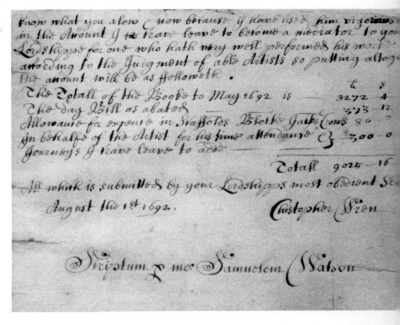

A page from a report signed by Christopher Wren in 1692 assessing the cost of work so far completed

The Library, containing part of the famous Chatsworth Collection of books and manuscripts. Formerly the Long Gallery, it was transformed in 1815 by the sixth Duke and Wyatville

opposite Looking down the terraces of the Great Cascade from the temple. The house can be seen at the foot of the cascade on the right

A painting by Jan Siberechts showing the appearance of Chatsworth from the south-east in about 1710, shortly after it was finished

opposite The Temple at the top of the Great Cascade containing the series of fountains and jets by which the cascade is fed. It was constructed in 1703, probably by Thomas Archer

stone statues in them and in the middle of each Garden is a large fountain.' The painting and this breathless description confirm each other exactly. Celia Fiennes was not so interested in the façades as she was in the garden and the interior, but her omission makes no difference, since three out of the four stand almost unchanged to this day. They have a noble classicism, which is enlivened by much exterior decoration, but decoration so restrained and well-proportioned that it appears part of the architectural concept of the whole. Of the three, the south front is the plainest, the west the grandest and the north the most original. That they were designed by different hands in different circumstances has not affected the external unity of the house. It was not until the early nineteenth century, when the sixth Duke and Sir Jeffrey Wyatville refaced the east front and added a long wing to the north, that Chatsworth suffered from any incongruity in its appearance from outside.

But the interior was less successful. Let it be admitted, with the reservation that one is here applying the highest possible standards, that the major rooms at Chatsworth are unworthy of it. The private apartments, redecorated by the present Duchess, are quite charming. But the state-rooms strain after an effect which only a totally new building, conceived as a whole by a single mind from the very start, could have achieved. Its odd history, so well disguised outside, becomes apparent within. The north entrance hall, previously the kitchen, is an attempt by the fourth Duke in about 1755 to bring the front door into closer relationship with the main staircase: the two are connected by a short length of passage parallel to the inner court, but the arrangement is still rather clumsy. The courtyard itself, which could have been a significant feature of the house, is little more than a well within it, and adds nothing to the outlook and little to the lighting of the four wings. The state-rooms, moreover, are all placed on the top floor, instead of forming a *piano nobile* on the ground or first floor, which Italian, French and English architects, after long experience, had found to be the best place for it. You are therefore obliged to climb a tall and steep staircase to reach them. Even allowing for the wonderful view from the windows, the rooms when you eventually reach them do not make quite the impact intended. The visitor feels that he has seen all this before, better done. The rooms are very grand, of course, and while they could not be expected to be in any sense intimate, since from the earliest days they were primarily show-rooms for the family's superb art-collection, they lack charm and even swagger. 'The Great Apartment,' wrote Horace Walpole in 1760, 'is vast but trist. Inlaid woods and floors, and painted Ceilings and unpainted wainscot darken the whole.' Modern eyes may agree with his, particularly if they are unsympathetic to the huge ceiling-paintings by Laguerre and (in one case) Verrio which press down upon the spectator. It is certain that the sixth Duke thought Walpole right. Some of his attempts to improve the rooms were disastrous: his gilded leather on the

walls of two of them, for instance, or his substitution of huge plate-glass panels for the original windows which have now happily been replaced. But in one case, he and Wyatville created between them the most attractive room in the public part of the house, the library. Partly it owes its success to the finish and colour of the book-cases and furniture, and to the books themselves; partly to the excellent proportions of the first Duke's anachronistic Long Gallery from which it was formed; but most of all, perhaps, because it looks usable and used, a merit which it shares with the untouched and beautiful chapel. The other state-rooms are so obviously designed for display that one begins to pity George V and Queen Mary, to whom the whole suite was allotted during their visit to Chatsworth in 1915.

The surroundings of the house are as little dull as it is possible to conceive. Its natural situation is a beautiful one, with the river pulled out into straightish lengths immediately below and parallel to the west front of the house, the valley cushioning it on either side. Capability Brown was called in by the fourth Duke, in 1761, but less than usual is due to him, for the early paintings make clear that even in the days of the first Duke, the park, while not so extensive as today, was by no means barren of trees, particularly on the east side. The garden, as we now see it, is in the main the creation of the sixth Duke of Devonshire, Wyatville and Joseph Paxton. The formal *parterres* of the seventeenth and eighteenth centuries became lawns, and on the upper slopes furthest away from the house, elaborate woodlands, mingled with flowering shrubs, were planted with the utmost forethought. In the middle of these glades one comes across endless surprises – fountains, temples, rustic pavilions, lakes, serpentine hedges, grottoes, and the foundations of the vast conservatory which anticipated Paxton's Crystal Palace. Yet it is none of these things that catches the visitor's eye at first: for within easy sight of the house are two enormous waterworks, the Emperor Fountain and the Great Cascade. The first was contrived by Paxton himself for the sixth Duke in 1843, and its single jet of 290 feet is still the second highest, after Geneva's, in Europe. The second is a waterfall of staggering proportions, which dates back to 1696 and impressed Celia Fiennes in the next year almost as much as the water-closets which had been newly installed inside the house.

These are two of Chatsworth's triumphs. But the house itself is the triumph of a man deeply involved in his country's politics, harassed by enmities and debts, who nevertheless managed to find the time and energy to create a masterpiece.

above The Wellington Rocks and waterfall created by Joseph Paxton in the mid-nineteenth century

right The bridge over the river Derwent completed in 1762

opposite The view across the south lawn to the Sea-horse fountain, the Emperor fountain beyond, and the canal. In the foreground is the copy in bronze of Canova's *Endymion with his Dog*, in the Sculpture Gallery

MOMPESSON HOUSE

WILTSHIRE

A lovely stone-faced house in Salisbury Close

Here is the smallest house described in this book, and if one excepts Brighton Pavilion, the only town-house. Yet in Salisbury Close you have no feeling of being in the centre of a town. It is a village green on which has risen unexpectedly the tallest and one of the loveliest of English cathedrals. The houses which surround it on the north side are toylike beside the great grey church, and their architecture, as if by the common consent of seven centuries, has remained modest and almost rural. The effect is heightened by the green lawns which run up to the very foot of the cathedral walls (we owe this to Wyatt, who overcame heaven knows what opposition to the removal of the gravestones) and by the dominant cherry-pink brick in which many of the Canons' houses were reconstructed. The general layout of the Close has remained unchanged since the Middle Ages, but immediately after the Civil War it became a rubbish dump, a children's playground, a market-place and a butchers' slaughterhouse. Its present appearance dates from roughly the turn of the seventeenth century, when the mess was cleared up and Wren was called in to advise. At the same period the finest house of them all, Mompesson House on the north side of Choristers' Green, was given its second and almost final form.

Around this square of grass is ranged an exhibition of English architecture from the fourteenth to the eighteenth century. Only one house, Mompesson itself, could be called a masterpiece, but collectively there is no lovelier sight in Britain, except perhaps the Great Court at Trinity College, Cambridge, which owes its harmony to the same haphazard fusion of several English styles. No attempt was made by the cathedral authorities of those days to impose a common building or roof line. The little houses sit good-naturedly side by side, some canonical, some secular, one a former schoolhouse, another the residence of its headmaster; a few hide their Gothic muddle behind a decent frame of Georgian brick, others are patched with flints and brick-nogging; some are lit by windows arched and cusped, some with sashes and cornices; there are front doors of every variety, and gardens everywhere.

From this attractive jumble Mompesson House stands out with serene dignity. It is princess of the Green, as the cathedral

Looking through the windows of the morning room across Choristers' Green towards Salisbury Cathedral

opposite The entrance to Mompesson House. Charles Mompesson's cypher appears on top of the wrought-iron gates and his coat of arms divides the pediment over the front door

171

is queen of the Close. But it does not dominate the others snobbishly. True, it is the only one faced with stone, and the only one with an imposing doorway, iron railings and gate-piers. But that the builder's intention was neighbourly is made quite clear by the modesty of the façade. The stone is creamy-white with a touch of yellow, enhanced by the green of a magnolia which has been allowed to cover part of it. The tall windows, four of them subtly narrower than the rest, a cornice with dentils below, the doorway and a strongly hipped roof, are almost the only elements in an utterly satisfying design.

Mompesson House was built in two phases. In about 1680, Sir Thomas Mompesson, a Member of Parliament and an important figure in the affairs of Salisbury, rebuilt the family's older house on the same site, and 'his new dwelling house' can have been little different in size and internal arrangement from that which we see today. Its original appearance from outside can be guessed from the neighbouring brick stable-block which Sir Thomas erected almost simultaneously, and which survives unaltered. But in 1701 – the date appears on the rainwater-head – his son, Charles Mompesson, refaced the main house with stone and inserted the sash windows, giving it substantially its present appearance. Here, then, we have an unspoiled example of a perfect Queen Anne house. Its architect is unknown. Its former attribution to Wren was based on nothing more than its excellence of design, and should be disregarded except as further evidence of his fame and influence.

The interior of the house has been furnished and redecorated by its former owner and present occupant, Mr Denis Martineau, in a manner that does full justice to the outside. Much of the original decoration remained, if by the term 'original' one can marry the 1700 panelling with the 1740 plasterwork and fire-places which Charles Longueville, a brother-in-law of Charles Mompesson, added at the later date. There are only four rooms on the ground floor of the main house, and they can be des-cribed better by the accompanying illustrations than by words. Between them is a hall which seems full of light even when clouds hang heavy overhead. At the far end of it is a staircase, the most delightful feature of the house. It rises in two flights separated by a half-landing. On the right-hand walls as you ascend, are swags and picture-frames of white plaster against a blue background. The banister-rail is supported on each tread by three exquisitely turned wooden balusters and is finished at the hall end by a sweeping curve as graceful as a curtsy.

Mr Martineau presented Mompesson House to the National Trust in 1952, and remains there as the Trust's tenant. He is by profession an architect, and every corner of the house and its garden reveals his understanding of the period and his affection for the place. If one held an architectural identification parade in reverse – to pick out the one non-rogue building from a line of rogues or semi-rogues – Mompesson is the house to which every finger would unhesitatingly point.

A detail of the plasterwork from the ceiling of one of the bedrooms

opposite top Mompesson House from the south-west. On the right is the archway to the stables

opposite bottom The dining room with panelling dating from 1700. The fireplace is an eighteenth-century original replacing a Victorian insertion

The carved wooden staircase dating from the early eighteenth century

POWIS CASTLE

MONTGOMERYSHIRE

A border stronghold with the finest garden in Wales

The castle lies on the border between England and Wales, a mile or so on the Welsh side beyond the River Severn. The actual boundary is not the river, as it would have been between two English counties, but the hills to the east of it, emphasizing that this was once a military frontier as well as a civil. You can see the castle quite clearly from the watershed. Steely strips of the river glint from the floor of the intervening valley, and half-way up the wooded slopes on the far side is a dark mass of stone, irregular in outline but large and solid enough to promise substantial fortifications. Seen from this distance, it could be a ruin, like most of the border-castles; but approaching closer, you find that its walls are sound, its windows intact, its park and garden in perfect condition. It is quite clearly a castle which has become a house. Nor is it a nineteenth-century reconstruction. Powis is the greatest house in Wales, not in size merely, for there may be others larger, but because it has been added to, patched, adapted, redecorated and embellished with consistent good-workmanship from the thirteenth century until the present day. Chronologically Powis could have been placed almost anywhere in this book: it has been given to the early eighteenth century because then the garden was given its shape and the castle was rescued from the crisis that could have toppled it into ruin.

It is not difficult to spot the earliest work. On the north and bleakest side (but 'bleak' is here a relative term, for Powis in sunlight is a fairy-tale castle), the fourteenth-century curtain-wall of the Barons de la Pole swings its semicircular bastions along the edge of a steep ridge, below which was dug a moat. On its inner side the wall helps to form a forecourt, previously the outer bailey. Its western portals were built by the third Baron Powis after 1667, but at the eastern end one is switched back again to the fourteenth century. Two massively rotund towers squeeze between their cheeks an entrance doorway which is lengthened into a corridor by arch upon arch of coiling stone. This entrance is further prolonged into the heart of the house by a narrow courtyard open to the sky, and leads out again on the far side by further gates terminating in a broad flight of stone steps. It is still possible to obtain a good idea of the mediaeval character of Powis by opening all these gates from one end of

The south front seen from across the garden. The ten conical yews were planted in the early eighteenth century. Below them are the terraces which are the most famous feature of the Powis garden

opposite The main entrance approached by a flight of steps and curving balustrade added in the time of Charles II

The forecourt, originally the outer bailey of the thirteenth-century castle, looking towards the entrance to the inner bailey set between the mediaeval towers

The south front in 1700, when the three upper terraces were complete, but the water garden below them had not yet been constructed

the castle to the other. One can imagine a friend wending his way on horseback between the vast stone walls; an enemy left snarling on the threshold of the outer bailey. It was clearly a tough nut to crack, the mansion of a very powerful family.

At every turn one finds evidence of the attempts made by succeeding generations to increase its convenience and comfort. Although the rooms retain their irregular shapes, they have been given classical face-lifts by panelling and larger windows, and in the last quarter of the seventeenth century a staircase of palatial grandeur was added within the north-west corner, leading up to a set of state-rooms that ring the interior courtyard on the first floor. Some of these rooms, like the dining-room on the ground floor, were modernized by G. F. Bodley in the early years of this century, and he chose a mock-Elizabethan style which conforms well enough to the central period of the castle's long history. But the most pleasing rooms are the Long Gallery built by Sir Edward Herbert, who bought the castle in 1587; the State Bedroom, with decorations of the time of Charles II; and the Blue Drawing-room, which dates from the early eighteenth century. These three rooms, spread over a century and a half, have been fused by time into a unity of subdued colour, and the whole is further bound together by furniture, tapestry, books and paintings that would not be out of place in any interior except the most modern. To wander through the rooms at Powis is to telescope one's impressions of seven centuries of British civilization. The strong old walls were equal to any modifications within them: a watch-tower became a bathroom, a dungeon a wine-cellar, a guard-chamber was transformed by Chinese wallpaper into a drawing-room, a passageway lifts by short flights of steps over an awkward inner bulkhead, the purpose of which has long been forgotten. From the windows there is a view of fields and woods so soft that they seem touched in by a painter's brush. Even the little town of Welshpool assumes from the distance of a mile the character of a scene from Grimm.

Almost every old house has been the victim of a regrettable lapse. At Powis it was the reconstruction of the windows in the late nineteenth century. The stone of which the castle was built is the ruddy rock on which it rests, almost indistinguishable in colour from Georgian brick. The stone was rough-hewn, giving the walls a pleasantly variegated texture, but when the Elizabethan windows were repaired, the stone was smoothed and cut with a harsh regularity that time has not yet softened. In spite of it, Powis wears as romantic an appearance as any connoisseur of border-castles could desire. Its situation, castellation, circular chimneys, bold rounded projections and irregularly disposed turrets, lift the huge building high over the countryside as if to announce that the Princes of Powis would brook no interference with their patrimony. In later ages, the castle's aloofness was mitigated by the structural changes already described, but most of all by its garden.

A detail of one of the panels illustrating the Fall and Expulsion from Eden on either side of the main fireplace in the Long Gallery

The Long Gallery built by Sir Edward Herbert, who bought the castle in 1587. The plasterwork ceiling dates from 1592

The Blue Drawing Room hung with seventeenth-century Brussels tapestries. The panelling and much of the furniture date from the eighteenth century

The lead statues of shepherds and shepherdesses which stand on the balustrade of the second terrace

Along the south-east front the ridge drops sharply away to a valley. Originally this was merely a boulder-strewn slope with a marsh at its foot, stiffening at intervals into bare walls of rock rising to the platform on which the castle lies. In the late seventeenth and early eighteenth centuries the Earls of Rochford, a Dutch family who occupied the castle during the exile of the Powis family from 1690 to 1722, began the transformation of this slope into six terraces. A print dated 1700 shows that the three upper terraces had been constructed by that date, and well before 1742 the whole scheme was completed by the second Marquess of Powis after his reinstatement. A Dutch water-garden, now a large rectangular lawn, was formed in the valley floor; above it rose the terraces, the back of one forming the platform of the terrace above it, right up to the castle walls. The four upper terraces survive, the lower two, which were merely grass walks, having reverted to banks covered by flowering shrubs.

The terraces look their best when seen individually from the level of each in turn. When they are viewed from the mount on the far side of the valley, banked one above the other, the pattern is to some extent blurred, the flowers are indistinguishable and the wonderful view towards the English border is of course lost. The finest viewpoint of all is from the second terrace looking down on the third. A row of urns stands on the balustrade of each, and on the centre of the lower balustrade, opposite the orangery, are four lead statues of shepherds and shepherdesses in Tyrolean attitudes probably by John Van Nost of Dublin or Henry Cheere, a pupil of Scheemakers. It is extraordinary how these statues steal the show. They are not very large, and there is much else to attract attention. But the vigour and charm of their execution and their perfect siting give the whole auditorium of the terraces a centre-point to which the visitor's eye will turn again and again.

On the east side of the terraces are hedges of yew over thirty feet high, gnarled by age inside but presenting outwardly a fresh apron of yellow-green shoots from top to ground. Further yews have grown from the little soldier-bushes shown in the 1742 print into huge conical trees at the foot of the castle walls. Lower down, the great lawn, flattened in the eighteenth century for the water-garden, now runs like a vast stadium into the curve of the hillside, which is covered by a wilderness of ornamental trees and flowering shrubs. At its eastern end there is a further drop in level to the old kitchen-garden, transformed by the late Lord Powis into a quieter garden of box hedges and short avenues of pyramid apples.

To many people the garden at Powis is its chief attraction. It is of equal interest to the botanist, the student of the history of garden design and the person who only wishes to enjoy a summer's afternoon on its terraces and steps. But castle and garden should be seen together, as a superb use of the opportunities which the lie of the ground presented to the border-barons of the fourteenth century and their more subtle successors in the eighteenth. What the first found sturdily convenient, the second rendered attractive. In their own ways, each succeeded brilliantly.

The view from an upper terrace, constructed in the early eighteenth century, looking across to the 'long mountain' which divides England from Wales

CASTLE HOWARD

YORKSHIRE

Where Vanbrugh 'hugely turned to architecture'

There is room to spare in this broad shoulder of Britain. The fields, like the views, are generous in size. As you approach the area of Castle Howard – and 'area' is the right word to apply, for it is more than a site – you notice that something is happening to the countryside. A sense of expectation is being created, as by the tuning of an orchestra before the curtain rises. The roads become more taut, the farms more regular. The impression is heightened by the silver splinter of a lake, an avenue dead straight for five miles, a column and an obelisk standing stiffly among the trees. From one direction you see suddenly the circular Mausoleum, lonely on its bare hill; from another, a pyramid squatting in the plough; from a third, you pass through curious outworks: a stone gateway, heavily rusticated, with flanking pyramids, battlements and towers; next, to right and left, a curtain-wall broken by turrets, in shape circular, pentagon, octagon or square; then another gateway, with a further pyramid, much larger, sitting over its arch. All this is not immediately intelligible, and was not intended to be. The mixture of motifs and periods – Roman, Egyptian; mediaeval, Tudor – announce the work of a daring innovator and a rich patron, neither of whom was tied by fashion or the fear of ridicule. Then, on the base of the great obelisk, comes hard information. An inscription proclaims the following:

Sir John Vanbrugh (1664–1726) by Godfrey Kneller. Soldier and playwright, Vanbrugh designed Castle Howard as his first experiment in architecture

If to Perfection these plantations rise,
If they agreeably my heirs surprise,
This faithful pillar will their age declare
As long as time these characters shall spare.
Here then with kind remembrance read his name
Who for posterity perform'd the same.

Charles the III Earl of Carlisle
Of the family of the Howards
Erected a castle where the old castle of
Henderskelfe stood, and call'd it Castle-Howard.
He likewise made the plantations in this park
and all the out-works, monuments and other
plantations belonging to the said seat.
He began these works
In the year MDCCII

The date, curiously enough, is wrong. The first drawings for

opposite The Temple of the Four Winds designed by Vanbrugh between 1724 and 1726

181

opposite The centre block of the south front. The
dome and part of this front were restored after a
fire in 1940

Castle Howard were made during the last year of the seventeenth century and work began not in 1702, but in 1700. The
architect was Sir John Vanbrugh. Space must be found to retell,
familiar though it is, at least the outline of the strange story of
his commission. Vanbrugh had never built so much as a garden-
shed before he embarked upon the design of the greatest private
house of its day. He was not an architect at all: he was a soldier
turned playwright. But just as he had sat down one day in 1695
to write *The Relapse, or Virtue in Danger*, with no previous knowledge of the theatre, and found himself acclaimed overnight a
rival to Congreve, so he was immediately accepted by the young
Lord Carlisle as his architect on the strength of a few sketches
for a great house which Vanbrugh had roughed out for little
more than the fun of it. The sketch, as it happens, was not particularly good, and lacked many of the more striking features,
including the dome and outlying courtyards, which were to
make Castle Howard the most original building of its age. Nor
had Vanbrugh any technical knowledge of how to translate his
ideas into stone:

> 'Van's genius,' wrote Swift, 'without thought or lecture,
> Is hugely turn'd to architecture.'

Three things combined to turn it. Vanbrugh's personality –
a friendly, gaily adventurous young Captain's manner – which
made him a favourite in the Kit Cat circle of Whig landowners
and intellectuals of which the Earl of Carlisle was himself one of
the most engaging members; the breach between the Earl and
the more tetchy William Talman, the architect of Chatsworth
until the Duke of Devonshire had found him too difficult to work
with (in fairness to Talman it must be repeated that one reason
was the Duke's inability to pay the bills); and the friendship
which had grown up between Vanbrugh and Nicholas Hawksmoor, Wren's chief assistant.

Seldom can there have been a happier professional relationship than between these three men. Not a hint of jealousy
marred their correspondence, and it was all the more remarkable in the case of Vanbrugh and Hawksmoor than of Wren and
Vanbrugh. Wren's reputation in 1699 was established un-
shakeably at the top, while Nicholas Hawksmoor, three years
older than Vanbrugh and twenty years a practising architect,
might have resented the exchange of a genius for a talented
amateur as his master, when he was already proving himself an
artist in his own right by his unassisted design for Easton Neston
in that very same year.

Vanbrugh handled this delicate situation with great tact. In
the words of Laurence Whistler's summing-up, 'Hawksmoor was
far from being a mere subordinate. It was he, an excellent
draughtsman, who turned Vanbrugh's sketches or rough elevations into working-drawings, and it is possible, and even probable, that a great part of the detail was his own.' Vanbrugh

opposite The north or entrance front. The right
wing, designed by Sir Thomas Robinson in the mid-
eighteenth century, is wider than the left wing
and does not include Vanbrugh's curved colonnade

The Gate House with a pyramid standing over the
archway. In the distance is the obelisk which
stands at the crossroads of the north-south and
east-west avenues leading to Castle Howard

The Satyr Gate designed by Vanbrugh as one of
the entrances to the walled garden

The Mausoleum designed by Nicholas
Hawksmoor, Vanbrugh's collaborator at Castle
Howard. It stands on a bare hill half a mile east
of the castle

opposite The garden front. The huge Corinthian
pilasters on the central block are repeated in
the smaller pilasters of the wings

never surrendered to Hawksmoor the credit for Castle Howard,
and Hawksmoor did not claim it. Their relationship throughout, as later at Blenheim, was that of senior and junior partner.
But Vanbrugh never made a decision without consulting Hawksmoor on its technical feasibility and was careful to explain to
Lord Carlisle that this was his practice. To their collaboration
one must add one other: that between the two architects and
Lord Carlisle himself. Mr George Howard, the present owner
of the house, has paid this wholly deserved tribute to his ancestor: 'There are a number of flattering references to his genius,
both by George London when speaking of the gardens, and by
Hawksmoor himself when writing of work on the house. These

184

often tend to be dismissed as the usual tactful compliments to a patron, but I suspect that they may mean more than that, and that he really was directly responsible for much that has been praised as the work of others.'

The changes that were made in the design as the work progressed have been described in detail by Mr Howard, Laurence Whistler and Kerry Downes. There is no need to repeat the tangled story here before coming to a description of the house as it stands today. Let us start with the south or the garden front; for although this is not the larger of the two main fronts, it is the more magnificent, the less altered and the more pleasing. A central block is crowned from behind by a high dome and flanked by two one-storey wings, as light as orangeries, supported on a rusticated basement. These are the essentials of the design. We can ignore the slight asymmetry which was due to Sir Thomas Robinson's mid-eighteenth-century 'completion' of Vanbrugh's western wing, for the fact that the two terminal pavilions are quite different in design, and that there is one more window on the west side than on the east, is not immediately apparent. The Corinthian pilasters and the dome take command of the whole façade. Talman had already experimented with external pilasters at Chatsworth a few years before, but here they come in two sizes, huge on the face of the central block, miniature by comparison on the wings. The effect is like a line of guardsmen trooping their regimental colours. One of the secrets of the façades is the alternation of plain surfaces with decoration, and rectangular window-openings in the basement with arched on the main floor. The deep fluting of the pilasters makes a series of vertical stripes which combine with the generally horizontal lines of the building to give it a wonderful balance when viewed from almost any distance. Even without the dome, as can be seen by placing a thumb over it in the photograph, it would still be a building of beautiful proportion, and indeed the dome was one of Vanbrugh's afterthoughts. Remarkably, it enhances an already self-contained façade, and when one remembers that this was the first dome to be designed in England (just after St Paul's and contemporary with Greenwich) and the first on any private house, its maturity and boldness are quite astonishing. It makes no apology for its presence. It is pulled out from the centre of the house on a tall drum like a section of a telescope, and its brilliantly gilded lantern shines out over the park like a beacon. A word of caution and credit should be added here: this is not the original dome, which was totally destroyed by fire in 1940. It is a careful reconstruction by Mr Howard, and he added the gilding on the evidence of paintings in the house which unmistakeably show that the original dome was thus enriched.

On the north side of the house is an even more grandiloquent display. Not only do the wings on this side break forward to contain a terraced forecourt, but on each flank there were to have been a kitchen-court on the east and stables on the west,

opposite Lady Georgiana's bedroom, wife of the sixth Earl. She died in 1858 and the painted four-poster bed with yellow hangings, together with much of the furniture and the prints on the walls, remain as she left them

The Tapestry Room, so called because it formerly contained the Four Seasons tapestries which now hang on the staircase. The paintings are by Reynolds, Romney and Gainsborough

One end of the Antique Passage which is characteristic of Vanbrugh's interior designs

fronted by archways and crowned by smaller domes which made them an integral part of the house and trebled its width. The whole scheme can be seen in the etching from *Vitruvius Britannicus* reproduced as the end papers to this book. In fact only the eastern extension was built, and the west side of the entrance court was left uncompleted on the Earl's death in 1738, and was finished by Sir Thomas Robinson in 1759 to a different and wider design. The entrance archways and outer forecourt were likewise never executed. But even the incomplete work is staggering in its originality and size. From a distance it passes every test; it is noble, dramatic, splendid and in scale. From a closer view, there is almost nothing in British architecture to match the explosive vigour of its soaring stone. Only from the middle distance does this front appear to some eyes slightly lacking in cohesion. There is a weakness about the articulation between the main wings and the kitchen court. The low lid-like domes on the four corners of the court sit a little unhappily on their dishes, and less care has been taken with the detailed design and construction of these buildings, probably because they would seldom be seen from within or from outside the house. A further awkwardness in Vanbrugh's original design was well disguised by Robinson fifty years later. The elevation of the west front is now an excellent and unbroken Palladian façade. In Vanbrugh's plan there would have been a deep and rather shapeless indentation behind the south front, as the *Vitruvius* plan makes clear. But here again, had the stable-court been built as planned, the west front would not have been visible as a whole.

Castle Howard is a house on the very largest scale of private building, but apart from the mid-eighteenth-century Long Gallery, its rooms are surprisingly small. There was no suite of state-rooms distinct from the family's quarters. The Carlisles lived in the main rooms along the south front, and the bedrooms were in the west wing and on either side of the Saloon. The reason for this is that the 'orangeries' are in effect only one storey high, and the greater part of the central block is taken up by the huge entrance hall. It could be said therefore that comparatively little has been made to go a very long way. This is greatly to the advantage of the house. It does not overawe like Blenheim. It catches up the visitor and retains his affection. The long internal corridors, in which Vanbrugh delighted, consist in arch beyond arch, linked by vaulted ceilings, and create an impression of great distance and coolness. The same is true of the hall itself. Here is architecture on a vast internal scale, but the hall remains astonishingly light, both in the clarity of every part of it and in the lack of any heaviness. This effect is achieved partly by breaking up the two side-walls above the fireplaces by openings into the staircase wells; and partly by the delicate base to the dome, from which angels should be blowing trumpets. Standing immediately beneath its central point, one looks up into the recently repainted underside of the dome, and cannot imagine a more successful or a more daring combination of strong uprights and circular bands.

The photographs must be allowed to speak for the ornamentation of the park and gardens. It must be emphasized that each of these beautiful stone buildings was placed in its present position with the utmost forethought for the effect which it would create from the windows of the house and the terraces. It would be difficult to choose between Vanbrugh's Temple of the Four Winds, Garrett's bridge over the river and Hawksmoor's Mausoleum. Each in its own way is a masterpiece of delicacy contrived from heavy blocks of stone. The Mausoleum is a building of very great originality, both inside and out, and removes any lingering doubt that Hawksmoor was an architect of the first order. The Temple destroys at one stroke the legend that Vanbrugh was incapable of gracefulness, while the bridge, which leads merely from one field into another and never had a road across it, is a reflection of classical design with which even the Palladians could find little fault; Garrett indeed, was a protégé of Lord Burlington.

These three buildings are the most important in a whole group which surround Castle Howard to a distance of a mile or more. The modern visitor to the house leaves it with an enduring impression that the minds of several great men have met here to create what is without question the finest memorial to the short-lived age of the English baroque.

Looking down the length of the Antique Passage which is lined with statues and casts

The hall, looking across from one staircase to the other. The fireplace is the work of two Italian stuccoists and the profusion of frescoes of mythological scenes on the ceiling and walls are by a contemporary Venetian painter, Pellegrini

ANTONY HOUSE

CORNWALL

A finely proportioned Queen Anne house

Some houses, like some people, are immediately likeable: others take time to know. Antony belongs to the first category, and its charm remains as fresh to those who have spent a lifetime in it as to the visitor of a single day. The impact which it makes is as instantaneous as that of an exceptionally pretty woman seen suddenly across a crowded room. That the eye can distinguish the minute variations of feature which make the difference between a pleasing and an unpleasing face, a pleasing or unpleasing façade, is one of the more enjoyable of human faculties. One calls it 'a sense of proportion', and although that does not explain all, one can be persuaded when confronted by Antony to believe that a science of aesthetics must really exist. Antony could be dissected element by element, but if such an analysis could answer the question How?, it can never quite answer the question Why? Why does it give us such delight? Why does one know that so long as men enjoy beautiful things, a house like this will be recognized as a perfect example of its kind? And there is another question. Why is Antony so unmistakeably English? After all, it shares with every famous old house on the continents of Europe and America the same classical ancestry. Its tall windows are by origin French, its pediment Greek, its door-frames Italian, its dormers Dutch. But it is sited, put together, composed, in a manner that justifies the English boast that for short snatches of time, one of which was the late seventeenth and early eighteenth centuries, loosely called 'Queen Anne', we achieved an indigenous style of architecture that has no rival in the world.

Antony was built by an unknown architect between 1711 and 1721 for Sir William Carew, whose family had lived for centuries in an older house nearby, the exact site of which has been forgotten. It is deceptively simple in appearance. Its two main façades, north and south, like the two side-elevations, are identical. Nine windows extend along the first storey, eight below, with a doorway under the central window, and six dormer windows set into the hipped roof above. The chimney-stacks are plain up-ended boxes spaced unapologetically at equal intervals against the skyline. The surface decoration is reduced to a minimum. There was no true porch on either side

Richard Carew, great-grandfather of the builder of Antony and historian of Cornwall. The exact site of his original house is now lost, but it stood close by. A portrait painted in 1586

opposite The main house seen through the wrought-iron gate at the entrance to the forecourt. The porch was added in the mid-nineteenth century (the present *porte-cochère* at the entrance front is an addition of about 1840), but merely a simple grouping of shallow pilasters and a cornice to frame the doorway. The central bay projects by no more than twelve inches. The angles of the house are slightly emphasized by rusticated quoins, there is a string-course marking the floor-level of the first storey, a strong plain pediment above the door and smaller pediments above the dormers. That is all. The secret of Antony's dignity and welcoming appearance lies in the spacing of these different elements, and in the silvery colour of its slate roof and Pentewen stone. Even the small square panes of its white sash-windows are an essential part of the design, for they add a touch of intimacy, a diminution of scale at precisely the right point, promising warmth and hospitality within, without in any way minimizing its fine appearance from outside.

If one wished to give a lesson in the principles of proportion, there could be no better way than by comparing the reality of Antony with the painting made of it by a local artist soon after its completion. It is recognizably the same house, but an error of drawing has fractionally increased the height of the building and reduced the scale of its windows so that nobility has become mere elegance. Alternatively, take the Borlase etching, which shows the true proportions, and cover up the pediment or eliminate for a moment the angle quoins, and you have something which the least sensitive observer will immediately know to be incomplete, even if he could not explain why. Antony is indeed struck true and firm from its die.

The central block or pile (but both words are too gaunt to describe a temple dedicated to domestic bliss) could stand in any company on its own – in a cathedral close, for example, or in eighteenth-century Piccadilly. But because this is the country, the architect could afford the space to enclose the forecourt by two wings which frame the house and add to its variety. He did so with exceptional daring. Within the general Wren context of the building, the wings are treated quite differently from the main house. The material is brick, not stone. There is much greater freedom of movement in the two colonnades, which anticipate by their tall arches the motif which we shall find constantly repeated inside the house. On the four corners of the court are set spiked cupolas which add a note – the only note – of frivolity, entirely successful in the case of the front pair, but they are seated a little uneasily on the corners nearest to the house, where one would have preferred a repetition of the two front pavilions by continuing the colonnade through to the garden instead of closing the vistas by a wall. Above the central part of each colonnade rises a second storey, a laundry on the left, a kitchen on the right. Originally there was also a row of dormers in each roof – they can be seen in both early drawings here reproduced – and the roof itself was flattened at the top to avoid any competition between the wings and the house. A low wall closes the fourth side of the courtyard. The combination

A painting, by a local artist, of Antony in about 1721, shortly after it was completed

The south or entrance front in about 1790 by William Borlase, showing the temporary disappearance of the circular drive, which has now been restored

The forecourt from the south-west corner. In the foreground is one of the four cupolas set at each corner, and the interior of one of the colonnades which flank the courtyard on each side

The north front from across the lawn. This façade is identical with the south front, apart from the terrace steps which replace the forecourt

of the brick wall and stone piers binds together the different elements of the composition most attractively. The circular drive within the courtyard, the statue (now replaced by a sun-dial) at its centre, cupolas as light as meringues to right and left, the curved iron gates and the twenty arches on either side, give the front entrance exactly the spring and colour needed to accentuate the pale simplicity of the façade.

One expects to find the interior equally light and graceful. There will be plaster swags on the walls and ceilings, perhaps a delicate circular staircase and fireplaces of restrained elaboration. The great windows must surely fill the rooms with sunlight and open them up to the superb view of which one has already caught a glimpse from the drive. This is true of the first floor, where charming bedrooms lead off a central corridor framed by tall open arches continuing down its length. But the ground floor was conceived quite differently. With the country so immediately available, the emphasis is on coolness and seclusion within. The rooms are small and intimate, facing north and panelled in dark Dutch oak. Only one, and that the smallest, has windows in more than one wall. All of them are arranged round a central hall with an eye to convenience and privacy more than for effect. The staircase rises from the hall in two broad flights, the turned balusters, three to a step, compensating for its rather heavy construction. Here again one finds tall arches dividing the outer from the inner hall, which give the interior movement – the only characteristic that it has in common with the contemporary conceptions of Vanbrugh and Hawksmoor.

For all these reasons the rooms at Antony probably look their best at night. They require, and have been given, low lighting, wood fires and heavy curtains. The excellent series of family portraits (some of the best are by the young Reynolds, who was born not many miles away) and the fine furniture, porcelain and books appear to perfection in this subdued atmosphere. Antony is a house to be lived in, wholly and continuously: it needs bustle, flowers, comfort and affection. It receives them all from Sir John and Lady Carew Pole, to whom the property has come by unbroken descent from the fourteenth century.

One further aspect of Antony needs to be described, its setting. The house stands halfway down a long slope leading at about a mile's distance to one of the many estuaries which ultimately combine to form Plymouth Sound. The wooded combes, half-sea, half-river, on the borders of Cornwall and Devon are ready-made for the landscape painter, and even more for the landscape gardener. Capability Brown had no hand here, but even in its natural state it could have inspired his unique contribution to the English scene. West of the house are hedges of clipped yew, tall, dark and widely spaced. Eastward lie farm buildings which share something of the serenity of the house. But to the north the view is open to the gently falling valley, with glimpses of water and farmlands beyond.

'Rich the robe, and ample let it flow,' quoted Humphrey Repton ecstatically when he was called in to advise Reginald Pole-Carew at the end of the eighteenth century. 'It is worth considering,' he added in a pencilled note to his employer, 'how far future generations may be benefitted by a disgusting eyesore [of new plantations] for the present.' Happily they chose to sacrifice present amenity to future glory. Clumps of trees were planted, vistas cut through the woods and the rigid lines of earlier avenues and stone walls were swept away. Today Antony – the very name reflects its masculine grace – is cushioned in firm hills and lies palely beautiful against a background of meadows and trees.

The library with a portrait of Sir Alexander Carew, who was executed by the Roundheads during the Civil War in 1644

EASTON NESTON

NORTHAMPTONSHIRE

An elegant classical house by Hawksmoor

Nicholas Hawksmoor built from scratch and his own invention only one country-house, and it was Easton Neston. It was not completed as he intended it, perhaps fortunately, for the wings and entrance-screen that he later proposed to add were imitative of Vanbrugh, and among the many virtues of the house is that it stands in time as a very individual creation, and in space as a breathtakingly pale and self-contained building which any additions would have spoilt. Hawksmoor himself would not have shared this opinion. He as deeply regretted that his full design was never executed as Vanbrugh despaired of Lord Carlisle's loss of interest in building the stable-block at Castle Howard. No doubt if we could see in stone the full array of Easton Neston as Campbell illustrated it in *Vitruvius Britannicus*, we would not wish to part with any of it. But it would not have made the same impression. Walking through the park to the point where Hawksmoor optimistically built his entrance-piers, one looks back to see the south front of the Petit Trianon miraculously translated to Northamptonshire. It anticipated Gabriel's little masterpiece by over fifty years. But everything that has ever been said in praise of the Trianon applies equally here. There is the same creaminess of stone, the same lift of the Corinthian pilasters, the tall windows, the rusticated basement, an almost identical balustrade on the flattened roof, and, most significant of all, the same proportions. Easton Neston has been called an example of the short-lived English baroque, and so it would have been if the full design had been carried out. But in its present imperfectly perfect state it foretells the full flowering of the eighteenth century in the century's first years. Externally it was finished in 1702.

Hawksmoor, said Sir Reginald Blomfield, 'was incessantly trying to translate Vanbrugh in terms of Wren.' As Hawksmoor was Wren's master-draughtsman at Greenwich and St Paul's and Vanbrugh's junior partner at both Castle Howard and Blenheim, it made a neat and damning summary of a great man's work. Even Laurence Whistler quoted it with approval in his biography of Vanbrugh. But with Easton Neston at the beginning of Hawksmoor's independent career and the Castle Howard mausoleum at the end of it, this judgement cannot be

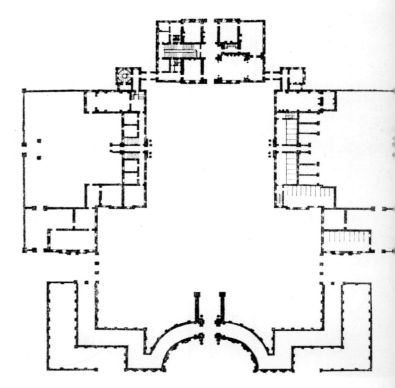

The original plan of Easton Neston showing Wren's wing on the left and the stable block on the right, which was built, but demolished in the late eighteenth century. The elaborate courtyards and huge forecourt were never built

opposite The centre of the west or entrance front. The giant Corinthian columns support the arms and motto of the Fermor family, for whom Hawksmoor designed the house

197

opposite The entrance front looking towards the Wren wing on the north side. The two wings were probably designed by Wren in about 1680, but the main building, begun in 1696, was entirely the work of Hawksmoor

below Part of the wooden model of Easton Neston made by Hawksmoor himself in about 1694. It shows the ground floor only with the first floor and roof removed

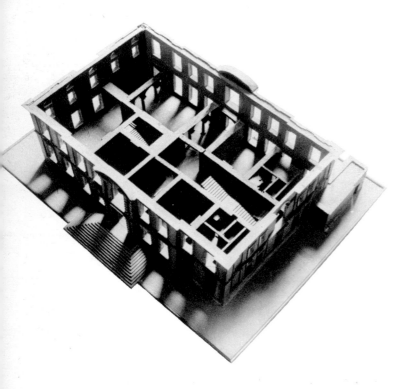

opposite The piers, which are all that was built of the huge forecourt which Hawksmoor intended as the approach to Easton Neston

allowed to stand. The commission to build Easton Neston for Sir William Fermor, Lord Lempster, fell into Hawksmoor's lap at exactly the moment when his artistry could profit from it most, for Wren's influence on him was beginning to fade and he had not yet met Vanbrugh. By 1696 Wren had picked out Hawksmoor from among his young pupils as the one whom he could most readily trust with original and unaided work, and he recommended him to Lord Lempster to complete the house on which Wren himself had advised some fifteen years before. Two wings of 'Wren's' building (the inverted commas are necessary because it is unlikely that Wren even visited the site, and he probably did little more than sketch a design to please his relation-by-marriage) faced each other across an empty forecourt, and one of them survives. It is a decent brick building with stone facings to the doors and windows, one-storey high externally, with dormers so mean that it seems probable that they were inserted later. Hawksmoor himself described the wings, in an untypically disloyal phrase, as 'good for nothing'. Such forthright condemnation was undeserved, but there is no doubt that the building which Hawksmoor erected between them completely overshadows the earlier work in scale and quality.

It is not known how Wren would have completed the building, if indeed he ever drew out the full design. In about 1682 – the letter is dated by the month only, and not the year – he wrote to Sir William that he hoped the house would soon be making progress, and added, 'I will, if I can, set it out.' Probably it would have been a stone-faced building not unlike Stoke Edith or Antony. But for reasons that can now only be guessed, the central block was never built by Wren. The wings stood isolated for years on top of a gentle rise, like the wings of Mellerstain before Robert Adam, and Sir William Fermor continued to live in the Tudor house of his ancestors a short way down the southern slope. Shortage of money is the most likely explanation of the delay, for in 1692, the same year in which he was created Lord Lempster, Sir William married an heiress as his third wife and his architectural ambitions then revived significantly. He took Wren's advice to call in Nicholas Hawksmoor, and the building was under construction by 1696 or 1697.

No written documents have yet come to light to illustrate the evolution of Hawksmoor's ideas or the relations between him and his patron. But something even more dramatic has survived: Hawksmoor's original oak model. This chunky doll's house, which stands in a corridor at Easton Neston, takes to pieces. The entire roof lifts off, and below it there are little lids, like those on breakfast-dishes, that can be removed to expose various rooms, and the whole first-floor section slides out to reveal the ground-floor plan. Internally the model shows the house almost exactly as it was built. But externally, between the model-stage and the actual building, changes were made to the two main façades which greatly enhanced their originality and appearance. The model carries in the centre of both entrance and garden fronts a

Looking east across the formal garden, with the
ornamental pond in the foreground and the canal
and park beyond

opposite The staircase which rises in two long
shallow flights to the first floor. The delicate
wrought iron balustrade is in the style of Tijou

double row of superimposed orders – rusticated pillars on the
garden side and engaged Corinthian columns on the entrance
side, the latter reminding one irresistibly of the main temple
façade at Petra. In execution Hawksmoor made three alterations: the building was slightly heightened and narrowed; the
double columns became pairs of pillars or pilasters rising almost
the entire height of the house; and between the windows and at
the corners he repeated the pilasters round all four sides.

The effect is quite astonishing. It is a palace in miniature. The
first impression, in much more than the hygienic sense, is of its
cleanliness. The Helmdon stone is the finest of all English building stones, for it is unmottled and unveined, as clear as liquid,
but where it is rounded, as in the two vast columns on either side
of the front door, it acquires a certain swarthiness, like a lion's
pelt. It can be carved with a crispness which more than two
hundred and fifty years of weathering have not dulled, and the
Corinthian capitals, the only one of the classic orders that can
turn a corner effectively, are as sharp as freshly-cut acanthus
leaves. Hawksmoor matched the elegance of his material by an
arrangement of doors, windows, external staircases and subtle
recessions that clothe the glowing skin of the façades with the
minimum of fuss or ostentation. Not a rainwater-pipe is allowed
to mar the composition of the main fronts, and when the pattern of windows and pilasters is varied, it is by curvature so
simple that it does not destroy the overall effect.

The park is Hawksmoor's, with its canal on the axis of the

A corner of the Drawing Room. The elaborate plasterwork was added after the room had been completed by Hawksmoor

The Dining Room, formerly the central part of Hawksmoor's hall, which was closed in during the nineteenth century and the ceiling lowered

garden door; but the view in the other direction was Wren's, or Wren's deputy's, for the house was sited frontally to face at two miles' distance the lonely spire of Greens Norton church, one of the few instances where the late seventeenth century acknowledged the existence of any period of English civilization previous to its own. The garden, however, is modern, the creation of Lord Hesketh, who died in 1944. A paved terrace, set with yew toadstools and snail-like patterns in box, overlooks a pool surrounded by roses and terms grinning from a hedge. On a June day, when the accompanying photographs were taken, the controlled fecundity of this garden, its gently stirring water that always seems about to overflow but never does, the abandon of the roses and formal curves of yew, form a bower that is scarcely a lesser work of art than the house itself?

The golden light is let in to all the rooms of the house. Not only are the main windows almost as high as the ceilings, but Hawksmoor contrived through the centre of both floors a long gallery that opens them to the views on each side. He has been gently chided by Kerry Downes, his biographer, for 'treating the interior like a box, giving it a number of large stately rooms, and filling up all the remaining spaces with as many small rooms as possible'. But what is any house but a set of boxes within an outer casket, and if the casket be noble, what does it matter that the boxes be of different shapes and sizes and differently orientated, provided that each is a delight in itself.

The rooms at Easton Neston pass this test without fault. Partly it is due, of course, to fine furnishing, pictures, chandeliers and tapestries, but also to Hawksmoor's original conception, evident in the photograph of the model stripped to its ground floor, that rooms must vary in shape as they vary in purpose, and that their arrangement must hold in reserve some surprises. His staircase, which rises in a long flight that turns back on itself to complete the slow climb to the first-floor gallery, imposes on the house a certain stateliness of rhythm. But the rooms themselves do not suffer from any excess of grandeur.

The one heavily-decorated room, the drawing-room, was the work of a local plasterer in the mid-eighteenth century who let himself go in a riot of picture-surrounds and a ceiling in high relief that would have shocked Hawksmoor, a man uncommonly lacking in humour, but has delighted its occupants ever since. The present appearance of the dining-room, too, would cause Hawksmoor to throw up his hands in despair, for it has been formed from the lower half of the central section of his Great Hall. The change, made in the late nineteenth century, was undoubtedly the right one, for Hawksmoor's hall, with its bare upper walls and lower 'vestibules' on each side, was one of his few unsuccessful innovations. But to end on a note of criticism of this great architect is quite inappropriate to a description of a house which gives the visitor such intense pleasure. Easton Neston is without equal for its grace, its sunlit dignity and its architectural audacity that transcends the mere piling of stone on stone.

The garden front from across the ornamental pond. The main living rooms look out over the gardens, which were laid out in the 1920s

MELBOURNE HALL

DERBYSHIRE

An early Georgian house overlooking a remarkable garden

This delightful country-house only just avoids being classified as a town-house. It stands at the edge of the little town of Melbourne, eight miles south of Derby, and there is nothing to prepare you for the sudden change of atmosphere from urban to rural. The town does not fade out into fields, but the raw main street gives a quick twist at its western end to translate you from ugly stucco and uglier shop-signs to decent Georgian brick and Norman stone. Among this group of buildings stands Melbourne Hall. It is at first difficult to find the entrance in the spread of stable-yards, church-yard and cottage gardens, and two piers, seemingly the gate-posts of the house, lead unexpectedly to a great lake which has no immediate connection with the house itself. Melbourne keeps its surprises hidden. Having eventually found the front or back door – the first has scarcely more pretensions than the second – you pass through part of the house onto the garden terrace. Then, for the first time, you acknowledge that the house deserves its reputation. Behind you is an early Georgian façade, more charming and homely than distinguished or grand, and before you is a garden flanked by vast yew tunnels and descending to an ornamental pond with green hills beyond – a more intimate version of the great garden at Powerscourt in Ireland.

The topsy-turvy lay-out of Melbourne, with its set-piece façade neither on the entrance front nor at the opposite end of the house, but on one of its sides, is due partly to the lie of the land and partly to its history. On all but this side the house is hemmed in by the road, the lake and the town, and as it also happened to be the direction in which the ground falls away, it provided the keen gardeners who have inhabited Melbourne for centuries with great opportunities for landscaping which they did not want to miss.

By origin Melbourne was a dependency of the Bishops of Carlisle. The Bishops let it to Sir John Coke, 'the last of the Elizabethans', who was Principal Secretary of State to Charles I immediately before the Civil War. It speaks well for Sir John's incorruptibility and modesty that he neither could afford to build a country-house of his own nor wished to rent one more in keeping with his high office. The house in which he lived until

The 'Four Seasons' monument, the great lead urn which is the centre of a number of radiating avenues in the garden at Melbourne

opposite The east front at Melbourne, begun in 1722 by Sir Thomas Coke. It replaced an earlier Elizabethan house which he had inherited

The Front Hall, divided from the inner hall by two Georgian arches

A plan of the gardens at Melbourne in about 1710, before they were altered by Henry Wise, and before the building of the present house

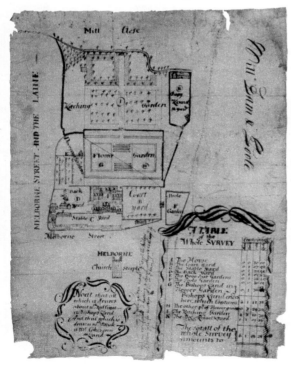

ejected by the Parliamentary forces was a plain Elizabethan building on the E or H-plan, with two wings enclosing a narrow forecourt. Its three other elevations were composed, to judge by a rough contemporary sketch, of a jumble of gables and chimney-stacks that betray the mediaeval and ecclesiastical origins of the site, if not of the building itself. The house was still standing unaltered as late as 1714, and the Bishops were still the landlords. A few years later, Sir John's great-grandson, Sir Thomas Coke, Vice-Chamberlain to Queen Anne and George I from 1711 to 1727, bought the house and decided to transform it.

The puzzle about Melbourne is why Sir Thomas did not make more radical changes if he was in a position to rebuild it almost entirely. Why did he not alter the awkward entrance and ground-plan to provide an approach as dignified as his new east front, and a new arrangement of rooms that would make it unnecessary to go outside or through the kitchens in order to pass from the west wing to the east? That he did rebuild the house almost from its foundations, and not merely the east façade, is clear from an examination of the roof, the cellars, the window-frames and interior doors. Only in one corner, facing the stable-court, is there any sign of the original Elizabethan work, and the interiors are all early Georgian. The rebuilding was prolonged a considerable time, since the lovely laundry building is dated 1710 on an outside stone, and the rainwater-heads on the main house carry the date 1744.

The Drawing Room. The two large portraits by Kneller are
of Queen Anne and George I, to whom Sir Thomas Coke,
builder of the house, was Vice-Chamberlain

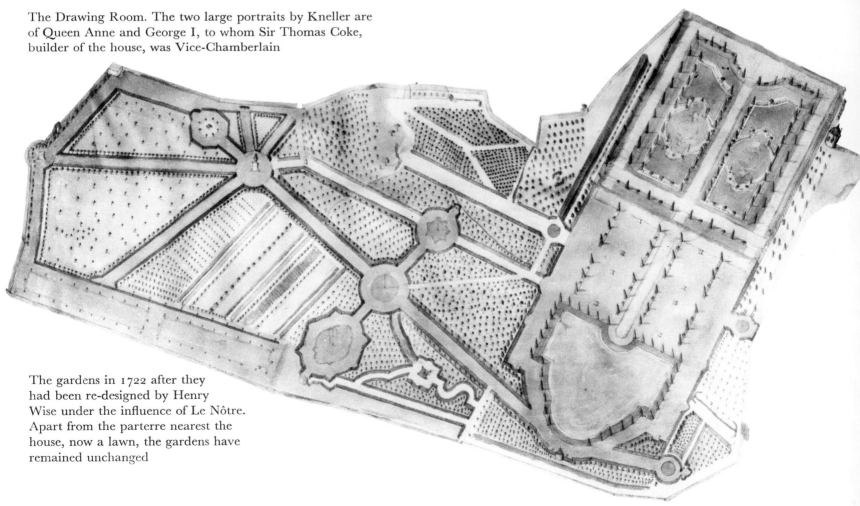

The gardens in 1722 after they
had been re-designed by Henry
Wise under the influence of Le Nôtre.
Apart from the parterre nearest the
house, now a lawn, the gardens have
remained unchanged

The product of all this activity is a house which could be described as elegant and very cheerful. It is full of light and pleasant comfort, more typical of country squires or, for that matter, of the rectors to whom the Bishops had earlier assigned it, than of two courtiers in the seventeenth and eighteenth centuries. There is dignity about it but no ostentation. The staircase rises in clean flights with nicely balanced balusters from the inner hall, and the dining-room is lined with small panels that must have been re-used from the earlier house, or like the overmantel, imported from outside, since they are at least a hundred years earlier in date than the windows and fireplace. Elsewhere the decorations are modest but well-proportioned, a perfect setting for the many works of art that the house contains, particularly the exceptional series of family portraits, from the Cokes to the Lambs (Melbournes), the Melbournes to the Cowpers, and the Cowpers to the Kerrs and Lothians. The house has never passed by sale since the seventeenth century, and the change in family name is due only to the marriages of the heiresses.

The greatest glory of Melbourne is its eighteenth-century garden. Before the end of the seventeenth century there was already a considerable flower and kitchen garden on the east side, but in 1722, in anticipation of his rebuilding, Thomas Coke commissioned Henry Wise to transform it into a garden of avenues and ornamental ponds of a splendour which far surpasses that of the house itself. Today the formal *parterres* immediately in front of the house have been replaced by lawns sloping down to the valley, but the groves, fountains, avenues and ornaments of the wooded garden beyond are preserved intact, and are only rivalled by those at Blickling. There can be no more agreeable experience than to wander through these glades early on a May morning, and rediscover the pleasure with which Coke and Wise arranged their periodic surprises – lead statues of boys fighting or playing, a superb urn by Jan van Nost presented to Sir Thomas by Queen Anne, a 'bird-cage' in wrought-iron by Robert Bakewell, and kitchen-garden walls of rosy brick lying aslant the avenues. In a hidden corner is one addition of later years: a shell grotto containing a mineral-water basin. It is not a thing of beauty, but the curious visitor will find inside it a tablet inscribed with a few doggerel lines of verse, signed 'C. Lamb'. That naughty, delicious, eccentric Caroline, who, in spite of everything, held Lord Melbourne's affections to the end, has left her mark on this lovely place, and one cannot regret it.

opposite A detail of the 'bird-cage', a folly in wrought iron designed for Sir Thomas Coke by Robert Bakewell in about 1725

right Lead statues of cherubs – one of the many pieces of eighteenth-century statuary scattered about the garden

above Looking across the ornamental pond at the foot of the lawn towards the bird-cage

BLENHEIM PALACE

OXFORDSHIRE

Vanbrugh's magnificent tribute to the Duke of Marlborough

The fashion for rewarding national heroes with great houses has passed, but the next best thing is to be born in one, as Winston Churchill was born at Blenheim in 1874. A hundred and seventy years earlier his ancestor, John Churchill, first Duke of Marlborough, had defeated Louis XIV's Marshal Tallard at the Danubian village of Blindheim or Blenheim, and the people received him on his return to London with an ecstasy that recalled the rejoicings after the defeat of the Spanish Armada. Queen Anne took the lead in proposing that the most suitable mark of her and the nation's favour would be a house, castle or palace (Blenheim has been called all three, but later generations have settled for 'palace', the only one in England that is not royal or episcopal), and as a site for it she gave the Duke her royal manor of Woodstock.

The Duke was invited to choose his own architect. He chose Vanbrugh. The choice was not the natural one, for Sir Christopher Wren was Surveyor of the Queen's Works, and Vanbrugh, his junior in age and rank, was still known only as the architect of Castle Howard and the author of some amusing plays. The Duchess of Marlborough pressed Wren's claims for this pearl of a commission, and one might have expected the Duke to capitulate from distrust of his own judgement and a wish to please her. But he showed unexpected vision. Wren would have designed a lovely brick palace like his great addition to Hampton Court or his unexecuted rebuilding of Whitehall – very neat, very gentlemanly, very English. But Vanbrugh alone had the capacity to translate a Roman triumph into stone.

He and the Duke met at Woodstock in February 1705, only six months after the battle of Blenheim. They selected as the site for the palace an elevated platform on the side of the Glyme valley opposite the mediaeval manor. The foundations were being dug by June of the same year, and by 1707 the east wing was ready for its roof. Few buildings can have been begun under happier auspices. Marlborough and Vanbrugh each recognized in the other the highest qualities of their respective professions; Queen Anne was more than delighted with the design; Vanbrugh had persuaded Hawksmoor to help him with the detailed execution of the work; Marlborough continued to win victories;

The East Gate. The inscription records that Blenheim was a gift to the Duke of Marlborough from Queen Anne. In fact he bore much of the cost of the building himself

opposite The entrance front looking west across the Great Court

211

An aerial view of Blenheim Palace from the
north-west, showing the huge extent of the
buildings and courts which cover seven acres

opposite The centre of the west front. In the
foreground is the beginning of Duchêne's water
garden, designed at the beginning of this century

and there was no lack of money. Only one person was not
pleased: the Duchess.

If ever there was a woman bent on mischief, it was Sarah Jennings, Duchess of Marlborough. She conceived for Vanbrugh a
loathing from which nothing would deflect her. Her vindictive-
ness stemmed from the rejection of Wren, but it soon became
clear that she and Vanbrugh had totally different conceptions of
what Blenheim should be. She wanted a comfortable country-
house. He saw it as a building in which convenience and elegance should take second and third places to monumentality. She
was worried about the cost of his grandiose designs, for she wisely
foresaw that the royal favour might not always shine so brightly
and that the Marlboroughs might have to pay. He regarded the
commission much as Le Nôtre might have regarded Louis XIV's,
as a licence to spend whatever was necessary to achieve the most
glorious effect. The basic incompatibility in their points of view
led to quarrelling so bitter that it is a wonder that the palace was
ever finished at all.

The scale of Blenheim was very large. Much more was made
of the two side courts, which had entrance towers and façades of
much greater regularity than those of Castle Howard, and these
courts were withdrawn from the sides of the main house to give
it an east and west front as well as a north and south. Perhaps
Vanbrugh was dissatisfied by the way in which the service-
courts at Castle Howard obscured the sides of the house and

The south or garden front seen from across Capability Brown's lawn, originally a formal parterre

opposite The Grand Bridge built by Vanbrugh despite repeated protests from Sarah, Duchess of Marlborough. Originally it crossed three canals running under the three arches. Now it spans Capability Brown's huge lake constructed in 1764

An engraving of the east front made in 1717 while the house was still under construction

Sarah Jennings, Duchess of Marlborough, by
Sir Godfrey Kneller. She quarrelled bitterly with
Vanbrugh over the designs for the Palace.
A portrait now at Althorp

were articulated to it, and there is no doubt that the side-
elevations of Blenheim are more satisfactory. On the other hand,
many people will prefer the two main fronts of Castle Howard.
There is nothing at Blenheim so immediately engaging as the
dome over the central building of Castle Howard. Instead, we
have a columned portico which appears slightly too high for its
width, topped by a curiously chunky affair of stubby pillars and
broken arches above the pediment. To the right and left there is
a curved porch, again heavily surmounted by a rectilinear
second storey behind it, and at all four corners a great tower of
deliberately outlandish design. Then begin the Tuscan colonnades. The whole façade is angular, massive, stern. All the
obvious aids to elegance have been rejected. Even the decorative
features are intentionally bizarre, like the finials to the towers, a
duke's coronet perpetually burning in the flames of a grenade.
Robert Adam, who admired Vanbrugh more than any of his
predecessors, felt compelled to comment, 'His taste kept no pace
with his genius, and his works are so crowded with barbarisms
and absurdities, and so borne down by their own preposterous
weight, that none but the discerning can separate their merits
from their defects.' The Great Court at Blenheim, like the
garden-front at Holkham, has left 'the discerning' at logger-
heads. Horace Walpole could call it 'a quarry of stone'. Voltaire
remarked *que c'était une grosse masse de pierre, sans agrément et sans
goût.* But Sir John Soane wrote, 'This work alone may be said to
stamp Vanbrugh the Shakespeare of architects'; and Sacheverell Sitwell, that it is 'one of the most extraordinary feats of
architecture'. That the finished result should continue to arouse
controversy would no doubt have pleased Vanbrugh. He did not
set out to delight, nor even to shock. He was constructing the
back-drop to a Wagnerian opera. The heaviness of the stone,
the thick duplication of the central part, the massed battalions
of columns, make the building intensely dramatic and challeng-
ing. It is like a declaration of war.

Moving round to the garden fronts, you find something of
much more immediate appeal. It is true that the military sym-
bolism is maintained by a huge bust of Louis XIV, a trophy
from Tournai mounted centrally above the south portico, the
eighteenth-century equivalent to exposing the severed heads of
your enemies on your gates. But on this side Vanbrugh's treatment of the huge masses was quieter and more conventional. On
the two side-fronts he allowed himself a certain grace of movement, now greatly enhanced by the formal gardens laid out by
the ninth Duke and his French architect Duchêne in the early
years of the present century.

The same consideration had its effect upon the design of the
inside. Vanbrugh has often been accused of sacrificing his interiors to the exteriors, of condemning his patrons to live in draughty
halls and move with guttering candles through endless corridors.
But the criticism cannot be sustained by the same person who
finds Vanbrugh's rooms small and mean. The truth is that

Blenheim and Castle Howard were both designed for a way of life that no longer has much meaning for our own generation. There had to be an entrance of overwhelming magnificence and a reception room equal to the dignity of the privileged few who were likely to be invited there: hence the Great Hall and the Saloon, the first painted by Thornhill, the second by Laguerre. But there must also be intimate rooms for the family, where the scale was reduced to closets where conversation could burgeon and one would not be too overawed to lay down a pipe. Blenheim is not often praised for its interior, apart from the icy blue emptiness of Hawksmoor's Long Library, perhaps the finest room he ever designed. But to dismiss the rest as immemorable

The memorial to the first Duke of Marlborough in the chapel. Designed by William Kent and executed by Rysbrack, it is considered by many to be the finest piece of English baroque sculpture

The Great Hall 67 feet high. The stone arches are typical of Vanbrugh's style

Looking through into the Saloon from one of the State Rooms

far right The north front seen from beyond the bridge. The monument in the foreground marks the site of the original Woodstock manor house

right The Long Library designed by Vanbrugh as a picture gallery, but finished by Hawksmoor to house the Sunderland Library, sold in 1872. The fine stucco ceiling is by Isaac Mansfield

is to do Vanbrugh less than justice. You find, to your surprise, that a habitable house has been built within a temple.

Vanbrugh is equally to be credited with his forethought for the surroundings, which provide an English setting for the baroque palace without bringing one into conflict with the other. His vast *parterre* on the south front has been swept away, but round the other three sides he transformed the royal hunting forest into a park of dimensions appropriate to the scale of his architecture and as green as baize. The vast bridge, which became the biggest bone of contention between him and the Duchess, lacks its superstructure, and from the house appears little more than a causeway across a deep valley. But walk to one side and you will see at once that this 'wasteful' edifice is in fact a master-stroke. It was to be 'the finest bridge in Europe'. Wren had prescribed something far less pretentious, but Vanbrugh's persuasiveness and sense of the magnificent won the day. There it stands, Appian in its stupendous bulk, and, like the palace, a symbol of triumph. He made only one mistake: in his day it crossed a slender canal, and it was left to Capability Brown to form the lakes on either side which gave the bridge something worthy to surmount.

The south corridor opening off the Great Hall. The cloistered effect is typical of Vanbrugh and it recalls the Antique Passage at Castle Howard

MEREWORTH CASTLE

KENT

An English adaptation of Palladian villa

The house which Colen Campbell designed at Mereworth for John Fane, later seventh Earl of Westmorland, in 1720–3 was a close copy of the Rotonda, or Villa Capra, which Palladio had built in the mid-sixteenth century for Paolo Almerico, a town official of Vicenza. This capsule of concentrated information can be swallowed whole or dissected, and dissection appears the better course, for why a Scottish architect who had never been to Italy should choose to erect an Italian villa in the Weald of Kent for a patron who had likewise never set eyes on the Rotonda, demands some explanation.

The story should begin with Andrea Palladio himself. He achieved in England a reputation that surprises Italians even to this day. His work was derivative from earlier Renaissance buildings which themselves derived from Imperial Rome, and by his time the style had been almost exhausted of its possibilities. But his famous volumes *I quattro libri dell' architettura*, first published in Venice in 1570, had been Inigo Jones' Bible and were republished in an English translation by Nicholas Dubois in 1715 with plates specially redrawn by Giacomo Leoni. Among the illustrations were an elevation, a cross-section and a ground-plan of the Rotonda, probably the most famous of the many villas which Palladio erected in the Venetian plain. Undoubtedly Campbell, the originator of the English Palladian style, worked from these drawings when he came to design Mereworth. As Palladio was Jones' idol, so was each of them Campbell's. He admired but rejected Hawksmoor and Vanbrugh in favour of what Summerson calls 'the search for absolutes', that purity of style which the Romans originated and Palladio followed. Of course Mereworth was not an exact copy of the Rotonda any more than Palladio built exactly as the Romans did. Concessions were made by both to contemporary tastes and comforts. The Rotonda was a Roman temple in form more than a Roman villa; and Mereworth is an English Palladian house more than an Italian *villegiattura* resort. Nevertheless the artistic descent from Rome to Kent is direct.

Colen Campbell, in the third volume of his *Vitruvius Britannicus* (1725), drew attention to the changes which he had made in translating the villa from Vicenza to the neighbourhood of

A cross section and elevation of Palladio's Rotonda at Vicenza, on which Colen Campbell modelled Mereworth. An engraving from the 1715 edition of *The Architecture of Palladio* by Giacomo Leoni

opposite The north or entrance front

Maidstone. 'I shall not pretend to say,' he wrote, 'that I have made any improvements in this plan from that of Palladio for Signor Almerico, but shall only observe the alterations which I humbly submit to my learned Judges.' These alterations were significant. Mereworth lies towards the bottom of a wide shallow valley and until the late nineteenth century was surrounded by a moat; the Rotonda stood on a tumulus. Mereworth has an outside staircase on two sides only, the north and south; the Rotonda on all four sides. Mereworth has a smooth outer dome of lead; the Rotonda's was layered and tiled. Mereworth's twenty-four chimneys are ingeniously fed through the shell of the dome into a single chimney at the top, disguised as a lantern; the Rotonda's chimneys emerge as obelisks on the outer walls. In the Rotonda the porticoes have arches at the sides; at Mereworth the sides are columned. Inside, Campbell also departed from his pattern by retaining only one of Palladio's four vestibules that linked the porticoes with the central hall and so managed to fit in a drawing-room extending the unbroken length of the south front. 'And if I may add,' concluded Campbell, 'the great difference both of dress and materials, the whole ornamental parts being of Portland stone, and as much enriched as the Rules of our Art can admit.'

All this amounts to quite a difference, and judges, learned or not, are likely to admit that each change was an improvement. Still, Mereworth remains an imitation and a tribute. Other

The west front. This, and the opposite east front, are not approached by steps, but otherwise all four façades are identical. The house was originally surrounded by a moat, removed in the nineteenth century

houses were built in England after the same model, notably Lord Burlington's villa at Chiswick and, at one stage removed, Lord Herbert's in Whitehall and Stourhead, Wiltshire, but Mereworth is the most faithful to the original. Nobody would have built like this unless compelled by admiration for a shape. It is a symmetrical shape that manages to achieve great variety. Here is a square two-storeyed block surmounted by a dome with an identical pedimented portico on each side. Those are the essentials of a composition visible from every direction. Yet the wonder of Mereworth is that you can walk round its outside without monotony. This is due not only to the change in the fall of light and shadow – and Mereworth must for this reason be seen in sunlight – but to the continually changing spatial relationship between porticoes and house. Each step backwards or forwards alters the relative position of the columns, as can never happen when mere pilasters are flattened against a formal façade. Portico is seen in relation to portico, at least two at a time, and when the house is viewed frontally, three. All of them are beautiful combinations of stateliness and ornamentation. Their ceilings are of great richness, but they are only discovered from within, like those of the Parthenon peristyle, and the eye is constantly choosing between the decoration of these porticoes and their plainness. The dome, of course, is unchanging from every direction, and its ornament is its structure – prominent ribs and a lidded cupola. The latter at first seems to need glass panels at the sides (which it cannot have, because it also does duty as a chimney) or failing glass, gilt, on the analogy of Castle Howard's. But on second thoughts one comes to agree that Mereworth is not a house that should glitter: the glitter is inside. It is a house of profiles and silver stone mottled like a bird's egg.

Campbell makes no reference in his book to the two exquisite pavilions that stand one on each side of the entrance front, and it now seems certain that they were not built until about 1736–40, about fifteen years after the main house was finished, and perhaps by 'Athenian' Stuart. Not only are they pretty buildings in themselves but they are perfectly sited in relation to the house, close enough to frame it but not too close to cramp it nor to interfere with the dignity of the stepped approach. Had it not been for the porticoes and the moat, the architect might have followed the Palladian tradition of linking the pavilions to the house by curved and colonnaded wings, and we can count ourselves fortunate that this mannerism was not possible here. It was also a happy notion to place arcaded loggias on the sides of the pavilions that face the house and porticoes on their inner fronts, so that the rhythms of the house are maintained but not repeated, and extra views from and towards the house are created. Although the moat is lost, Mereworth still seems to swim. It is a very light structure. The dome might be gas-filled, anchored by its square base to the ground.

Every chance passer-by must want to go inside. For how, he asks himself, can people live in such a place? Is there a room

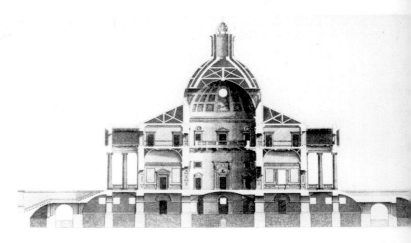

A cross-section of Mereworth from *Vitruvius Britannicus* showing the ingenious way in which the twenty-four chimneys are fed through the shell of the dome into a single chimney disguised in the lantern

Looking across from the portico of the west pavilion to the east pavilion. These pavilions were added in 1736–40, about fifteen years after the main house was completed

The dome seen from the circular hall beneath.
The elaborate stucco decorations by Bagutti are
contemporary with the building of the house

The doorway from the entrance vestibule into the
hall. The stucco work and figures over the doors
representing the arts and sciences are by Bagutti

within the dome? And what happens at the angles where
straight walls meet curved? The answers, in their order, are as
follows: that they live very comfortably; that the dome forms a
hall in the form of a half-egg, rising from floor-level to the base
of the cupola, with a gallery ringing it at the level of the first
floor; that spiral staircases fill two of the corners, a lift the
third, and a small cloakroom the fourth. The structure and
ground-plan are very ingenious and can best be followed in the
cross-section here reproduced from Campbell's book. But not
even the best photograph can convey the total impression made
by the lovely circular hall in the centre of the house. Campbell
called it a Saloon, but it is doubtful whether it could ever have
been used as a living-room since its only windows are the circular recesses at the base of the dome, and it is a place where
furniture is superfluous. The present owner, Mr Michael Tree,
has had the happy inspiration of painting the inside walls in
terracotta, slightly roughened in imitation of the colour and
texture of the walls of an Italian villa. Against it lies the white
stucco of Bagutti. This takes the form of swags of flowers and
fruit, allegorical figures and boys reclining above the doorways,
busts on wall-pedestals or cupped in shells, enriched soffits to the
gallery, plaques, friezes and pilasters. Thus catalogued, the

stucco may sound overdone. The photographs prove that it is not. The circular shape makes possible the continuity of the pattern without a break, and the height – who does not first look upwards when entering a domed hall? – lifts the eye away from the drum below. Horace Walpole, who visited Mereworth with John Chute in 1752, called the hall 'a dark well'. Even making allowances for his bad temper at the time, of which his letters give ample proof, no judgement could be more ridiculous. But of the rest of the house he had more good to say. 'I must own,' he concluded, 'that it has recovered me a little from the Gothic.' From Walpole that was high praise.

The other downstairs rooms are richer than the hall. The doors and doorways are as sumptuous as Holkham's, and not a square inch of the coved ceilings is unadorned by paint or gilt except where they were left unfinished. They are nonetheless extremely habitable rooms. Partly this is because they are inhabited – humanized by the comfortable clutter of a family's daily life; and partly because the colours, though rich, are fused to the gentle tones of tapestries. The long drawing-room is so immediately attractive that the visitor finds himself guilty of looking around it before greeting his hostess; while the smaller rooms vary between ornamental closets and state-rooms that can still be used to sleep, eat, write, play billiards and even bath in without feeling that one is doing these things in surroundings that demand a special behaviour. The climb upstairs by the spiral staircase to the gallery affords a unique pleasure: until the last moment you are hidden from the renewed surprise of looking down on the hall from the base of the dome.

Mereworth is a house of paradoxes. By following after a fashion the antique rules of temple architecture, it breaks the rules of house-planning. A villa in descent, it is a castle by name. A house that could be freakish in its Kentish context, is immediately recognizable as a great work of art. Rooms that belong to a palace never overawe. Mereworth is a remarkable incident in the long flirtation between Italy and the Gothic North.

The fireplace in the dining room, formerly the west bedchamber. The walls are hung with Beauvais tapestries

The Drawing Room which runs the full length of the south front

HADDO HOUSE

ABERDEENSHIRE

A William Adam house transformed by Lady Aberdeen

Three people made this house: William Adam, who built it; Lord Aberdeen, the Victorian Prime Minister, who developed the park; and his grandson's wife Ishbel, who added to the house and redecorated its rooms. That is a telescoped version of a strange collaboration between people whose lives and tastes barely overlapped, but who managed to create between them an extremely pleasing entity. Ishbel, for example, appears not to have known or cared that Adam was the architect of Haddo, for she never mentions his name in her description of the house and thought it poorly planned; while the Prime Minister frankly disliked the place until his tree-planting began to loosen the stiff muscles of his imagination.

That the house makes a totally different impression on the present-day visitor is mainly because the trees have now grown up around it and the rawness of the new buildings and freshly decorated rooms has been softened by time. But it is also because we have come to recognize the excellence of William Adam's design, which shines through all subsequent additions to it. The distinguished father of more distinguished sons, he and Colen Campbell were the only true Palladian architects that Scotland ever produced. He was commissioned in 1731 to build the house for William, second Earl of Aberdeen, to replace the old House of Kellie which had been the family house of the Gordons of Methlick for centuries. He constructed a central pedimented block, with exterior staircases to the first floor on both the garden and entrance fronts, and two wings enclosing the entrance forecourt, one for the stables and the other for kitchens, linked to the main house by curving one-storey corridors. At Haddo the idea was executed to perfection. The high central building, Wren-like in its general style, has a commanding presence and its proportions are correspondingly severe. An English architect would probably have added another window on each side of the pedimented centre and heightened them by an extra foot. But in compensation for any northern angularity, there were the elegant curves of the original outside staircase and the charming low corridors. It was more than a decent house for an Earl. It was an integrated work of art, and it is almost inconceivable to our eyes that anyone could have thought it gaunt.

The Dining Room, originally two rooms, hung with portraits of the Aberdeen family. The ceiling is Adam-style dating from about 1880

opposite The garden front. The external staircase from the Drawing Room into the garden was added in the nineteenth century and replaced William Adam's original structure

227

The north or entrance front. The main structure is as William Adam designed it in 1731, but a number of changes and additions were made in the 1880s

Inside, William Adam's arrangements were less happy. The idea of a *piano nobile* on the first floor approached from outside was more suited to Italy, where it originated, than to the northern parts of Great Britain. In such a climate it was not agreeable to descend from your carriage in rain or snow and be confronted by stone exterior steps instead of by a welcoming front door and hall. As you mounted them, exposed to a gale whipping round the corner of the house, you must have wondered where the entrance was. You found yourself creeping through a window off the first-floor terrace into a living-room, with no obvious place in which to lay your dripping coat and hat. Splendid though the staircase was as a platform from which Queen Victoria and Mr Gladstone could show themselves to the tenantry (each did so on more than one occasion), it had been designed for effect and not for convenience. It had the further disadvantages that the heavy perron darkened the ground-floor rooms, which were therefore made over to the servants, and that the house lacked a main internal staircase.

For a hundred and fifty years the Gordons accepted these drawbacks. It did not even occur to Lord Aberdeen, the Prime Minister, to alter them, although after his first visit he wrote of 'the desolation of the exterior [by which he meant the surroundings] which is only equalled by the appalling badness of the house'. Instead of doing something about it, he planted fourteen million trees. His character and the life he lived there were not, however, ill-suited to its austerity. He maintained the formality of a minor court, with a somewhat rigid etiquette. The house was darkly panelled in conformity with this grim régime.

William Adam's elevation of the entrance front, showing the horseshoe staircase and the curving corridors, to which another floor was added later, linking the main house to the wings

All was transformed by Ishbel, wife of the seventh Earl, who died in 1939 at the age of 82. Her disappointment at her first sight of Haddo drove her into activity, not despair. In the early years of their married life the Aberdeens ('WeTwa') completed the chapel on one side of the house, added a nursery wing (since burned down) on the other, created an entrance hall and staircase on the ground floor and rebuilt Adam's outside staircase to a wider, bulkier design. The convenience of the house, if not its appearance from outside, was thereby greatly improved. The interior was utterly renovated. Lord Aberdeen had given his young wife *carte blanche* to redecorate it as she wished, and she chose the Robert Adam style of her father's house, Guisachan in Invernesshire. The work was completed in the 1880's.

When he hears this, the visitor expects the worst. In fact the rooms are delightful. There are few more successful examples of the Palladian style allied to late-Victorian. The decorations are not of course a match for Adam originals, and two Wedgewood fireplaces in the library, presumably brought here from Guisachan, immediately catch the eye for the greater fineness of their design and execution. But Ishbel's bold bay-windows, the clean colours and garlands of the ceiling, the pleasantly gilded pilasters of the morning-room, the Victorian water-colours and chintzy furniture everywhere, make it a house of great personality and, one is tempted to say, vigour. Haddo is the house of people who have known what they liked – a house for children, flowers, and cherry-jam for tea. Today we must add music, for Mrs David Gordon has made Haddo a centre for the most successful choral society in this part of Scotland.

The Drawing Room which overlooks the garden. The ceiling decorations in the Adam style were completed in the 1880s

A green jasperware Wedgwood fireplace in the library, depicting the apotheosis of Virgil. It was executed in 1786 and brought to Haddo by Ishbel, Lady Aberdeen

HOLKHAM HALL

NORFOLK

The finest Palladian interior in England

Looking south through the columns of the portico towards the obelisk

Above the inner side of the front door at Holkham is an inscription more modest in its proportions than in its claims. 'This seat,' it reads, 'on an open barren estate, was planned, planted, built, decorated and inhabited the middle of the XVIIIth century by Thos. Coke, Earl of Leicester.' A pedant could comment that not all these statements are quite true. The estate, far from being barren when Lord Leicester inherited it at the age of ten, was rolling sheep-country and had supported for over a century a large and distinguished family who lived not more than a few hundred yards from the present house. He had the controlling hand over the design and execution of his new building, but he was assisted by friends and professionals even more knowledgeable than himself, and by an army of skilled craftsmen. He did not live in more than a corner of it, because he died five years before its completion. But such carping criticism would be out of place at Holkham. Lord Leicester should be allowed his note of triumph. By inspiring the idea of Holkham, by seeing it through twenty-five years of its construction (1734–1759) and filling it with the books and works of art that he had collected in his youth, he was the author of one of the greatest memorials to the Palladian age.

Holkham makes an immediate and overwhelming impression of stateliness; but it also strains the critical powers to the utmost. For its exterior is not, in the facile sense, attractive. It is built of a yellowish brick, as near a copy of the Roman Renaissance brick as the Norfolk kilns could manage, and its south elevation lacks that liveliness and balance which one has come to associate with the prettier achievements of Palladianism. Its relieving features are the great portico, the Wilton-like caps to the corner towers of the main block and the triple-pedimented façades to the wings. That is all. The eye searches for pleasing colour, and finds it only in the great red curtains of the central windows; it searches for the more obvious signs of grace and movement, and finds them in the arches of a large orangery and the curves of a garden balustrade, only to recoil with something like guilt from these Victorian additions. The windows flanking the portico appear lost in the expanse of brickwork above them, and the basement windows are as plain as port-holes.

opposite The Marble Hall, rising to almost the full height of the house, and modelled by William Kent on the design of a Roman basilica. The great columns are in fact of Derbyshire alabaster

The south front, a carefully thought-out
adaptation of the Palladian style. It is 344 feet
long from wing to wing

opposite The Saloon. The walls and furniture are
covered with the original red Genoa velvet. On
the left is Rubens' *Return from Egypt*, the most
famous painting in the house

right Thomas Coke, first Earl of Leicester, the
builder of Holkham. A contemporary print
showing him with the house in the background

A drawing of the south front made by William Kent in about 1735. He originally conceived the house rusticated up to the eaves and with a double staircase leading from the portico

opposite top The gallery of the Marble Hall looking towards the doorway of the Saloon. The huge alabaster columns are copied from the Temple of Fortuna Virilis, Rome

opposite The ground plan of Holkham showing the careful balance of the design. The doorways of the rooms facing south (top) are so perfectly aligned that it is possible to look from one end to the other through the keyholes

The question which then forms in our minds is why the incomparable trio who created Holkham – the Earls of Leicester and Burlington, and William Kent – adopted this austere external manner. It is not convincing to dismiss it as ugly or a mistake, nor to suppose that they were incapable of more 'stylish' architecture. The south front goes beyond mere elegance. It is an attempt to sum up in brick the ideals of an age: stoic rejection of frivolity in the essentials of a man's character and conduct, secular robustness and common sense. The placing of the windows was partly dictated by interior design: there are great voids behind those blank walls which were left empty to accommodate high ceilings and the reverse sides of the internal apses. But if a second storey had been thought necessary to the façade, it could have been contrived. Its omission was deliberate. If the house at first appears as functional as a Prussian riding-school, contemplation of the relationship between its different components convinces one that here is an organization of masses and planes which has few equals in the country.

Lord Leicester, we are told by his executive architect, Matthew Brettingham, was insistent on 'commodiousness' throughout his house, by which he meant comfort, ease of access and excellence of construction. Over two hundred years later his care is still apparent. To our eyes there are certain deficiencies, such as the great distances between the kitchen-wing and the dining-room, and the comparative poverty of the servants' quarters which made it necessary for footmen to sleep four to a bed (not unusual in the eighteenth century) and for the maids' rooms to be split up into attic-cubicles as late as the 1930's. But of the soundness of construction there can be no doubt at all. The craftsmanship of the ceiling and other decorations was worthy of their designers. Almost nothing has had to be changed or repaired since the 1750's. The gilding of the cornices, the doors and window-frames, the carpets and wall-hangings, are the originals. Only in a few rooms has even the paint been refreshed in modern times. At Holkham, therefore, one sees a house of the utmost distinction exactly as its creator desired it and his widow completed it.

Here is a Roman palace reinterpreted by the English eighteenth century. Its astonishing maturity, its restrained voluptuousness, its coolness, grandeur and disdain of the tawdry, leave no room for doubt that centuries of experiment and artistic creation have led up to this point. It comes as a shock to realize that almost nothing about Holkham except its site can be called basically English. In the official account of the house, published shortly after its completion, every part of it was attributed to its Roman or Italian prototype, or to Jonesian derivations from them. Yet nothing could be less plagiaristic. To take the outstanding example of the entrance hall, the idea of which was credited by Brettingham to Lord Leicester himself. In essence it is a Roman basilica with an *exedra*, surrounded by Ionic

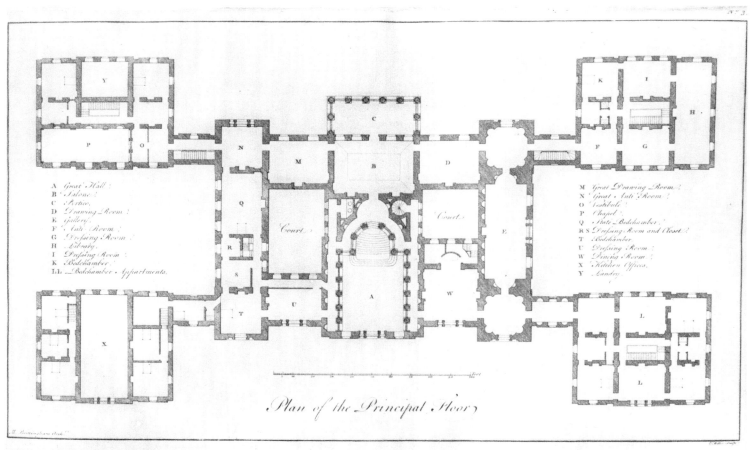

A Great Hall.
B Salone.
C Portico.
D Drawing Room.
E Gallery.
F Anti Room.
G Dressing Room.
H Library.
I Dressing Room.
K Bedchamber.
LL Bedchamber Apartments.

M Great Drawing Room.
N Great Anti Room.
O Vestibule.
P Chapel.
Q State Bedchamber.
RS Dressing Room and Closet.
T Bedchamber.
U Dressing Room.
W Pensira Room.
X Kitchen Offices.
Y Laundry.

Plan of the Principal Floor

The Long Library, which runs the full length of the south-west wing. It contains the collection of books acquired by the first Earl on his Italian tour

columns. But the splendour and grace of this vast hall lies in the device of mounting the peristyle on a podium the depth of the basement floor, and in making the columns out of Derbyshire alabaster, a material which is used again in the facings of the podium and gives the hall its only colour apart from the stair-carpet. It is not in the least like a temple, though it owes its origins to temple architecture. As Arthur Young observed, it is more like a bath-house of the utmost magnificence.

In the rooms that compose the state-suite on the first floor, there is the same absence of fuss. The materials, like the furniture, sculpture and pictures, are of the highest quality, but they are used with such chastity (the word is James Lees-Milne's)

The North Dining Room which takes the form of a cube, with an apse for the serving table. Over the fireplace is a bust of Lucius Verus

236

that it was possible to decorate the smaller private rooms in the same style without oppressing them. The long library in the south-west wing is one example. It is Kent's untouched work, a beautiful room which owes its subdued colour to the calf bindings of Lord Leicester's editions of the classics and to wall-gilding which only becomes apparent as each part is examined in turn. The sculpture gallery, a favourite eighteenth-century room, is one of the few in existence which seems habitable as well as a perfect setting for marble statues. The dining-room expresses perhaps best of all the ideal of classical purity to which the eighteenth century aspired but so seldom attained in their private lives. Though it must often have been the scene of revelry and debauch, it could surely also stimulate a high level of conversation, just as the cricket-ground between the north front and the lake makes a hero out of every village Bradman.

That such a house should have descended to the greatest agricultural reformer of his day, 'Coke of Norfolk', first Earl of Leicester by the second creation, may seem anticlimactic, but only if one pictures an aristocratic yokel clumping up and down these rich rooms. He was not in the least like that. As he pretended to no knowledge of the arts, he had the good sense not to Adamize or Gothicize his great-uncle's legacy during the sixty years of his ownership. 'I shall never venture rashly to interfere with the result of years of thought and study in Italy,' he said, and Holkham could not be more concisely described.

The Statue Gallery running the full width of the house from north to south. It was specially designed to hold the collection of Greek and Roman sculpture acquired by the first Earl of Leicester in Italy on the Grand Tour

Looking west from the Landscape Room down the length of the south front through the sequence of inter-connecting rooms. This room takes its name from the paintings by Claude and Poussin with which it is hung

SYON HOUSE

MIDDLESEX

One of Robert Adam's greatest interiors

Syon is the last of the great patrician houses around London to remain in the hands of its original owners. The rest have been institutionalized or preserved in the aspic of State ownership. The house is still occupied for several months in the year by the Duke of Northumberland and his family, but its closeness to the metropolis, which swirls round its park on three sides (the fourth is mercifully edged by the River Thames with Kew Gardens on the opposite bank), and the apparatus of guard-ropes and drugget carpets necessary to protect the rooms from prying fingers and stiletto heels, diminish its seclusion and turn some of the most charming rooms to be seen anywhere in England into corridors for tired feet.

The visitor who is ignorant of its contents is not likely to be enticed to Syon by its appearance from outside. Outwardly it resembles an arsenal more than a house. A square battlemented block of brown stone with angle-turrets, its garden front surmounted by a great lion, suggests a Wyatt house more than something basically Tudor. Yet Tudor it is to its bones. The house was raised in about 1550 by Edward Seymour, Duke of Somerset, Protector of the Realm during the reign of the boy-king Edward VI, who made use of the walls of an earlier Bridgettine nunnery that had stood on the site since 1431.

The early history of Syon is an appalling succession of disasters. The house drew to itself people at the crisis of their lives, and passed from one failing hand to another with a rapidity that suggests a curse upon it. The nuns were ejected by Henry VIII in 1534 on a trumped-up charge that their relations with the friars were more than cordial: one of the priests was quartered, drawn and hanged, in that gruesome order. Henry VIII confined his Queen Catherine Howard at Syon during the months before her execution, and his own corpse was mauled by dogs as it lay there in state on its way from London to Windsor. Protector Somerset himself was beheaded in 1552 before the new house was completed, and he was followed to the block by his successors at Syon, Lady Jane Grey, her husband and father-in-law, who had forced the Crown upon her for a reign that lasted no more than nine days. Henry Percy, the ninth Earl of Northumberland, was fraudulently implicated in

Robert Adam, the designer of Syon. A portrait by an unknown artist

opposite The Entrance Hall. In the foreground is a fine copy of the *Dying Gaul*, and at the opposite end a copy of the *Apollo Belvedere* stands under a half dome inspired by Roman originals

239

The garden front. Syon retains the four square plan and original walls of the Tudor house built *c* 1550. The lion came from Northumberland House at Charing Cross, demolished in 1874

Detail of the ceiling and gilt stucco panels in the Ante-Room, including one of the gilt statues of gods and goddesses which stand on the entablature

the Gunpowder Plot, and imprisoned in the Tower of London for fifteen years because he could not pay the £30,000 fine imposed upon him. Syon was for a time the prison chosen by Parliament for the children of Charles I. It came in the late seventeenth century to the three-year-old Elizabeth Percy, who was married at twelve, widowed in the same year, re-married at fourteen to Thomas Thynne of Longleat who was almost immediately assassinated in Pall Mall by the order of a disappointed rival, and married for the third time at the age of fifteen to the Duke of Somerset. From that moment Syon at last found peace. It is strange that a house with such a history should have survived at all. It is even stranger that it should contain the finest expression of the imagination of Robert Adam.

In 1760 Adam had not long returned from a tour of Italy, his mind filled with the possibilities of recreating the Roman style in terms of eighteenth-century refinement. He was on friendly terms with the Duke of Northumberland, for whom he helped to redecorate Alnwick Castle, and straight from Alnwick was commissioned to refashion Syon 'in the antique style'. Adam was delighted with the commission. 'I endeavoured to render it a noble and elegant habitation,' he wrote, looking back with satisfaction on his work, 'not unworthy of a proprietor who possessed not only wealth to execute a great design, but skill to judge of its merit.' But Adam was not allowed to do all that he wanted. He was instructed to preserve the original Jacobean layout of

opposite The Ante-Room, one of the richest rooms created by Adam. The twelve columns of verd-antique were dredged up from the Tiber and brought to Syon in 1765

the rooms, one running into the next around the four sides of the first floor, and he was not permitted to build over the central courtyard the large circular room, capped by a cupola, from which he intended that all the outer rooms should radiate. He finished only five of the rooms, occupying two-and-a-half sides of the building, but they remain exactly as he designed them, laid out like five playing-cards round the courtyard.

Adam complained that his difficulties were increased by the fact that the entrance hall, probably the old refectory hall of the monastery, was on a lower level than the other rooms. Yet this difference of level imparted variety to an otherwise rather bleak hall, for he was able to introduce steps at each end, increasing the 'movement' of the design, and arousing expectation of what might lie beyond. To some eyes the hall is nevertheless the least successful of the rooms, for its walls and ceilings are unrelieved by colour and the antique statues make it seem cold rather than cool. It is the only one of the five which looks better in a photograph than in reality.

The Ante-Room, approached by the short flight of steps on the right of the hall, is by contrast one of the richest and noblest rooms that Adam ever created. It is quite small, but an effect of Roman splendour is achieved by the twelve columns of verd-antique dredged from the bed of the Tiber and brought to Syon in 1765. What a discovery, and how splendidly Adam turned it to advantage! The columns are ranged round the room against the walls except on one side where they are brought forward to give it the semblance of a square, and standing on the Ionic capitals are statues of dull gold which look downwards from just short of the ceiling. The whole room, for which the word 'gorgeous' is for once not inappropriate, is Adam at his most adventurous. Gone is the 'lace and embroidery . . . Adam's filigree', at which Horace Walpole unfairly mocked, and in its place is bold design, architecture carried indoors, mingled with an unashamed use of strong colours. The floor of yellow, red and blue scagliola work, the ceiling and the gilt stucco wall-panels in the form of trophies, combine to make the Ante-Room

The East Door in the Red Drawing Room

opposite The Red Drawing Room hung with Spitalsfield silk. The coved ceiling decorations are by Cipriani

Syon House in 1752 by Canaletto
Photo 'Country Life'

a triumph of grandeur on the scale of a private house. It was never a living-room, but was used as a waiting-room for servants – those pipers and Swiss porters whom Walpole observed with a shrug of the shoulders as evidence that the Northumberlands 'live by the etiquette of the old peerage', and were likely to end in financial ruin.

Turning the corner of the house, one enters the dining-room, a treble-cube room sixty-three feet long by twenty-one feet wide and high. Four statues in niches face the windows, the whole finished in gilt and ivory, almost clinically, for Adam believed that dining-rooms in England were places where men liked to linger over their meals talking politics, 'more detached from the society of the ladies' than was the custom in France. So there must be no wall-hangings, not even curtains to the windows, which could retain the smell of food and smoke. For the same reason, the drawing-room must be a sort of insulation chamber to protect the ladies in the Long Gallery from the sound of revelry in the dining-room. The Red Drawing-room, so called from the lovely red Spitalsfield silk which covers its walls, is in fact a great deal more than an air-lock. It is a beautiful room with a coved ceiling painted by Angelica Kauffman in round paper medallions set in gilded octagons, and a carpet, the finest of its sort in existence, woven by Thomas Moore from Adam's designs in 1769. On the fireplace and the doorways (the latter doubled for the sake of his much-cosseted ladies) Adam lavished his most exquisite filigree, a form of classical rococo. The long narrow panels of ormolu on a background of ivory are the perfect expression of that 'variety and gracefulness' which he considered essential ingredients of a gentleman's house.

The fifth and last Adam room is the most astonishing and satisfying of all. Here is the eighteenth-century solution to the residual problem of the Jacobean Long Gallery. The room is 136 feet long, with a width and height of only fourteen feet, and eleven windows ranged along one side. How was Adam to adapt it 'for the reception of company before dinner or for the ladies to retire to after it'? He finished it, he wrote, 'in a style to afford great variety and amusement'. The three doors and two fireplaces, the bookshelves and highly ornate ceiling expand its apparent width, while the groups of pilasters give it extra height. The furniture, all of Adam's design, helps to break up the great length of the gallery. But the first and lasting impression is of its colour, a very pale green enriched with gilt like a *pot-pourri* of lavender and faded rose-petals.

Looking back on these five rooms one is conscious of their variety and inventiveness. One is led from the highly enriched classicism of the entrance rooms, which anticipate the style of the French Empire by a generation, to the restful, habitable dignity of the Long Gallery. Syon is a supreme example of the art of decoration. But as Adam said, 'a proper arrangement and relief of apartments are branches of architecture'. Syon is one of those houses which only truly begin at the front door.

The Boudoir Room off the north end of the Long Gallery. The birdcage is a typical Adam conceit

A richly decorated capital and architrave in the Dining Room

opposite The Long Gallery, adapted by Robert Adam from the original Jacobean gallery, and with furniture specially designed by him. The grouping of the pilasters, the position of the doors and fireplaces, and the design of the ceiling were intended to give the appearance of greater width

KEDLESTON HALL

DERBYSHIRE

A neo-classical house with a fine Adam interior

One of the few forms of self-discipline which great men of the mid-eighteenth century imposed on themselves was a willingness to undergo discomfort and ugliness for the sake of a finished result that they might never live to see. There was a perfectly good house at Kedleston in 1758 when Sir Nathaniel Curzon, later Lord Scarsdale, decided to rebuild it completely on the same site. It was not more than seventy years old. But all had to be pulled down in the interests of fashion and architectural adventure, and for years Sir Nathaniel can seldom have been out of earshot of hammering and shouted instructions. The park was cut up by the transport of huge loads of building materials, a whole village had to be removed because it lay too close to the house, and the turnpike road was diverted by special Act of Parliament.

Sir Nathaniel showed equal courage in his choice, and change, of architects. Kedleston is the product of three men, not working in collaboration but replacing each other as the building progressed and as their patron considered their powers of invention to be exhausted. The idea of a Palladian mansion connected by curving arcades to four detached wings or pavilions was conceived by Matthew Brettingham, who had been the executive architect of Holkham under Kent and Lord Burlington. It was he who built the north-east, or family, wing at Kedleston in 1758, which allowed Sir Nathaniel to pull down the Restoration house before the work advanced further. Then James Paine

Kedleston Hall painted in about 1770, shortly after the house was built. On the left is the bridge, and on the right the fishing lodge, both designed by Adam

opposite top The south front, the work of Robert Adam. Two further wings were to have been added on this side of the house but they were never constructed

left The north or entrance front, designed by James Paine. The church on the right is all that survives of the village swept away by Sir Nathaniel Curzon to make room for his house

247

KEDLESTON HALL

Effigies of Richard de Curzon and his wife in Kedleston Church. They are seen through 'portholes' made when the floor level of the chancel was raised

Looking through two of the columns of the Marble Hall to the fireplace. Above it are some typical Adam decorations; even the grates, fenders and fire irons were specially designed by him

was called in to complete the whole building in a more magnificent style, and to him we owe the north front. He was the most distinguished architect of his day, and it needed determination on the part of Sir Nathaniel and a dignified withdrawal by Paine, before Robert Adam could replace him in 1760 without any apparent friction between the three of them. Kedleston is known today as an Adam house, one of the first and major works of his career, and he endowed it with all its originality and most of its distinction, inside and out. But in taking over other men's work he altered little of what they had completed, and both Brettingham and Paine should have some share in the credit.

This double change of architect might have had a disastrous effect on the appearance of Kedleston. In fact, it lost nothing by it. This was partly because each of the three was working in the same general neo-classical context; and partly because it was possible to treat the north and south fronts quite differently, as neither would be visible in juxtaposition to the other. A third reason is that Kedleston lies in the middle of a rolling park so lovely in itself that almost any stone building of the appropriate size would be enhanced by it. The plan, however, was not quite completed. For reasons not now known, Brettingham's two southern wings were never built. It has been suggested that the omission of these two wings was due to a last-minute economy. But that is unlikely, since Adam was commissioned to build an even larger stable-block nearby, as well as garden temples, a bridge over the lake, several lodges, a fishing-pavilion and the Home Farm. Nor can Adam have advised the change in plan. His south front was dependent upon the wings for the extra liveliness that they would have imparted to it, and the east and west elevations would also have gained greatly from them.

The great north front, which one sees first when approaching the house from across the lake, is a grandiloquent Palladian façade of simple and (by that time) conventional design. A double exterior staircase rises to a portico formed by six columns mounted on a base of rusticated arches. This was Paine. On each side run the curved colonnades linking the main house to the family wing on the left and the kitchen wing on the right. This was Paine-*cum*-Brettingham. The only hint of Adam so far is his dome peeping over the top and five roundels which he added to the back wall of the portico above Paine's statue-niches and front door. But on the other side of the house Adam entered into his own. He applied to this front his principle of 'movement': that is, a combination of different shapes in three dimensions – columns with arches, domes with architraves, circular sweeping shapes with plain uprights and horizontals – breathing life throughout the building like a lung. It has been compared to a triumphal arch, both to its discredit and in its praise, but this is only one element. It is not Roman, but it borrows Roman ideas and transforms them. It is sturdy but

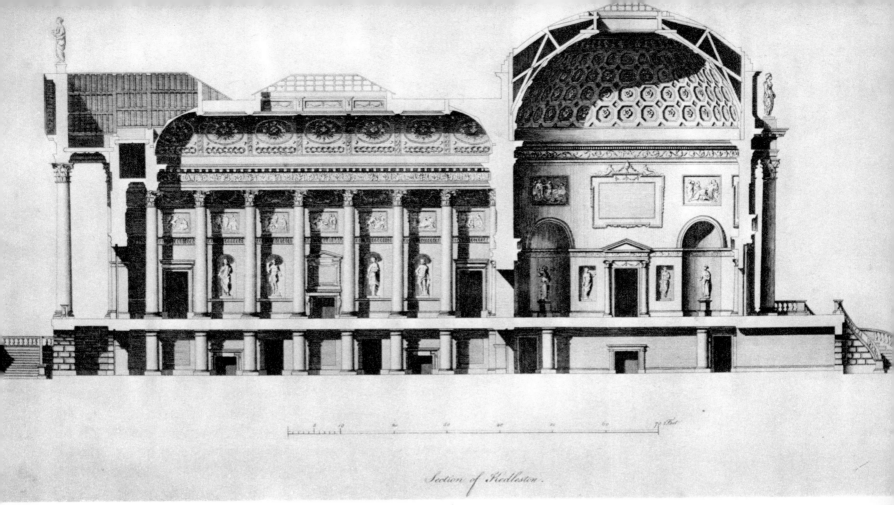

Section of Kedleston.

below The Marble Hall, the ceremonial entrance on the first floor, approached by an external staircase. Statues of Roman gods and goddesses stand in the niches round the walls. The huge columns are of Nottinghamshire alabaster

above A cross-section of Kedleston Hall from *Vitruvius Britannicus*, showing the marble hall (left) and the domed saloon (right)

The mantelpiece in the State Drawing Room

decorative, firm but graceful. It is astonishing that something so heavy could contain something so light. It was quite revolutionary for its day, and Adam was barely thirty when he built it.

The interior of Kedleston is almost all Adam's work, and illustrates his monumental style to perfection. Having returned from his long visit to Italy only a couple of years before, his mind was full of Roman splendour, either in its original Augustan form or in Renaissance derivatives from it. His Marble Hall at Kedleston is an attempt to reproduce the effect of a Roman *atrium*, and his circular Saloon the *vestibulum*, in eighteenth-century terms. The twenty fluted monoliths of Nottinghamshire alabaster dominate the hall by their solemnity. It was not simply a place in which to leave your hat, but the still heart of a great house. In Elizabethan times such a hall would have been the centre of household life, but not at Kedleston: voices were not raised in this stupendous room, and functionally it had no purpose. 'Movement' was discarded, apart from the coved ceiling and three round skylights: even the fireplaces on each side were Adam's later additions. It is cool and superbly empty, as if the very air which it encloses is an essential part of the design.

The Saloon, almost equally vast, makes quite a different effect, though it too is monumental in character. Here there is more decoration, less majesty. The coffered ceiling, rising sixty-two feet into the dome and lit by a spider's-web skylight at the apex, is the most satisfying geometrical design that can be seen anywhere in Adam's houses. The finish and spacing of the furniture, the lamp-brackets and Rebecca's chiaroscuro paintings, have been thought out with infinite care, and even the cast-iron stoves form pleasing silhouettes in the alcoves. The photographs must be allowed to speak for the other rooms on the main floor. They illustrate Robert Adam's inventiveness, his acute sense of what best fits a particular purpose, his capacity for quick variation between the grand and the domestic, between the elaborate and the merely pretty, and the obvious enjoyment with which he turned from one material to another – alabaster, marble, bronze, iron, wood, stucco, plaster, paint – contriving his exquisite designs from each in turn. They also illustrate the care with which the Curzon family have looked after this priceless possession.

opposite The Saloon. The ceiling is formed by the dome which is such a feature of the south front. The decorations and furniture in this room were personally designed by Adam, even including the locks on the doors

left A detail of the organ-pipes in the Music Room, by Robert Adam

MELLERSTAIN

BERWICKSHIRE

The combined achievement of William and Robert Adam

That one of the Adam family should have built your home is a boast which every owner would be proud to make. But that two Adams should have collaborated on it at an interval of nearly fifty years is more than any man, even a Scottish nobleman, has the right to expect. Yet this in brief is the story of Mellerstain. William Adam began to build it for George Baillie in 1725. Robert Adam, his more famous son, finished it for Baillie's grandson (also George) in about 1770–5.

Of the two, Robert Adam has left on the house the deeper impress, not only because he built the larger part of it, but because he applied to its main rooms the infinite grace and care with which he touched everything that came under his hands. The interior, therefore, is the main attraction of Mellerstain – the interior and the garden. The exterior is in a sense a double disappointment. It is disappointing because the father was unable to complete the whole house as he designed it; and because Robert Adam chose for his additions the castellated style of which he never became so great a master as in his own version of the classical.

The contrast between William's work and Robert's is immediately seen on the northern, or entrance, front. The two wings which flank the forecourt are William Adam's; the main block which joins them is Robert's. The former are self-contained buildings, nearly square in shape, with cupolas rising over tiny internal courtyards. They are very simple, their rough walls as mealy as porridge and virtually unornamented, but instantly satisfying in their homeliness and proportions. The east wing was the family's house, the west the stables. The family wing is so modest that it contains not one room that can be identified as the main reception room, and the staircase is an apologetic stone spiral of which the turret juts out so awkwardly into the courtyard that it denies the latter any architectural distinction that it might have possessed. Even the horses in the other wing were more elegantly housed than this. But the simplicity, even humbleness, of these wings is explained by William Adam's drawings of the central block which was never executed. Here indeed was a noble pile, more in the Wren tradition than Vanbrugh's (with which William Adam was experimenting at the

The iron cage at the top of the newel of the spiral staircase in William Adam's east wing. An excellent example of eighteenth-century ironwork

opposite The Library, one of the finest rooms designed by Robert Adam

The entrance front at Mellerstain. The two wings –
the family house on the left and the stables on
the right – were built by William Adam in 1725
for George Baillie. The central block was added
about 1775 by Robert Adam for his grandson

opposite top The south or garden front. The
austere façade shows little trace of the elegance of
the interior. The garden terraces were added
between 1900 and 1909

opposite Looking south across the gardens to the
ornamental lake

same time at Hopetoun), and it is easy to understand how easily
the little wings would have lain alongside the main building.

One of the mysteries of Mellerstain is why William Adam's
main house was never built. George Baillie the elder was rich,
well connected, politically influential and married to a charming
woman, Grisell Hume, who left upon contemporaries an impression of determination, efficiency and taste. She was a woman of
high moral and physical courage, a poetess in her own right, and
a formidable housekeeper. Yet she ruled over nothing more than
one small wing. Between it and the stable block was a void, 'the
intended house', as Richard Pococke described it after a visit
to Mellerstain in 1760. The problem deepens when we learn that
during the whole of the interval between the beginning and the
finishing of the house a majestic park was being laid out around
it with a vista southwards over a great lake cupped in beautifully
wooded hills. Its appearance can be guessed from a plan of the
grounds made four years before Pococke's visit. To the north is
a starred and tonsured wood; to the south the rectangle of the
lake. In the centre is the terminating circle of the approach
drive. Miniscule below its bottom arc, are two hatchured blocks:
these are the wings. Between them extends 'the intended house',
a gravelled continuation of the drive, a mere emptiness.

Whatever the reason for his grandparents' strange system of
priorities, George Baillie determined to fill the gap soon after he
succeeded to the estate in 1759. He called in Robert Adam. So

A general view of the Library, one of the most beautiful eighteenth-century rooms in Europe

left A bust by Roubiliac of Lady Grisell Baillie, wife of the first owner of Mellerstain, over a door in the Library. It was carved in 1746 when she was aged 81

opposite top The centre of the Library ceiling with musical trophies and a painting of Minerva in the style of Angelica Kauffman or Zucchi

opposite One of the plasterwork panels of classical scenes which decorate the frieze in the library

The eastern end of the corridor which extends the whole length of the house behind the southern rooms. It is vaulted in an Adamesque version of the Gothic

opposite The Small Drawing Room, one of a suite of rooms by Robert Adam that runs the length of the south front

Adam the younger designed for Baillie the younger a large house which incorporated his father's wings but bridged them by a domesticated castle instead of by the classical building which his father had intended. The building is stern, even tough; an anachronistic throwback to Border pele-towers. It is not in any sense Gothic, in which the Adam brothers showed little interest even when it became the fashion of the times; it is not even romantic, like Adam's Culzean Castle in Ayrshire; it is more Georgianized Tudor, faintly reminiscent of the exterior of Syon, where Robert Adam had been working ten years before. The walls are so roughly finished, with quoins and window-labels of odd sizes set at careless angles and without a single swag or medallion to gratify what we have now come to expect of him, that one suspects that they may have been intended as a base for a stucco finish. Some doubt could exist whether it was really Adam's work, did not his original designs survive in the Soane Museum to prove it.

The second mystery of Mellerstain is why it is so thin. It is one room, and one corridor, wide, with bulkier angle-towers and a thickened centre for the hall and staircase. There was space on its platform for a house of more normal proportions, and one can only guess that the Baillies desired a house that would look bigger from outside than it actually was, and would remain manageable without too large a staff. The result is that the main reception rooms extend in a long line all along the south side, leading one into the other, with a connecting corridor running the full length of the house behind them. The pattern is repeated on the bedroom floor above. On the top storey of the central tower is the largest and one of the loveliest rooms in the whole house, a long gallery as splendid as a ballroom, with superb views over the garden and the lake.

Each of the main living-rooms was decorated by Robert Adam with a delicacy that holds the visitor in thrall to his superlative talent. The rooms do not depend upon his usual contrast between straight lines and curved, coved ceilings and flat. The only departures from the rectangular shapes are the apses of the entrance hall, and the Ionic screens and coved ceiling of the long gallery. The other rooms are basically boxes of different sizes. In no other of his houses is Adam's sense of colour more brilliantly displayed. The rooms are made by the decoration of walls, ceilings and fireplaces, but the reliefs of plaster and marble are so shallow that they would be almost insignificant but for their contrasted colouring. There is one room, Lady Haddington's private sitting-room, where the decoration is unpainted (perhaps deliberately, but more likely left unfinished or overpainted in white at a later period) and the most exquisite shells, harps, garlands and other devices seem as bleak as moulds without their gilding or background painting. But in the library, undoubtedly the finest room in the house and among Adam's very greatest creations, the reliefs spring to life. One would know it immediately for an Adam room and yet one finds

A detail of Robert Adam's ceiling in the Music Room

opposite The Music Room. The mantelpiece representing War and Peace and oxen ploughing is a later addition

in it decorative inventions that have no parallel in his work elsewhere, particularly the broad friezes above the bookcases containing long panels of Homeric scenes and busts set in recessed circles framed by squares. This wonderful room also illustrates how well Adam's decorations combine with present-day furniture. Such rooms need the addition of solids like sofas or the larger type of writing-desk, for without them the decoration can sometimes appear over-sweet, like icing without its accompanying plum cake.

Mellerstain, in short, is a jewel set in a block of rough-hewn stone, and the stone is laid on a carpet of incomparable texture and variety. The contrast between the garden, the house and the rooms will strike every visitor. The first and the third are the products of the subtlest design: the house is by contrast of little more than academic interest. But the combination of the three is a memorial to two generations of two families who worked together to create something of enduring value.

ALTHORP

NORTHAMPTONSHIRE

An Elizabethan house reconstructed in the seventeenth and eighteenth centuries

Fifteen generations of Spencers have inhabited this house, and it is in the present ownership of the sixteenth. Allowing for brothers succeeding brothers, and the same men holding in succession two different titles, there have been at Althorp, since the early sixteenth century, five Knights, three Barons Spencer, five Earls of Sunderland, seven Earls Spencer and one Duke of Marlborough, and the descent has never wavered from the direct male line. Many of them have been distinguished in public life. The second Earl of Sunderland was Charles II's and William III's leading Minister; his son, the third Earl, who married the great Marlborough's daughter, was Secretary-of-State to Queen Anne and George I; the third Earl Spencer led the House of Commons during the Reform Bill debates of 1830–4; and the fifth Earl Spencer, having held a number of high offices in the later part of the reign of Queen Victoria, was leader of the Liberal Peers from 1902 to 1905. Almost every one of them, to a greater or less degree, has been an enlightened patron of the arts, and two, the third Earl of Sunderland and the second Earl Spencer, assembled libraries which were among the most famous of their times.

The house reflects the Spencers' artistic interests and their marriages with other great English families more than their political activities. There could scarcely be room for both. The furniture, sculpture, books, porcelain and, above all, the pictures fill the walls, and many of the rooms were designed or remodelled to show them off to best advantage. This description is not directly concerned with the works of art, though they will be evident in the photographs. They are the chief glory of Althorp, forming one of the greatest family collections in the world.

Althorp, like the family's history and art-collection, is the product of the slow assimilation of changing fortunes and tastes. It has been the same house for more than four centuries, in the sense that the site is the same and the basic structure is Elizabethan. Parts of an even earlier but smaller house, built of the local orange stone, is hidden in its core, the house which the first Sir John Spencer bought in 1508 and which dated back unfathomable centuries. It was surrounded by a moat, which survived until 1790. Early in the reign of Queen Elizabeth I his

The memorial in Great Brington Church to the first Earl Spencer who was responsible for buying some of the finest paintings at Althorp, including many of those in the Marlborough Room

opposite The Marlborough Room on the ground floor of the north front. This was formerly two rooms and is hung with a fine collection of family portraits by Reynolds and Gainsborough

263

The entrance front. The original mediaeval manor house was reconstructed in 1573 when the two projecting wings were added. In about 1790 the whole house was re-faced by Henry Holland and two corridors were added on the side of the forecourt and also the pediment over the entrance

Althorp in 1677 by John Vorstermans. This shows the appearance of the house soon after its reconstruction in the Restoration period. The Elizabethan brickwork and pre-Tudor moat are still visible

grandson, another Sir John, greatly enlarged the manor-house which he inherited, adding the two wings which still enclose its forecourt, a long gallery (now the Picture Gallery) and other rooms around an open central court, on the far side of his Great Hall. The whole was built in red brick with stone dressings, concealing the mediaeval stone and timbering behind its central part. When the present hall was recently repaired, roof-timbers, possibly dating from the fourteenth century, were found above it. Although it is possible by a process of mental X-ray to discern the Elizabethan buildings behind the present façades, nobody could guess without investigation that this is one of the most continuously occupied sites in Northamptonshire, or indeed in the whole country. It looks like a splendid product of the two grand centuries of English architecture and landscaping, the seventeenth and eighteenth, and such, in effect, it is. The changes that were made to the house externally have stamped it with an Augustan character, although its origins were a great deal earlier.

The Vorstermans painting of 1677 well illustrates the transition between the old and the present appearance of Althorp. The moat still ran round all four sides of its platform, and the main walls were still of sixteenth-century brick. But when the picture was painted, the Elizabethan house had recently been transformed by the second Earl of Sunderland into a palace 'disposed after the Italian manner'. The gable-ended wings had been

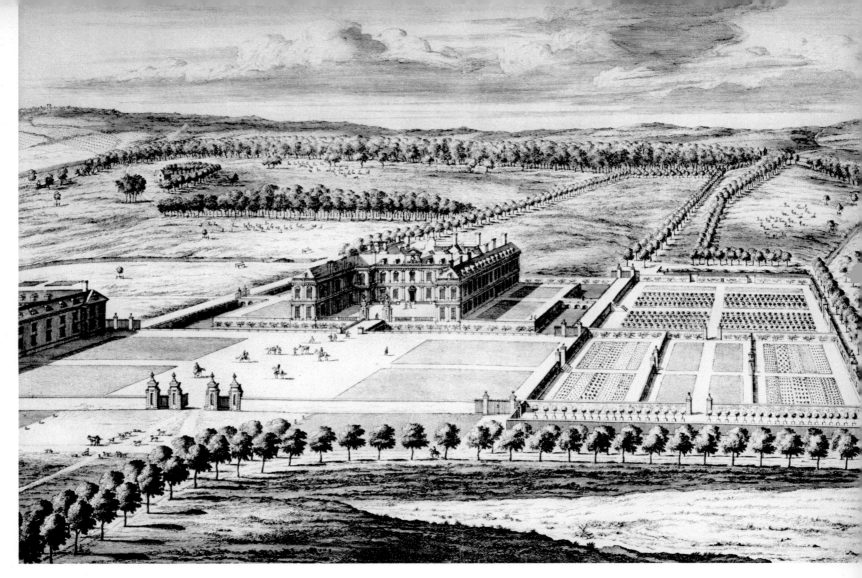

altered into typically Restoration hipped roofs with a balustrade, the upper windows were topped by arched pediments, and classical pilasters clung to the wall between them. To the east, formal walled gardens stretched outwards towards the park, in the design of which André le Nôtre is said to have had a hand. Internally the Earl modernized the house by improving the staircase within the central courtyard and laid out the state-rooms on the first floor of the north side, comprising the Saloon or Great Room, two large bedrooms at each end, a waiting room and a dressing-room.

It was one of the few houses to meet with the approval of Duke Cosimo of Tuscany's courtiers in 1669. It 'may be said to be the best planned and best arranged country seat in the kingdom', they reported. 'For although there may be many which surpass it in size, none are superior to it in symmetrical elegance.' John Evelyn was equally enthusiastic:

The house or rather palace at Althorp is a noble uniform pile in form of a half H, built of brick and freestone balustered and *à la moderne*; the hall is well, the staircase excellent; the rooms of state, galleries, offices and furniture such as may become a great prince. It is situate in the midst of a garden exquisitely planted and kept, and all this in a park walled in with hewn stone, planted with rows or walks of trees, canals, and fishponds and stored with game.

When Celia Fiennes visited the house in 1702, the year of the second Earl's death, she described it as 'like a Prince's Court of brick and stone very fine, with a large Parke wall'd in of a good

An engraving by Kip showing Althorp in the late seventeenth century with the formal gardens said to have been designed by Le Nôtre

The gardener's cottage built by the fifth Earl of Sunderland in about 1730

above The Entrance Hall as re-designed in the
early eighteenth century. The hunting pictures
are by John Wootton

opposite top The Long Library at the north end of
Holland's suite of rooms

opposite bottom The Yellow Drawing Room, looking
through to the South Drawing Room

The Staircase Hall hung with portraits of different generations of the Spencer family

A family group by Angelica Kauffman.
Right, George John, second Earl Spencer, with his two sisters Georgiana, later Duchess of Devonshire, and Henrietta, later Countess of Bessborough

extent'. Already it was filled with many of the most valuable pieces of its art-collection, for the second Earl, during his travels in Italy and Holland, and as Ambassador in Paris and Madrid, had many opportunities to indulge his tastes as a collector.

The next stage came in the early eighteenth century, when the fifth Earl of Sunderland, later third Duke of Marlborough, altered the entrance hall, possibly with the advice of Colen Campbell, and commissioned John Wootton to paint the huge hunting pictures, which, like those at Longleat, show the continuous interest taken by the family in field-sports. He also built the splendid stable-block of local stone with two classical porticoes at its north and east sides, and the charming gardener's cottage with its three-arched porch. But the Elizabethan-Restoration façades remained until nearly the end of the eighteenth century. Their mellowed red brick glowed richly across the park.

When George John Spencer succeeded as the second Earl Spencer in 1783, part of the house had exhibited alarming signs of disintegration, and repair work was urgently required. He called in Henry Holland to advise him. 'At first,' wrote the Earl, 'we thought we must be content with making the apartments we live in weather-proof and saving the house from tumbling down. We have got Mr Holland here who has brought his plans with him. I have a notion that they will be very clever ones . . . but the Quomodo is the difficulty.' Holland was a young man of talents, exceptional good looks, grace of bearing, charm of manner and unusual powers of persuasion. He was not content merely to prop up a beautiful house, but induced his patron to alter it inside and out, at an eventual Quomodo of £20,257, by a transformation as radical as any since the additions of the second Earl of Sunderland over a hundred years before.

Holland's main external change was to cover up the Elizabethan brick with silvery-white facing tiles, known technically as 'rebate-tiles' but popularly as 'mathematical-tiles', with which he refaced Sloane Place, his own house in London. His motives were two: as a protection against the weather, which they assuredly were; and because a prejudice, originated by Isaac Ware in 1756, had condemned plain brick as a surfacing for country houses of the noblest kind. 'The colour,' wrote Ware, 'is fiery . . . and in summer has an appearance of heat that is very disagreeable.' Moreover, 'there is something harsh in the transition from red brick to stone, and it seems altogether unnatural.' Compton Wynyates, Blickling, Weston! So Althorp, to its present disadvantage, was refaced by brick-tiles. Behind them are the original Elizabethan bricks, and behind them again are the stone and half-timber of the pre-Tudor house. Althorp was assuming its present appearance. Holland added pediments to the centre of the entrance and garden fronts, and tall pilasters to the former. He filled in the moat, widened the windows and built corridors along the inner sides of both wings, which narrow the forecourt but add greatly to the charm and convenience of the interior. Furthermore, in 1790 he completely remodelled the reception rooms on the ground floor of the west wing by throwing the Long Library into the Yellow Drawing-room and South Drawing-room. Later, exceptionally wide doors were added which can be left open to form a long gallery of great variety and friendliness. These three rooms are the most pleasant in the whole house and contain many of its finest possessions. When the ceilings were refashioned in 1864 by Broadbent of Leicester, Victorian standards scarcely dropped below those of Holland himself.

Althorp is a house of the greatest interest in its history, owner-ship, architecture and contents. Its setting between formal gardens and in the middle of a park that is the quintessence of all that is loveliest in the Midland countryside, make it a house that deserves contemplation, just as if it were a picture on one of its own walls. It has a ready-made dignity which immediately proclaims it to be the house of a great family, but its charm is much more subtle. Even Holland's brick-tiling, must originally have glowed in the sun before it became discoloured. The rooms are large, numerous and some of them grand, but one can still agree with Cosimo's companions that it is the 'best-planned and best-arranged seat in the kingdom'. At every doorway one experiences a sense of surprise, of delight, but never of shock. It is a good-mannered house, and its present owner, the seventh Earl Spencer, has cherished it and loved it as all his many ancestors did before him.

The Picture Gallery which runs the length of the west front on the first floor and almost certainly occupies the position of the Elizabethan long gallery. It was re-panelled in the late seventeenth century and the paintings include Lely's 'Beauties of the Court of Charles II' on the left, and many pictures by Van Dyck

HEVENINGHAM HALL

James Wyatt's masterpiece of decoration

An old print of Heveningham reproduced on a plate from a dinner service made in Paris towards the end of the eighteenth century. A modern copy of the original plate

opposite The Entrance Hall designed by James Wyatt in the style of Robert Adam

If a modern child were asked to draw his conception of a grand house, he would draw something very like the north front of Heveningham. Thus far has the intention, and the achievement, of Palladianism penetrated our subconscious. Its grandness is due not so much to its size as to its pride: and in the mid-eighteenth century pride was architecturally expressed by a combination of rusticated arches and great porticoes rising in firm outlines from a park. If the lie of the land made it possible to set the house on a hill, so much the better. If a lake could be formed at its foot, the flat dish of water would mirror the house and double its impressiveness. It was ostentatious architecture. It made no attempt to charm. It was even rather repetitive. If done badly, it could become gross; done well, it conveyed an impression of certainty – certainty of status, certainty of design. At Heveningham it was done well.

The architect was Sir Robert Taylor, his patron Sir Gerard Vanneck Bt MP, and the date of the commission about 1778. But Sir Robert had no hand in the interior decoration. It was entrusted to a man of very different taste and temperament, James Wyatt. It is not for Taylor's exterior that Heveningham is renowned, for it was merely competent and by that time traditional; but for Wyatt's interior, which here achieved a dexterity in the Robert Adam manner that Adam himself never surpassed.

Sir Robert Taylor had made some progress with his designs for the interior of Heveningham before the exterior was completed, and one can imagine with what annoyance he learned that his designs were to be thrown over for those of a much younger man (Taylor was sixty-six in 1780, and Wyatt thirty-four), and that the house was to be decorated thoughout in the Adamesque style which for twenty years had been thrusting aside older Palladian concepts.

Wyatt, who was neither an original artist nor a generous rival, affected to despise the work of Adam. He once said to George III, 'When I came from Italy, I found the public taste corrupted by the Adams and I was obliged to comply with it.' This remark was made in 1804, by which time Wyatt had gone Gothick and his outlook had been soured by drink. It is barely

The Palladian façade of the north front designed by Sir Robert Taylor in the 1770s

conceivable that he would have felt like this when he came to Heveningham soon after 1780 fresh from the triumphs of his Pantheon in London and Heaton Hall in Lancashire, both of which were decorated in the same manner. No man who felt contempt for another's style could have employed it with such assurance and obvious delight as Wyatt displayed in all three buildings; and there was no 'obligation to comply with it', since the fashion had many influential critics, led by Horace Walpole. The truth is that Wyatt embraced and adapted Adam's stylistic innovations so superbly that contemporaries could say that of the two, Wyatt 'employed the antique with more judgment'. But it remains undeniable, in the words of Mr Lees-Milne's summing-up in *The Age of Adam*, that 'Wyatt's constructional and decorative style is in all essentials an imitation of Robert Adam's.'

Wyatt, then, took Taylor's shell, left the outside untouched by a single additional swag (thus far he respected the architecture and feelings of the older man) and applied himself with gusto to the interior. His first task was to shape the rooms. Taylor had left him with rectangular Palladian boxes. Wyatt transformed them by semicircular apses, half-domes, niches, roundels and coves, giving the interior a cocoon-like softness, as if he wished to cushion the occupants as much by the walls and ceilings as by their furniture. This curving of the rooms also imparted to the house a vitality which makes nonsense of the often repeated

A detail of the staircase balustrade

opposite The staircase at Heveningham. In the background is a mirror by Wyatt reflecting the delicate wrought-iron balustrade

273

One end of the Saloon. The painted decorations
are by Biagio Rebecca

The Dining Room with shallow apses
characteristic of Wyatt's style. The dark red
medallions on the wall are set against a
Wedgwood blue background

gibe that the chief symptom of the change from Burlingtonianism to Adamism was a tendency to design in two dimensions rather than in three.

His colourings were everywhere soft – apple-green, biscuit, Wedgwood blue, madder. On these backgrounds he applied in paint or low plaster relief exquisite pictures 'from the antique', linking them together or framing them by scrolls, wreaths, fan-tracery and festoons of leaves and flowers. His superiority over Adam lies in the restraint with which he employed this intoxicating form of embroidery. The possible variants of the new art-form, being so limitless, led the artist on. If all the wall and ceiling surfaces were covered by it, only fuss would result. In his more exuberant moments Adam tended to fill every square inch, as one can see in the Long Gallery at Syon. Wyatt left large areas quite bare, thus drawing attention to the individual medallion, the isolated arabesque. When he formed a border of tiny repeated patterns, such as the Greek acanthus, he did not crowd it by juxtaposed reliefs which would kill it. He allowed it to stand out like a brocade border to a skirt. The loops of a garland, the circle of a wreath, a frieze of boys or griffins, always stop short in Wyatt's designs at precisely the right point.

In his larger compositions Wyatt demonstrated that elegance, even prettiness, could be achieved without loss of dignity. What could be more splendid than his hall at Heveningham – surely one of the most beautiful rooms in England – yet its impressiveness owes nothing to violent contrasts or strong colours. The butter-yellow of the Siena scagliola columns dominates the whole. The slightly roughened surface of the marble floor is a welcome contrast to the smoothness of the huge mahogany doors and the gentle curvature of the ceiling. One wonders at the ingenuity of the man who could foresee this room whole when considering the infinite detail of its several parts. Only

one thing has been added to the hall since Wyatt left it, a lion-skin rug snarling from the floor. Surprisingly, it is wholly appropriate, for the pale colour of the pelt, the smooth lift of the head, even the gleaming white teeth, are completely in tune with Wyatt's conception of dignity, colour and repose.

When one comes to look back at Heveningham, one sees it not in terms of splendour or even elegance, but as a romantic place in which artists have worked for the fun of it. These cool rooms reveal the light-heartedness with which Wyatt and his band of helpers toyed with the new art-form. To portray Shakespeare in *trompe l'oeil* as a cameo in paint; to decorate an entire room like the Saloon with pictures so fanciful and attractive that it is only afterwards that one realizes that it is almost unfurnished; to give the red figures of Greek vases a flow and vitality that the Greeks never achieved, and then call it 'Etruscan'; to set lead medallions within the iron framework of a balustrade, and paint it blue and white: all this was conceived by Wyatt with bravado and high spirits. But if one wishes to flavour to the full his youthful spirit, one must visit his Orangery. Here is Palladianism liberated from its severity. The slim pillars share the fragility of the glass behind, and even the Corinthian capitals are irreverently transformed into harvest-festival sheaves of foliage. In comparison, Lancelot Brown's serpentine brick wall in the neighbouring kitchen-garden looks almost heavy.

The interior of Heveningham is perfectly preserved. A fire in 1949 damaged part of the dining-room, but it has been repaired with a skill that only the post-war reconstruction of Brighton Pavilion can rival. For its crispness of detail, its purity of line and colour and the absence of all clutter, one might be tempted to call this house a monument to late-eighteenth-century taste, were not the word 'monument' quite inappropriate to a work of art so fresh, so endearing and so gay.

The Orangery, built by Wyatt in 1791. Its elegance contrasts with the monumental qualities of the exterior of the house

A doorway in the Etruscan Room

DODINGTON

GLOUCESTERSHIRE

An architectural bridge between two centuries

The back entrance to Dodington is only two hundred yards from a public road, but the visitor's approach is along a drive a mile long. The détour is well worth it. A classical rotunda known as Bath Lodge stands demurely just behind the entrance gates, and from that point onwards expectation mounts as the drive follows its winding course through a wood, around or over small knolls, across cattle-grids, down a valley and along its steep side. When the house is finally sighted, it is lost again further on and then rediscovered in the last few hundred yards. This teasing approach is most dramatic, but it was only partly an artificial contrivance. The south-west corner of the Cotswolds is troughed by deep and wooded vales, which closely resemble Derbyshire combes, and where one expects to find a ruined Abbey at the end, one finds a house. Capability Brown was here in 1764 and he made two lakes in the valley, one of which has been drained away to expose the natural stream on the approach to the house. The other has survived, and was extended by James Wyatt by a third on a lower level, fed from the upper lake by an aqueduct which passes through a Gothic turret and tumbles down in a dancing cascade. The house lies above the lakes. Its rather severe classical lines contrast with the bold swinging curves and romantic gulfs of its surroundings. Seen from a distance, Dodington looks exactly like one of Neale's 1820 prints of gentlemen's seats. All that is missing is Elizabeth Bennett walking with a parasol on the lawn, and a young man on horseback approaching along the drive discreetly shadowed by a groom.

This view and atmosphere were illustrated in a series of charming water-colours by Charles Turner of Oxford. They look as if they had been made all at one time, but the two here reproduced represent the scene at an interval of some twenty years, 1796 and 1816, before and after Wyatt had replaced the old house by the new. Either Turner sketched the old house from life and imagined the finished appearance of the new one from Wyatt's elevations; or, more likely, he drew the complete set in about 1816, and took as the model for his drawing of the Elizabethan house a sketch in an estate book of 1760 which shows it from exactly the same direction as his water-colour.

The Elizabethan house was built in about 1560 by Thomas

Two watercolours by Charles Turner, the first showing the original Elizabethan house at Dodington, and the second Wyatt's south and west fronts soon after the completion of the new house

opposite The Staircase Hall, completed by James Wyatt in 1812, and the outstanding feature of Dodington. The balustrade, originally from Fonthill in Wiltshire, dates from about 1760

277

The entrance front with its huge portico composed of six Corinthian columns in front and two pairs of columns behind. The conservatory curves away from the house on the left

opposite top The south-east angle of the house seen from above the lake

opposite The aqueduct between the upper and lower lakes, ending in a castellated turret through which the water falls. This may be the work of Wyatt, but in a different style from the house

Weekes who sold it to Giles Codrington soon after it was finished. It was a gabled house on the H-plan with a hall in the cross-bar, and for over two centuries it served the Codringtons well. Christopher Codrington, Governor of the Leeward Islands and founder of the Codrington Library at All Souls College, Oxford, made a fortune by careful management of his sugar plantations in the West Indies, and his descendant, Christopher Bethell Codrington, decided to rebuild the house completely. He did so with labour from his estate and out of income, so that the house took an exceptionally long time to finish. Wyatt, a man of lethargic disposition who took on more commissions than he could manage, was not displeased by the delay. He had the leisure to contemplate and alter his designs as he went along. There is every indication that his patron, himself an amateur architect of no mean gifts, took a keen interest in every detail.

Dodington is of very special interest in the history of architecture because it bridges the eighteenth to the nineteenth century in style as well as in time. A first and distant glance suggests that the house may be plain and rather conventional, for its stone is a dullish grey and the silhouette of the main block is austere to the point of starkness. On approaching closer, however, it begins to take to pieces. A great portico of six Corinthian columns, in the Greek more than the Roman style, reaching from pediment to ground-level without any supporting plinth or basement, stands clear of the house on the entrance side,

The Entrance Hall just inside the portico. The columns, made of porphyry scagliola, support a frieze set with lions' masks, and the pattern of the lavishly gilt ceiling is echoed in the different coloured marble and stone floor

leaving room for a carriage or Jaguar car to draw up at the front door within it. The portico fills two-thirds of the width of this façade, and from one corner a glass-fronted conservatory curves away like a horn. So different is it in feeling from the Palladian antecedents of the house, that it takes time to become reconciled to the idea that Wyatt designed and built it just like this. He was deliberately breaking with a tradition of orderliness that had grown stale, and the Codringtons, to whom a certain disarray has always appealed, approved his taste. The conservatory links the house with Wyatt's church, and this too is sited off the axis of the entrance front in the form of a Greek cross with a flattened dome. The whole composition of this front is of symmetrical units asymmetrically disposed, and it was essentially picturesque and puzzling in intention.

The other fronts are more conventional, and rely for their interest on the deep folds of the garden and the architectural novelties dotted about it. There is the bow-fronted east façade, similar to Wyatt's Plas Newydd in Anglesey, but here it overlooks the chain of lakes instead of an arm of the sea. There is the cascade, formerly attributed to Brown's reshaping of the park, but clearly it is Wyatt reverting to his castellated style, since neither it nor the lower of the three lakes is shown in the plan of 1770. There is a charming Dairy House, now separately occupied, with a semi-circular portico and oval rooms behind it, originally a prolongation of the east front of the house to which it was linked by a service wing, now pulled down. There is a fishing-pavilion on the lower lake; an ice-house; a pleasing stable block by Wyatt; the Bath Lodge already mentioned; and a grander gate and lodge on the other side of the park, known as Chippenham Lodge. Altogether, it was and is a seat of considerable magnificence, and every part of it is evidence of the most careful planning and execution.

Wyatt reserved for the interior his most dazzling effects and materials. There is barely a hint of his youthful flirtation with the Robert Adam manner, and the entrance hall is a much more sombre version of the Great Hall at Heveningham. But he made use in the old dining-room of the same yellow scagliola pilasters, now most successfully repositioned in the drawing-room, and the friezes of the cornices and fireplaces, the grille-fronted bookcases in the library, and, above all, the doors of veneered mahogany are all of great elegance in spite of a slightly coarser finish than Adam himself would have employed.

The set-piece of the house is the central staircase. A short time before these photographs were taken, Major Simon Codrington had had the whole of this magnificent hall repainted in white and powder-blue. The effect is intensely dramatic. The hall is day-lit only by a lantern in its roof and rises the whole height of the house. Its position comes as a surprise, because you do not see it from the entrance hall, and the size of the house and style of the rooms do not lead you to expect anything of such grace and splendour in its very centre. The staircase branches from a half-landing into two parallel flights joined at the top by a gallery along the fourth side, and the steps are cantilevered out from the walls with their undersides cut into S-shapes, so that the whole floats effortlessly upwards like a length of stiff paper pleated into strips and then re-opened. Fluted columns on the ground and first floors and in opposite openings in the upper part of the side-walls form galleries on three of the four sides, providing platforms from which to look or call down into the more shaded passages beneath. Part of the fun of this staircase is the wide choice of directions from which to photograph it, since from every angle the effect has been most cunningly foreseen. As if he realised that the wedding-cake lightness of its arcades was too fragile for the rest of the house, Wyatt roughened the floor, as he did in the hall at Heveningham, by paving it with lozenges of black marble and white stone. It is directly from this paving that the staircase, fitted with an earlier iron-work balustrade from Fonthill, begins its glorious ascent.

The story of the building of Dodington ends in a tragedy, not for the house, but to its creator. On 14 September 1813 Wyatt and Bethell Codrington were travelling back from Gloucestershire to London after inspecting the house in its almost completed state. Driving in Codrington's coach at high speed near Marlborough, they narrowly missed collision with a post-chaise, and the coach overturned. Codrington escaped unhurt, but Wyatt received a blow on the head which killed him instantly. His employer added the finishing touches in accordance with Wyatt's design, and it is the one piece of good fortune which we owe to Wyatt's premature death that all his original drawings are still preserved in the house. Turning them over one by one and comparing them with the finished work, you obtain the clearest possible idea of how this great work of art was evolved.

One of the fine mahogany doors in the Drawing Room inlaid with maple, satinwood, and ebony filigree

The Library completed in 1811 some time after the structural work had been finished. The bookcases are closed by gilt grilles

THE ROYAL PAVILION

SUSSEX

Nash's oriental fantasy for the Prince Regent

The Pavilion has become an accepted part of the Brighton scene. It goes with the elegant, indolent, faintly raffish atmosphere of the sunlit promenades. The last few hundred yards of the London road, before it is extended out to sea by the leaping extravagances of the pier, are enlivened by a gleaming pile of domes and minarets rising from a lawn. The dullest mind would wonder what it could be. An amusement arcade, a temporary exhibition ground, a fair, a folly? It is none of these things. It is a former royal palace. It is by far the greatest, almost the only, example of a style that flashed across English architectural history at the beginning of the nineteenth century to die out like a rocket in a trail of sparks. It contains decorations and furniture which for all their fantasy form the most brilliant expression of the revolt against classicism. It is romantic and exotic, Coleridge's pleasure-dome translated from Xanadu to an English seaside resort. Most remarkable of all – for such a building, one might suppose, could only have been erected by someone with more money to spend than position to sustain – it was built for the heir to the British throne and Empire by John Nash, the creator of the classic terraces around Regent's Park.

The Royal Pavilion had its origins in an illness and a romance. The Prince of Wales, later Prince Regent and still later George IV, first came to Brighton for his health in 1783, when he had been persuaded that sea-water was a cure for glandular swellings of the neck. Two years later he secretly married Mrs Fitzherbert, the twenty-five-year-old daughter of a Roman Catholic family, who had already been twice widowed, and brought her to Brighton in a hopeless attempt to economize (his debts already amounted to over half-a-million pounds) and to enjoy his unavowed marriage in comparative privacy. He rented a small farm-house in the Steine, a broad strip of lawn that ran down to the sea. In 1787, such was his ungovernable love of society, he decided to rebuild the house in a style fit to receive his friends. As his architect he employed Henry Holland, who between April and July in that year ran up a bow-fronted house in the classical manner, topped by a shallow dome. It was already known as the Prince's 'marine pavilion', as if to stress its primarily flippant intent. This house became the core of the vastly larger and more

An engraving of the Jummah Musjed, Delhi, published in Thomas and William Daniell's *Views of Oriental Scenery*. This work had an important influence on contemporary taste and on Nash's designs for the Royal Pavilion

opposite On the roof of the Pavilion, looking towards the great central dome which lies over the Saloon

The east façade which, unlike the other fronts, is perfectly symmetrical. Nash made brilliant use of fretted stonework which casts dappled shadows on the wall behind

The original Palladian house designed for the Prince Regent by Henry Holland in 1787. It was later absorbed into the structure of Nash's Indian pavilion

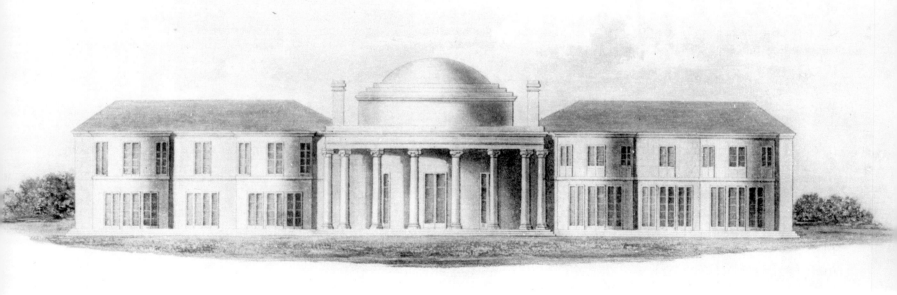

elaborate palace that was to be built around it. You can still see behind its oriental encrustations the shape of Holland's pretty Palladian villa. Its loveliest room, the oval Saloon, has survived structurally intact, though unrecognizable in its decoration. Somewhere embedded in the walls must be part of the original farm-house. Never can a yeoman's dwelling have undergone such a metamorphosis.

In the course of the next thirty-five years, Holland's building was transformed, slowly at the start and then with gathering speed. The first change was the addition of two further oval rooms at either end, and of green-painted iron canopies to the balconies, the originals of that charming Regency vogue that spread rapidly through Brighton and then to the entire country. In 1802 the Prince was given a roll of Chinese wallpaper, and he made for it a Chinese gallery in the northern wing. This was the beginning of the oriental decorations. Gradually Chinese motifs spread throughout the house. Chinese furniture was brought down from Carlton House, where the Prince had already begun experimenting with the style; Chinese mantelpieces and bamboo panelling were installed; works of art were imported from China itself, including more wallpaper, porcelain and huge pieces of highly coloured statuary. By 1803 the entire interior had been redecorated in this manner. The press and public scoffed, but the house was acknowledged by the ebullient circle of the Prince's friends to be an outstanding success. So entranced was he by its bazaar-like interior, that he toyed with the idea of encasing the whole house in a Chinese pagoda. William Porden was commissioned to do the designs.

Before Porden's plans had advanced beyond the stage of sketches, the Prince's Chinese tastes succumbed to his discovery of the Indian. He first allowed Porden to build an immense stable and riding-school in the Indian, or more properly, Moorish, manner, and then complained that his horses were better housed than he was himself. So first Humphrey Repton, and then John Nash, were invited to design a new exterior for the Pavilion which was to stand comparison not only with the stables but with the greatest monuments of Delhi itself. Repton's designs, to his great mortification, were not used, but they contained the germ of Nash's later and more subtle interpretation. In the final version, there was to be a great onion-dome over the Saloon with two smaller ones on each side, flanked by two other domes over a new banqueting-room to the south and music-room to the north. The building was started in 1815 and was almost finished five years later, the year in which the Prince Regent succeeded to the throne. The total cost had by that time amounted to over half a million pounds.

The Indian exterior does not clash with the Chinese interior because both were western conceptions of the Orient as a whole. The Pavilion could have been built in a Russian, Japanese, Persian or even Egyptian style without making much difference to the total effect. There was no literal imitation of anything.

A door in the Music Room, added at the north end of the Pavilion in 1817. It is decorated in the Chinese style which the Prince Regent favoured before he became king

The Banqueting Room, the most ambitious and elaborate of the chinoiserie decorations attempted by Nash. The wall paintings and the chandelier, weighing over a ton, are by Robert Jones

The Kitchen, an illustration from Nash's *Views of the Royal Pavilion*. The lantern roof is supported by four iron columns representing palm trees, with leaves of sheet bronze. Many of the original fittings have survived

286

The very shape of the onion-domes was a deliberate refinement of the Indian originals illustrated in Thomas and William Daniell's *Views of Oriental Scenery* which made so great an impact on contemporary taste. Those on the extreme north and south of the building had no prototype whatever east of Suez. As few visitors to Brighton were likely to go to India or China, there was little risk of pedantic comparisons, and the gaps in the architect's knowledge could be filled, to the building's great advantage, by his own fancy. Cobbett thought the Pavilion a copy of the Kremlin. William Daniell himself, one of the few critics competent to judge, exclaimed indignantly that 'there is not a feature great or small which at all accords with the purity, grandeur and magnificence that characterize the genuine Oriental style'. Hazlitt described it as a collection of stone pumpkins and pepperboxes; while to Sidney Smith has been attributed the most famous comment of all, 'The dome of St Paul's must have come down to Brighton and pupped.' Since then ridicule of the Pavilion has become as unfashionable as its style.

There is a marked difference in the two decorative phases of the interior. When the Prince's exuberance was at its height, he favoured a barbaric splendour that recalls the colour-plates of a children's edition of Marco Polo. The two largest rooms, the banqueting and music rooms, look as if they had been put up at a circus for the Christmas season, until one discovers the excellence of the materials and workmanship and the refinement of much of the detail. But those who find themselves appalled by such grotesque display will soon be reconciled to the Pavilion by the exquisite *chinoiserie* of the smaller rooms in the centre and upstairs. One does not need to have a taste for the Orient to appreciate these rooms; only an eye for decorative pattern and colour, and the imagination to recapture the excitement with which these new designs were conceived and executed. What fun they had! What shapes a dragon's tail could be made to assume, since nobody had ever seen one! What variations one could play on Regency Gothic, since the point of the building was that all existing rules should be broken!

Yet there remained a basic discipline. The east façade, one discovers with some surprise, is perfectly symmetrical. The fireplaces, though the chimneys be shaped like minarets, must not smoke. The kitchen, though decorated with cast-iron palm-trees, must serve banquets punctually and hot. If one of the huge chandeliers were allowed to fall, it might kill a king. Perhaps during the building of the Pavilion tempers became frayed, as during rehearsals of a harlequinade. It was a serious attempt at fun, and therefore full of pitfalls.

Now that the Pavilion is open to the public and much of its original furniture and decoration restored, it is seen to be the most magical house in Britain. The habitual glumness of custodians of public buildings is absent here; it is as if something of the Prince Regent's unashamed extravagance and delight in people and things has entered their souls and kept them perpetually amused.

The South Drawing Room, now restored to its original appearance. The ceiling is supported on palm tree columns decorated in gold and ivory

George IV's private suite, among the last of the rooms to be completed. It is less exuberant than some of the earlier rooms, although it owes much to chinoiserie

ACKNOWLEDGEMENTS

The author and publishers are greatly indebted to the owners or tenants of the houses for permission to include descriptions of them in this book, and in particular to the National Trust of England and Wales and the National Trust for Scotland. The names of the owners are given below in roman type. Where a house is occupied by a family or individual who have presented it to the National Trust, or who hold it on a long lease from the Trust, their names are given in brackets.

The photographs in this book were taken by Kerry Dundas with the exception of those identified below in italics. The author and publishers are grateful to the individuals and institutions mentioned for permission to reproduce photographs. (Numbers refer to pages)

ST MICHAEL'S MOUNT	The National Trust (Lord St Levan) *13 top, Aerofilms*
IGHTHAM MOTE	Mr C. H. Robinson
HADDON HALL	The Duke of Rutland
OXBURGH HALL	The National Trust (The Dowager Lady Bedingfeld) *30 bottom, J. K. St Joseph, by courtesy of the University of Cambridge*
COMPTON WYNYATES	The Marquess of Northampton
THE VYNE	The National Trust (The Hon Antony Lyttelton)
SPEKE HALL	The National Trust (Liverpool Corporation)
CRATHES CASTLE	The National Trust for Scotland *60 and 61 Country Life*
LONGLEAT HOUSE	The Marquess of Bath *65 bottom, British Museum; 66 bottom, Aerofilms*
SULGRAVE MANOR	The Sulgrave Manor Board *All photographs are the copyright of the Board*
MONTACUTE HOUSE	The National Trust *78 bottom, Aerofilms*
HARDWICK HALL	The National Trust *83 by courtesy of The National Trust; 84-5, 87, 88, 90 and 91 bottom, Edwin Smith*
KNOLE	The National Trust (Mr Lionel Sackville-West) *95 top, Aerofilms; 97 bottom, 100 Edwin Smith*
FOUNTAINS HALL	Mr Henry Vyner *104 bottom, Aerofilms*
HATFIELD HOUSE	The Marquess of Salisbury *All photos by Derrick Witty, except 111, 112, 113 A. F. Kersting*
BLICKLING HALL	The National Trust (Sir Jocelyn Lucas Bt MP) *116 Royal Institute of British Architects by courtesy of J. C. Prideaux-Brune; 117 Jarrolds, Norwich; 118 bottom, British Travel Association; 120 National Buildings Record*
WILTON HOUSE	The Earl of Pembroke *125, 128, 129, 130 bottom, 131 bottom, 132, 133 Derrick Witty; 124, 126, 131 top, Edwin Smith; 127 A. & C. Cooper; 130 by courtesy of Worcester College, Oxford*
GROOMBRIDGE PLACE	Mr S. W. Mountain
WESTON PARK	The Earl of Bradford *142 top, Aerofilms*
BELTON HOUSE	Lord Brownlow *148 H. Tempest, Nottingham*
UPPARK	The National Trust (Lady Meade-Fetherstonhaugh)
CHATSWORTH	The Duke of Devonshire *158, 167, 168, 169 Edwin Smith; 159 Airviews, Manchester; 162, 163, 164 T. S. Wragg; 165 S. W. Kenyon*
MOMPESSON HOUSE	The National Trust (Mr D. Martineau)
POWIS CASTLE	The National Trust (The Earl of Powis)
CASTLE HOWARD	Mr George Howard
ANTONY HOUSE	The National Trust (Sir John Carew Pole Bt)
EASTON NESTON	Lord Hesketh
MELBOURNE HALL	The Marquess of Lothian
BLENHEIM PALACE	The Duke of Marlborough *212 Aerofilms; 214 Ian Graham; 215 bottom, British Museum; 216 Lionel Bell; 217 left, 218, 219 top, Edwin Smith*
MEREWORTH CASTLE	Mr Michael Tree and Lady Anne Tree
HADDO HOUSE	Major David Gordon
HOLKHAM HALL	The Earl of Leicester
SYON HOUSE	The Duke of Northumberland *238, 240, 241, 243 top, 245 Edwin Smith; 239 National Portrait Gallery; 243 bottom, Country Life*
KEDLESTON HALL	The Viscount Scarsdale *246 A. F. Kersting*
MELLERSTAIN	The Earl of Haddington *256 top, 257 top, 259, 260 A. F. Kersting*
ALTHORP	The Earl Spencer *262, 264, 265, 266, 267, 268 top, 269 Lionel Bell*
HEVENINGHAM HALL	The heirs to the Hon Andrew Vanneck
DODINGTON	Major S. F. B. Codrington
THE ROYAL PAVILION	The County Borough of Brighton *286 top, A. F. Kersting; 287 top, County Borough of Brighton*